TECHNOLOGICAL MAN:
The Myth and the Reality

By the same author

AFRICA'S SEARCH FOR IDENTITY

TECHNOLOGICAL MAN: *The Myth and the Reality*

Victor C. Ferkiss

GEORGE BRAZILLER   *New York*

For Michael,
   Deborah,
   and Ethan—
and their fellow citizens
of the Twenty-first century

Preface

"The political scientist . . . must recognize in foresight a moral obligation, to be felt and taught,"* writes Bertrand de Jouvenel, one of the world's most distinguished social theorists. Yet foresight also includes evaluation: we cannot interpret without placing values upon the objects of our study; our very choice of concerns betrays us. So what began as an attempt to examine the interrelationship between technology and politics in the last decades of the twentieth century inexorably evolved into an attempt to point out at least the direction in which mankind must move if it is going to be able to deal with the new challenges put to the social order by technological change.

But just as ethical evaluation could not be avoided, it proved impossible to deal with the question at hand within the narrow framework originally envisioned. Aristotle held that politics was the architectonic moral science since it determined the total shape of society. Today we are all

* Bertrand de Jouvenel, "Political Science and Prevision," *American Political Science Review*, LIX (1965), 29–38.

forced toward agreement with him because technology has made human society into a seamless web, with mutual interrelationships that can be disentangled only at the peril of losing touch with reality.

To study politics today—and especially to study the politics of tomorrow—is to study all aspects of human life. In an era when academic specialization and ethical abdication are the hallmarks of virtue, any kind of interdisciplinary study centered on normative concerns opens one to reproach from many quarters—from those whose self-imposed limitations have been abandoned and those whose territory has been invaded, from those who view concern with values as a sign of approaching senility and those who simply regard your values as the wrong ones. But if one takes the task of the social scientist seriously, one must go where the problems are, and if one acts as a human being as well as a scientist, one must go where the relevant problems are. The result is a book that, because it is about everything, can be definitive about nothing; but one hopes it may help set readers on the track of the real issues facing mankind today.

Any book—especially one as wide-ranging as this—is the fruit of many encounters with individuals and ideas. But some debts especially stand out. Certain of my teachers, consciously or otherwise, spurred my interest in aspects of the subject at hand, most notably Carroll Quigley, Dwight Waldo and Harold Winkler. Leo Strauss and Hans J. Morgenthau have served as living reminders that the student of politics must be concerned above all with human and, ultimately, moral problems. Graduate and undergraduate students in my courses in technology and politics have provided both stimulation and continuing faith that the subject is important. The Department of Government of Georgetown University made available to me the services of Henry Kenski, now Assistant Professor of Political Science at the University of Arizona, as a research assistant during a crucial period of this book's gestation. John T. Schlebecker of the Smithsonian Institution provided much appreciated bibliographical assistance. My wife, Barbara Ellen Ferkiss, served not only in routine typing chores but above all as my literary and intellectual conscience, and the book owes much of what form it possesses to her. Edwin Seaver of George Braziller, Inc., manifested an ideal combination of anxiety and patience in seeing it through to completion, as well as encouraging me to begin it in the first place. The responsibility not merely for incidental errors but for the total viewpoint presented and above all for the *hubris* represented in such an undertaking is entirely my own.

V. C. F.

Contents

TECHNOLOGICAL MAN:
The Myth and the Reality

1

What Is
and What Is To Be

To the stars! Today, after uncountable millennia of existence bound to the surface of the planet we call earth, humanity is taking its first feeble steps toward the conquest of outer space. Men and women throughout the world thrill to the exploits of the individuals who represent mankind in this great adventure, seeing in their triumphs not simply victories for the United States or the Soviet Union, but for the human race itself. Yet many of us already have become accustomed to these marvels, taking them almost as much for granted as we do the electronic sorcery that brings them into our living rooms. The astronauts—cosmonauts if one speaks a different political language—are heroes to our children also, and they, too, have come to look upon them as familiar beings. But there is a difference. The young have a right to be somewhat blasé. Space travel is just one aspect of a new world, a world regarded by many adults with a mixture of tentativeness, uncertainty and fear, but which for the young of the advanced nations is simply the only world they know, or ever really can know. They are the men—and women—of the future, and they already are being trained for their roles in that future in a host of ways by school and society. For the future is already here.

By pure accident I encountered my first astronaut not too long ago. Since, despite Professor McLuhan's hyperbole, there is still a penumbra of reality that electronic media cannot reproduce, it was an enlightening experience. So much about the occasion symbolized and exemplified the advent of the new breed that rapidly seems to be taking over the world. James E. Webb, director of the National Aeronautics and Space Administration, retiring president of the American Society for Public Administration, had arranged for one of America's astronauts—his name does not matter, for he is the Everyman of the future—to be the unannounced speaker at the association's annual convention banquet, with his talk followed by color movies of the latest American space success, in which he had participated.

Here was the new man in the flesh, one of the few members of our species who had done what men throughout human history have dreamed of doing. He had seen our Mother Earth from afar, and looked upon the sun and stars from outside her mantle of atmosphere, not vicariously through the camera like his audience but with his own eyes. He had walked weightless—or virtually so—in the void of space. In him the human race had found a new freedom from limitations, had crossed, however haltingly, a new threshold.

What was he like, this new man, this hero of technological civilization? His speech—presented in the first person—could have been written by a sophisticated computer. He read it perfectly, with the enthusiasm and sincerity of a perfectly happy and well-brought-up child, the kind one seems to encounter these days only in films from mainland China. A politician seeking identification with his listeners would have deliberately fluffed a few lines; the astronaut was above that. A military man by formal profession, he seemed neither soldier nor sailor nor airman nor even warrior. He was obviously a supertechnician whose character combined keen intelligence, perfect poise and calculated courage. When he spoke of his own and his companions' reactions in space, he was, except for a sprinkling of personal humor deemed necessary and appropriate by those other technicians in public relations who had polished his text, perfectly clinical, even when discussing the most fantastic of exploits or the direst of perils. The tale he told was one of unbounded bravery, yet it was bravery of a different kind from that of the men who fought across Iwo Jima, who could have been his elder brothers, or those who sailed the uncharted seas to America in centuries past. It was a bravery compounded of knowledge and self-control, of perfect acceptance of reality, suggestive of the courage of the physician dying of a disease he seeks to conquer, who records clinically his own symptoms and emotions until the end.

He was an objective man, and only when he spoke of wonder felt or beauty observed did he seem close to striking a false note; emotional or aesthetic self-indulgence would have been his audience's reactions in space, but were they really his? This personable young man—who in appearance and manner could just as well have been a rising junior executive in any large American corporation—seemed so obviously at peace with himself and his world, so perfectly adjusted to the machines and the organization around him, knowing them and their capacities as well as he knew himself, finding in that knowledge peace and freedom. By every test of any number of political and psychological ideologies he should have been an almost perfectly alienated man, for had he not given his body, mind and soul over completely to the vast physical and human machine of which he and his fellows were the cutting edge? Yet it would be hard to visualize anyone who less fitted the popular modern stereotype of the alienated man, or who seemed more assured and serene.

What, one wondered, were his dreams like? Do (one assumes they do) NASA psychologists get an after-action report on these also? Significantly, in defending the space program, he did not mention the death of his friends and colleagues in the Apollo fire a few months previously—a sordid and trivial death, somehow also symbolic of the new civilization. But why should he, since in the new technological world such things should and normally will be prevented, and thus are, save for the victims and their families, of concern only to those who are charged with doing something to prevent them. Death is of no intrinsic interest, only its causes are. What is important is that the venture itself should not die.

For what he did not say, and what no one connected with the space program has said directly, though they say it under the guise of talking about scientific progress, is that if it succeeds the human race may not die. Earth may perish someday, but the universe, for all science knows, may be eternal. Mankind, on leaving earth, has taken what could be the first step toward escaping our planet's fate. A cosmic boundary has been crossed, not unlike that which our remote ancestors crossed aeons ago when they first left the seas to venture onto the land, an event that marked not only the conquest of a new environment and disassociation from the fate of the old but the beginnings of a change in the nature of the conqueror himself.

However, there is a difference between our situation and theirs, even leaving aside our uncertainty as to whether this new evolutionary thrust will be a successful or abortive one. For we are conscious of our strivings in a way that the sea creatures of old were not. Our men go not as individuals but as the agents of a huge social effort involving a large, deliberate commitment of the resources of human society. The astronauts are the culmination of a long process of social development, and they are but the most obvious and colorful representatives of a new race of humanity engaged in a new kind of interaction with its physical environment. For our technological triumphs are the creation of a dawning technological civilization, and the astronauts and their fellows not only represent this civilization but are helping to create it as well. They are not only the fruits of the labors of humanity but increasingly the arbiters of its destiny. Technological man, it would seem, has come of age.

This is considered one reality. But there is another.

By the end of 1945, the combined Allied armies had destroyed the military might of Nazi Germany and Imperial Japan. By then also, through a process that is increasingly a subject of dispute among historians, the major Allied powers—the United States and the Soviet Union—had come to regard each other no longer as friends but as potential and, in some areas, actual enemies. During the course of the war there had been two major innovations in military technology: the Germans had developed the V-1 and V-2 rockets and used them with devastating effect against Britain and the Allied installations in Europe; and a team composed largely of European scientists had enabled the United States to construct atomic bombs, which, dropped by conventional aircraft, destroyed Hiroshima and Nagasaki, resulting in loss of life from a single weapon unprecedented in human history.

The now hostile great powers become engaged in a scramble to combine the two new technologies of missilry and nucleonics, which had been important but not crucial in World War II, into a single weapons-system that would be decisive in any future war. Both made important use of scientists and technicians from defeated Germany to do so. The United States had the lead in nuclear weaponry, but the Russians soon captured the lead in certain aspects of rocket propulsion. As a result, the Russians were the first to send a satellite into space—the famous "Sputnik," man's first total conquest of the gravity that bound him to earth. This feat, which many reputable scientists had deemed unfeasible, was a by-product of a global struggle for political power between capitalist America and the heartland of Marxist socialism. Superiority in space technology was held to be an intrinsic part of over-all military superiority, and was intimately tied in with increasing advances in nuclear-weapons technology and the development of intercontinental ballistic missiles. The space race was part of the age-old drama—tragedy laced with farce—of international power politics.

Space technology had an important role to play in domestic politics as well. In the Soviet Union it enabled the political elite of the Communist party to keep their growing scientific community busy at congenial tasks and to utilize the productivity of their burgeoning industrial capacity without abandoning the garrison-state for a consumer-oriented economy with all its attendant economic instabilities and political uncertainties.

In the United States the space race performed even more necessary political functions. The United States had never completely pulled out of the Great Depression, even under the ministrations of the New Deal. World War II had given the economy an enormous boost. The postwar boom underwritten by repressed consumer demand was followed by the Korean war. Post-Sputnik technological rivalry with the Soviet Union insured that the economy could be kept going almost full blast without any major changes in the American economic or social system. Excess economic capacity could be siphoned off without distributing it among those who could not pay; the government would buy it and either blow it up or literally send it into outer space. The aerospace industry was a particular boon to the fast-growing and increasingly politically potent areas—Florida, California and the Southwest generally. The space race was controlled from Houston, and during the Johnson administration Texas moved from eleventh to second place among states in value of defense contracts received.

At the ASPA banquet at which the astronaut spoke, all about were signs that the millennium had not yet arrived, and man and his society had not broken with the past. Speaker and guests still ate the same convention roast beef; the technology that had sent man beyond earth's boundaries had yet to create a first-rate portable public-address system, as the narration accompanying the pictures of man's conquest of space demonstrated. It was obvious to even the most politically untutored that NASA-head Webb, a peculiarly American combination of visionary and con man, was using the occasion for old-fashioned political purposes. Aware that the American public seemed increasingly disinclined to see their money diverted from social services, deepfreezes and new cars to the conquest of the universe and man's next step up the evolutionary ladder, he hoped to convert his influential captive audience into supporters of a higher budget for NASA.

In writing of the Eichmann trial Hannah Arendt has spoken of the banality of evil.[1] The unparalleled horrors of the extermination camps had been enough to convince some Jewish theologians that the notion of the Jews as the chosen people of an omnipotent Yahweh was a vicious lie; such a God would be better dead or nonexistent.[2] How could one ascribe even a minor part of such earth-shaking atrocities to a bland nonentity like Eichmann? In the same way, how is it possible to ascribe a breakthrough in human destiny to NASA or its Soviet counterpart and their agents? Could this nice young man and his friends—with their demichic wives and scrubbed children straight out of *Better Homes and Gardens*, with their football and their scuba diving and their military-academy and engineering-school backgrounds; these thoroughly conventional and middle-class and essentially dull people, who would make such nice neighbors and such unlikely friends—could these be the supermen whom the race had struggled for a million years to produce? The mind boggles. One cannot but be struck that not only is evil often banal but glory also. The future would be like the present, only more so. The more things change . . .

Which of these realities is really real? To ask the question is to answer it. They both are. All that is real is real. This is the central fact that must be kept perpetually in mind if one is ever going to be able to understand the vast changes that are already beginning to transform human society, the dangers they portend and the triumphs they promise. Technological man is both myth and reality.

The Myth of the Future

Never before in human history has a civilization been so intoxicated with change. Most societies have been virtually static. Some, more self-conscious, have sought to return to a Golden Age that existed sometime in the past. Even the Renaissance, with all the forces for change that it loosed upon Western civilization, began as an attempt to revive the culture of classical antiquity.

At a fundamental cultural level, this intoxication with the future can be said to stem from the Christian element in Western civilization. Christianity provided a basis for believing that history had meaning, that events moved in a straight line: Creation, Redemption, the Last Judgment. This attitude superseded the cyclical view of the world, which the Greeks and Romans shared with the religions of the East, and which was in turn a sophistication of primitive man's acceptance of the cycle of the seasons and the unbreakable chain of birth-life-death and new life again.

The millenarian sects of the late medieval period revived the early Christian vision of the Second Coming and the Parousia. Combined with the belief in progress that stemmed from the post-Renaissance birth of modern science, this vision was later completely secularized into the creeds of democracy and, eventually, socialism.

But this belief that the future would be better and should be encouraged to come into being was implemented primarily through slow, piecemeal changes; or, in the case of major departures from existing practices, at least in logical additions to or extrapolations from what already existed. If engines could be improved, they were improved, buildings became bigger, transportation faster; new ideas and techniques were introduced and accepted if they seemed to be improvements on the old. Novelty and innovation were valued and accepted for their own sake certainly, especially in the United States, the example par excellence of a "forward-looking," "progressive" country. But despite abstract allegiance to progress, change for most men had to be self-justifying, and the future came piece by piece.

By contrast, contemporary culture literally has been invaded by the future. Sensitive men always have been troubled by the ethics of mortmain and have echoed Jefferson's belief that each generation must lead its own life, unexploited by dead men. But we increasingly live in a world in which the touchstone of cultural reference, and thus to some extent of political power, is the image of the future. Science fiction in the sixties has finally become a popular form of literature, rather than the province of a cult. The oft-remarked fact that American and Western science fiction generally, unlike that of the Soviet Union, has become increasingly pessimistic[3] does not seem to have disturbed the complacency of the general public, who approach science fiction primarily secondhand through motion pictures and television. For most men and women, the future is a promise to be fulfilled. Even fashions reflect the orientation toward tomorrow, and women dress not like their grandmothers but like their granddaughters. All of this poses the danger that when the future arrives no one will recognize it. Or, more seriously, that, although things will happen and time will pass, the future may in fact be prevented from ever coming into being.

That the new myth of the future—mythical because it combines elements of fantasy with new goals or meaning for life—is different in kind from the cult of progress of the nineteenth and early twentieth centuries, the musings of literary cranks and the idiosyncracies of artists[4] is evidenced by the fact that the future has become a serious and respectable object of study by culturally sophisticated and scientifically trained men. Indeed, it bids fair to become a new academic industry.

The science of the future, like so much in contemporary Western society, owes its origins to the military exigencies of the Cold War era. Like the theory of systems analysis, which is now vitally important to modern business and government and increasingly dominant in the social sciences, it issued from the womb of the RAND Corporation, forerunner of the "think tank" industry, which was set up by the United States Air Force to solve certain strategic problems. Air Force planners had to plan for aircraft that would fly and fight almost a decade later and to seek to incorporate in them features that would make them useful at that time. But to do this they had to make some predictions—to foresee what new materials would be available, what new defenses the enemy would develop, and what kind of warfare would exist—and all these predicted factors had to be interrelated and their mutual interdependences sorted out. Thus the techniques of systems analysis and the study of the future were born as twins.[5]

The Committee on the Year 2000, set up by the American Academy of Arts and Sciences under the leadership of the distinguished sociologist Daniel Bell, has been the most notable group concerned with the study of the future in the United States.[6] A similar group in England, with typical British understatement, focuses on the next thirty years, bringing its study up only to 1998. Herman Kahn and his associates in the "war game" have produced a massive tome, *The Year 2000*,[7] and the Foreign Policy Association has upped the ante by publishing a book entitled *Toward The Year 2018*.[8] In Europe the futurists are led by the noted political theorist Bertrand de Jouvenel and flourish particularly in Switzerland, France and the Netherlands.[9]

Precise techniques for prediction vary,[10] but all are especially concerned with predicting the future in terms of particular trends or events. All are aware that many predictable trends necessarily tend to cancel each other out: improved means of communication may decrease the pressure to improve transportation, for instance. All are convinced that certain basic trends will continue, in particular the growth of scientific knowledge and the growth of population, and therefore that humanity's choice is limited to a few possible "futures" depending on which current trends and predictable future events are dominant. But though certain technological, political and cultural trends are viewed as basic in determining what the remainder of the century will be like, the organized futurists tend to come up with sets of predictions that are eclectic in nature, futures in which a variety of often disparate and conflicting elements coexist.

Another group of prophets takes a fundamentally different tack, sometimes without wholly realizing it, since many of them are involved in the organized study of the future as well as in predicting on their own. This latter group seeks to find the key to the future in one single aspect of present trends, or a cluster of related aspects, and they view the future world as a new civilization based on a single integrating factor, as civilizations of the past were integrated by such institutions as feudalism or capitalism or such ideas as Christianity or liberalism. Thus Daniel Bell speaks of "post-industrial society"[11] based on the substitution of intellectual activity for primary production as the basis of economic life, and Zbigniew Brzezinski describes essentially the same purported phenomenon as the "technetronic age."[12] Many theologians speak of the age coming into being as "post-Christian" or marked by "the death of God," while Harvey Cox hails the advent of the "technopolitan" era.[13]

But for all these prophets of the future, technology is in some fashion or other the factor that is making the radically new civilization possible and necessary and providing its organizing principle. Some economists look upon the rise of technology and the technician as putting an end to traditional private capitalism; for J. K. Galbraith the "new industrial state" is dominated by the "technostructure."[14] Psychologist Kenneth Keniston finds the key to the alienation of many of today's brightest youth in their inability to meet the demands of the ego in a contemporary milieu that he refers to as "technological society."[15] Marshall McLuhan sees the new civilization as based on a single aspect of technology—the new electronic media, which he holds constitute not merely new methods of communication but a total new environment that will radically alter everything from politics to sexual behavior.[16] Jacques Ellul concludes that technology per se will determine the future; in Ellul's opinion we are entering into a new era of "technological society," wherein technology is no longer an instrument for pre-existing human purposes but has become an end in itself, controlling both men and their society.[17] All are agreed, however, that as a result of certain technological factors we are leaving the industrial era and bourgeois society behind and entering a radically new world. More than a decade ago a theologian who regarded with apprehension "the end of the modern world" even spoke of the coming of "technological man."[18]

Ideas have consequences. Millenarian ideas have a special kind of consequence. Those who believe that vast changes are about to occur can be pardoned for paying less attention to the minor, because passing, problems of the present. Religious believers who sought salvation in an afterlife have frequently been able to ignore worldly problems on the grounds that "this too will pass away." Granted their premises, they were correct in giving priority to what was more long-lasting and significant, even if this sometimes meant disregarding the immediate and temporary entirely. Myths about the future, which are after all in large part merely a secularization of religious expectations of an afterlife—the bringing of eschatology down to earth—have essentially the same effect as supernaturalism. Thus Marxian socialists with a belief in the eventual and necessary triumph of the revolution could be indifferent to day-to-day politics or might seek to manipulate them not in their own terms but in those of what they conceived to be the long-run meaning of history. This can be dangerous, as illustrated by the Communist equation of Nazism and decadent capitalism, which ended in the destruction of the German Communist movement in the 1930's. Sometimes the present has a vigorous life of its own.

Thus those who are convinced that a radical change is taking place in human society as a result of technological progress are often wont to denigrate the problems of the present, or at least to lead others to do so. If we are entering upon a new "epoch of universal technology,"[19] then the differences between the United States and the Soviet Union become insignificant. If the problem of the future is what to do with leisure in an age of automated affluence, then the apparent class struggle in the United States can be dismissed as of no long-run importance. Other problems are not so much dismissed as epiphenomenal as they are given new meanings that rob them of immediate political saliency. When one predicts that new technological advances will enable us to turn all the world into a garden, or to make the advanced nations so affluent that they can support the less developed out of their surplus, then the revolutionary ferment sweeping the Third World loses its importance. It is a mere growing pain of the new world civilization, and when the approaching scientific era realizes its potentialities, we will look back with amusement on those who thought that trade, tariffs and traditional technical assistance made a difference; figures such as Ho Chi Minh and Che Guevara will be as quaint as the Luddites.

Once one is intoxicated by the myth of the future—and whether one looks upon the future with hope or dread is irrelevant as long as one is transfixed by it—certain problems tend to disappear entirely. The Black Revolution in the United States and its counterparts elsewhere have no organic intellectual relationship to the coming of post-industrial society. It is true that automation has made the economic problems of the American Negro worse in the short run, but racial strife is as peripheral to the new vision of the future as national strife was to that of classical Marxism. Since the machine is color blind, any racial conflict that may occur in the coming technological era will necessarily be arbitrary and almost accidental, tragic perhaps, but peripheral to the main theme of future history.

This is not to say that the myth of the future is deliberately cultivated in order to divert attention from the day-to-day problems of the present—although there is a certain air of intellectual chic in dismissing such philosophies as Marxism, conservatism, or orthodox Christianity as *vieux jeu*. The futurists are by and large sensitive and moral men deeply concerned at a certain level of existence with today's mundane problems. But futurism has a natural tendency to disorient its adherents and sympathizers, focusing their attention on what is to come (in most cases with a certain presumed degree of inevitability) rather than on what is. If that were the only charge that could be leveled against it, any indictment would fall. For our society does have long-range problems, which, if not dealt with long before they become obviously pressing, may already have become insoluble. Would that we had been aware of the population explosion two generations ago. Would that we had predicted our problems of air pollution and urban decay before the automobile became basic to the American economy and culture! Those who see the future in advance should be looked upon as heroes.

But what if the future never comes? That is, what if the future is always more myth than reality? There is, we know, a natural human tendency to overanticipate as well as to fail to adjust to change. But the appearance of the first robin does not mean that one can abandon all sources of heat without danger of freezing. Nor does simple extrapolation make for sound prediction. The whaling industry grew rapidly for many years, just as the civil-rights movement once flourished. We must also beware of assuming that the advent of the new means the demise of the old. This sometimes seems to happen in the intellectual realm. Marx's rediscovery of the economic basis of politics (something which Aristotle after all knew) caused many to believe all life was economically determined. Freud shocked a rationalistic age by calling attention to the unconscious animal springs of human behavior, and since then many have held that all human behavior is subjective and irrationally determined. Yet reality may be far more complex—human life may be based on economic relationships and on the influence of infantile experience and on the Darwinian struggle for existence and on a broad-gauge rationality as well. The future will come into being, but the present will not die any more than the past has.

Existential Revolution and Social Inertia

Humanity today is on the threshold of self-transfiguration, of attaining new powers over itself and its environment that can alter its nature as fundamentally as walking upright or the use of tools. No aspect of man's existence can escape being revolutionized by this fundamental fact—all his self-consciousness that we call culture, his patterns of interaction that we call society, his very biological structure itself. At the same time there are certain patterns of human institutional and personal behavior that are almost as resistant to change as those of the lower animals and the social insects. Man is fundamentally oriented to scarcity, conflict, insecurity, fear, irrationality, self-centeredness and a host of social and cultural institutions that reflect these or seek to transcend the problems they are traditionally considered to pose. The juxtaposition of these two factors is not just an overwhelming intellectual paradox, nor is it simply a moral scandal. It poses both a danger and a hope of cosmic proportions.

In what sense is it meaningful to say that an existential revolution is taking place, that technological man is more reality than myth? To speak of reality in this context is to assume that the term itself has meaning, that there is some sense in which our perceptions of the world correspond to something "out there." Debating this question is a favorite and not completely useless occupation of philosophers, but for most of us we can act only as if our words and ideas had some objective meaning. It is less simple to assume that there are different levels of reality, yet our "common sense" seems to tell us that the invention of agriculture, the advent of Christianity, the liberation of atomic power were somehow events of profound significance, and not merely in terms of the numbers of persons directly affected. So, too, the transition from feudalism to capitalism is regarded as more important than the decline of the Hapsburgs and the rise of Prussia, the French Revolution as more significant than the freeing of Greece from the Ottomans. We know that beneath the surface of day-to-day events there is a beneath-the-surface, a larger context in which ordinary social and individual behavior takes place.

Since Darwin, we are all dimly aware that man was not always man, that there was a long process of ascent from something else, and that this was somehow marked by specific changes such as upright posture and the opposed thumb that were physical, and others—the development of speech, the use of tools and the discovery of fire—that were in a sense technological and social. But we have assumed that at a certain point in the distant past man became man and evolution stopped. Everything since then is of a lower order of significance in that human nature is fixed, and man's economic and political and cultural life, while admitting of change and perhaps great improvement, is fundamentally unchanging. Man is here and his relation to the world of nature, his place in it, is a given. All of his achievements, however great, are variations on a theme, incremental and in the last analysis not very important. He has always eaten vegetation and animals; used tools; constructed dwellings; lived in families, usually in the company of a relatively large group of other men; been ruled by a combination of persuasion, coercion and inertia; traded with others, whether in goods or services; amused himself, and sought to find meaning in life and to express it in cultural forms. With a fixed biological heritage, a limited choice among social forms and a limited control over his environment, he has gone on his way from birth to death. Death and Taxes—basic biological and social facts—are inevitable.

But from a more meaningful perspective on evolution, the above is simply not true. Man is still capable of fundamental change, since evolution has not come to an end. Biologically speaking, it is true that every newborn infant is a brother to the cave-man's child. In that sense there has been no change; "test-tube" babies will still be of the species *Homo sapiens*, and if Cro-Magnons or Neanderthals still existed presumably it would be possible for the "test-tube" men to interbreed with them. But this is not the whole story. Babies are born into society, and depend on it for their survival. Culture is part of the human inheritance even if it is not built into the genetic code. As a distinguished biologist puts it, in man there is "a fundamentally new sort of heredity, the inheritance of learning."[20] Changes in human culture can be changes so fundamental as to be of significance even on the evolutionary scale. Man can become a new kind of creature. This is the message of men such as Teilhard de Chardin, Julian Huxley and Sir Charles Sherrington: evolution is still taking place and man is aware of it and can consciously direct its course.

But what could take place in the realm of culture so fundamental as to alter the basic nature of the human animal? What discovery could rank with those forces that turned animal into man? No one thing, certainly. But a complex of events has altered the nature of man, the complex of discoveries and powers that we glibly speak of as modern technology. "Technology is altering life to its existential roots before our very eyes."[21] How? Simply by giving man almost infinite power to change his world and to change himself. In the words of Emmanuel Mesthene, director of the Harvard Program in Science and Technology, "We have now, or know how to acquire, the technical capability to do very nearly anything we want. Can we transplant human hearts, control personality, order the weather that suits us, travel to Mars or Venus? Of course we can, if not now or in five or ten years, then certainly in 25 or in 50 or 100."[22] The space race and atomic energy are not the most telling evidence for man's new existential position. More fundamental yet is what is going on in medicine and biology. "We cannot duplicate God's work," is a typical comment of the emerging new man, "but we can come very close."[23]

How close can man come? What is left to do to challenge his Creator? He must be able to create life out of non-living substances and to guide its development. Recent work on viruses and DNA brings him fairly close to that. He must be able to postpone death indefinitely. This he cannot yet do, but the existence of cryogenics (freezing bodies in the hope of reviving them after certain diseases have been conquered) is an index of how close some believe man has come. Actually, organ transplants may make the question meaningless. If the brain can be transplanted, especially if its contents can somehow be transferred to another, fresher brain, then death of the original body will have little meaning. Man is destined to be forever frustrated in not being able to create the world *de novo*; it is already there. But he is now close to being able to render the planet absolutely uninhabitable and perhaps to so skew its orbit as to cause it to be physically destroyed.

To the extent that man can do all the things that he can do and knows it, we are entitled to speak of the end of of the modern world and the advent of an existential revolution. For these new powers are not merely extensions of the old. The whole is greater than the sum of its parts, and absolute power over himself and his environment puts man in a radically new moral position. Throughout his history he has lived with certain concepts of freedom and identity. Freedom was doing what you wanted to do. You were restricted by other men or an intractable physical environment. But the degree to which other men could control you or restrict your freedom was limited by the fact that the environment limited their powers also. You lived in a society, an economy, a physical environment that was difficult to alter. If worst came to worst you could run away. You could hide. Or you could remain true to yourself to the stake. Identity, by the same token, was a limited problem. You were the result of a combination of circumstances—your childhood, your surroundings, your own desires. These might be determined by fate, but not by anyone else, certainly not by yourself.

In the era of absolute technology, freedom and identity must take on new meanings or become meaningless. Other men can change your society, your economy and your physical environment. Eventually, they will be able to force you to live in a world with neither trees nor oceans if they choose. Running and hiding become increasingly difficult. They can make you love them so that you need not go to the stake. They can alter your identity by controlling how you are brought up and what your experiences are; they can even program your children genetically in advance of birth. But perhaps more disturbing is the fact that you can do all these things yourself: you can change your appearance or even your sex, your moods and your memories, you can even decide what you want your children to look like. But if you can be whatever you want to be, how will you distinguish the "real" you from the chosen? Who is it that is doing the choosing?

Not all of these changes affecting the nature of freedom and identity are yet practicable, but all are implicit in the new powers being developed by modern technology. Not whether they can exist but how long it will be before these futures come into existence seems to be the only question. The fact that postmodern man knows that they are coming must already begin to alter his self-image and his actions. No, there is no doubt but that the era of the new man will soon be upon us. For the existential revolution is a reality. At the deepest level of human existence man as we have known him is on the verge of becoming something else.

Yet can this really be true? Men such as Hubert Humphrey and Richard Nixon still aspire to become President of the United States. The Flat Earth Society still holds meetings. The Dodgers continue to play, albeit in Los Angeles. Politicans are bribed by the Mafia, and schoolteachers complain about their pay. Television advertises candy and children quarrel over it. Books are banned in England as well as Boston. Muezzins still cry from their mosques, and the bush returns in triumph to the streets of Congolese towns. The stock market flourishes, as do fortunetellers and fundamentalist preachers. Dialectical materialism is still stuffed into the heads of Russian students, and Americans still vote against big government. The world we know is still as real as it ever was.

There are several senses in which one can think of realities as coexisting. One would be the situation in which differing worlds somehow coexist in the same universe without any points of contact save in abnormal or highly special circumstances, as in the relationship usually postulated between the natural and the supernatural. Such a dualism affords few difficulties since the interpenetration of the two realities is marginal or unpredictable.

There is another possibility. You may be on a hiking trip and return the next day to your base to find that nuclear war has broken out, most of the world has perished, and you will die the next day because of radioactive clouds coming your way. But everything about you, your clothes, the food or drink you have left, will be just as real as it ever was, made by men who may never have thought of the hydrogen bomb once in their lives. The missiles are in their silos as you read this. Such a dualism—between the routine of ordinary life and the possibility of unparalleled horror—is less manageable than the dualism of supernaturalism, since both realities exist within the same world-wide social system. Yet they still can be separated by most of us since one is immediate and the other, unless we are military or political decision-makers, is remote. Politics and economics must to some extent reflect the possibility of nuclear destruction, certainly more than they do that of the Last Judgment, but for most people most of the time the existence of atomic weapons is nothing they can or need take into account.

But the reality of present everyday life will continue into the era of the new man—is continuing already, for that era is already beginning—in a different fashion. The new civilization will exist side by side with the old, gradually re-placing it but never completely so, just as the Enlighten-ment never destroyed tradition. The survival power of old orders—their institutions, their ideas, their ruling classes—is simply enormous. Inertia is the most important factor in human society. Man is the animal who relinquishes noth-ing. He simply adds to what he already is and has.

This should not be surprising. Contrary to one's first impressions, evolution has destroyed very little. Newly dominant creatures shunted others aside, but few, save the dinosaurs, perished. The amoeba still exists, so do fish, in-sects, the lower animals. They are no longer the torchbear-ers of life, but most of them go about their business as if man did not exist. So, too, in human society there are found survivals of earlier societies and earlier types of men and cultures. Despite the world-wide triumph of industrial man, most humans are farmers living in villages even today. Most will be even after technological man (if he is allowed to come into existence) takes command.

What will this continuance of the old amidst the new look like? To some extent it will simply be a kind of superfi-cial social eclecticism. The world can exist as a crazy quilt of cultures—Amish and jet set side by side. Confusion seems destined to be a major feature of the world of tomorrow. Variety may predominate simply because of affluence. Since most people will not be needed to keep the produc-tive machinery going, they can be allowed to do what they please, to live not only as early-twentieth-century Ameri-cans but as self-created Bushmen if they choose. A wealthy civilization can afford its Hippies. The juxtapositions will be sometimes bizarre or tragic or sinister, and the result will be a culture of maximum disorientation and limited inte-grating power as far as its members are concerned. But it could be a viable one.

If social eclecticism were the only problem posed by

the failure of technological reality to triumph completely over social inertia, the future could be viewed with equanimity. But there are other possibilities. When one speaks of the advent of the new man on the existential level, one need not assume his triumph on the social level. Certainly the number of scientifically trained persons will increase and more and more thought will be given to the problems posed by man's new powers. But there is no guarantee that any of the fundamental realities of the social, economic or cultural systems will change. The new powers in man's possession may be in the hands of those motivated by greed, fear, superstition or the lust for power in the old sense. A heartless, cold and rational technological man is sometimes portrayed as the bogeyman of the future. Many hope that he may be induced to take on more of the humanistic virtues and use his physical powers in accordance with traditional moral codes. But what if he emerges as the thrall of the worst elements of the past? What if technology rather than becoming "autonomous" remains much as it is today, the tool of the salesman and the militarist? What if bourgeois civilization and its socialist counterparts remain dominant, and technology becomes merely another weapon in the arsenal of the drive for profit and power?

The prophets of the new reality may be right in stressing the vast powers available to the new society, but they may be wrong in estimating how different the new society will be. Modern man is far from slaying the beast within; why assume that the man of the future will be a completely new creature? What if the new man combines the animal irrationality of primitive man with the calculated greed and power-lust of industrial man, while possessing the virtually Godlike powers granted him by technology? This would be the ultimate horror.

2

Technology
and Industrial Man

Technology and Human Culture

Man is a technological animal, and technological change is the fundamental factor in human evolution. This is simply another way of saying that man is a cultural animal. Other animals have technologies (beavers construct dams and birds build nests), and they sometimes possess a rudimentary form of culture as well, passing on acquired knowledge from generation to generation (rats, for instance, teach their young about the new poisons developed by man). But only for man are tools and cultures central factors in his existence. Only man has evolved culturally to the point where he consciously can alter radically his physical environment and his own biological make-up.[1]

Yet to say that technological change is the central factor defining human existence is not to say that technology is the one autonomous, independent variable in human civilization. Technologies are created and used by men. Those who, like the French social critic Jacques Ellul, hold that we are becoming a technological society defined by the fact that technology has become an end in itself, subject to no external controls, are plainly mistaken. For we have the technological and scientific knowledge to eliminate grinding poverty, prevent the pollution of our environment and make the world generally a far better place in which to live, yet we do not do so. The new powers that man possesses are capable of many uses. Some of these uses are contradictory: biological and medical research can be used to produce germ warfare or to cure disease. And some of them, in practice at least, are mutually exclusive: the resources devoted to the space race cannot be used to create a "Great Society."

Indeed, the central danger facing humankind in the latter part of the twentieth century lies not in the autonomy of technology or in the triumph of technological values but in the subordination of technology to the values of earlier historical eras and its exploitation by those who do not understand its implications and consequences but seek only their own selfish personal or group purposes. The new man with his vast powers is coming into existence as the servant of neoprimitive man. The sorcerer's powers are in the hands of a vain and foolish apprentice and disaster threatens.

The idea that human culture is dependent on its technological foundations is at first startling or even offensive, yet reflection will show this to be as obvious as it is undeniable. Chartres would have been impossible without the craft of the stonemason; the discoveries of Galileo, which revolutionized man's view of his position in the universe, could never have been made without the skill of the lens grinder; the glories of Bach would not exist save for the manufacturers of musical instruments. All human societies —their economic and political structures and their intellectural cultures as well—are dependent upon their technological foundations. Alterations in ideas can bring about alterations in technologies just as changes in technology can cause us to change our ideas. But technology has perhaps something of an edge. We cannot yet do everything we can conceive of, though we are fast becoming convinced that anything we can imagine we will be able to do in some not-too-distant future.

The fact that technology sets limits to man's activities and in large measure defines his existence is no contemporary or recent phenomenon, although the scope of the powers bestowed upon him is. From the very outset of his existence man has been dependent on technology; in fact it could be argued that technology is what has made man man.

Friedrich Engels contended that "the generation of fire by friction gave man for the first time control over one of the forces of nature and thereby separated him forever from the animal kingdom."[2] Many anthropologists hold that the use of tools, made possible largely by man's opposed thumb, stimulated the physical development of the brain, and that the use of tools was both a cause and an effect of bipedal locomotion. Lewis Mumford, a contemporary critic of the role of technology in society, has argued against this view, holding that speech and man's consciousness of his dream life were more important than his ability to use tools in setting him apart from other animals and in providing the basis for human culture.[3] Others have viewed man's sexual habits as forming the basis for a distinctly human society and eventually of culture.[4] Actually, none of these factors acted in isolation. In the words of one anthropologist, "Tools, hunting, fire, complex social life, speech, the human way and the human brain evolved together to produce ancient man of the genus *homo* about half a million years ago."[5]

Similarly, throughout human history up to the present transitional period, technology has been a necessary but not wholly sufficient cause of the rise and fall of civilizations; technology conditions civilizations and explains much about them, but never completely determines them or acts in isolation or independently of human choosing. This ambivalent relationship of technology and culture goes far to explain the various controversies among social scientists about the relative importance of technology.

Many historians have been inclined to regard technology as of only incidental importance[6] and until recently have largely ignored its influence. Other students of society, such as the noted American sociologist W. F. Ogburn,[7] have, in effect, been technological determinists for whom technology controlled social forms and cultural norms. The anthropologist Leslie White states explicitly that "social systems are in a very real sense secondary and subsidiary to technological systems. . . . The technology is the independent variable, the social system the dependent variable."[8] Though Marxists are less clear on this point, it is plain that Marxist economic determinism is in reality a technological determinism, since control over the means of production —the basis for all economic and social systems, according to Marx—is ultimately a function of the changing character of the means of production.

Clearly—whatever else he is—man is a technological animal, and technology is fundamental to his humanity. But technology is more than toolmaking. As Daniel Bell, in speaking of the role of technology in the contemporary world, has argued, technology is "not simply a 'machine,' but a systematic, disciplined approach to objectives, using a calculus of precision and measurement and a concept of system. . . ."[9] With little alteration in substance, Bell's words could be applied to the agricultural and administrative technologies of ancient civilization. Irrigation systems, military formations and the organization of tax collection are as much technologies as are ways of building ships or bridges or weapons. In so broadly conceiving technology there is obviously the danger of falling into the trap of Ellul and other writers for whom technology is technique and everything is technique and therefore all human actions are technological. We can avoid this pitfall if we think of technology as a self-conscious organized means of affecting the physical or social environment, capable of being objectified and transmitted to others, and effective largely independently of the subjective dispositions or personal talents of those involved. Thus an opera singer exhibits "technique" but is not really utilizing a technology.

Agriculture and Civilization

The dating of the beginnings of agriculture is a matter of some dispute among students of prehistory, but it seems clear that by about 7000 B.C. in the uplands of the Middle East men were already living in settled agricultural communities. The consequences for humanity of the new technology were immense. The food surpluses created by agriculture and the problems and possibilities that these surpluses created provided the basis for specialization of labor, writing, the city, social classes, the state and civilization as we know it. These surpluses also made possible the first great population explosion in human history, raising human population to a new plane in a fashion not repeated until our own industrial era. By about 5000 B.C., according to one eminent archeologist, all the requirements for the birth of civilization were present; yet it did not occur. Why? Professor Mellaart suggests that "before further economic or technical progress could take place, certain political improvements were necessary—a complex social hierarchy . . . ; systematic urbanization; strong political control and adequate concentration of economic resources."[10] In other words, technology by itself could not create the conditions necessary for its own full use and development; new social and political forms were required.

The first great agricultural civilizations appeared in the fourth millennium B.C. in the valleys of the major rivers of the Old World—the Tigris and the Euphrates, the Yangtze and the Nile and the Indus—where rich alluvial soil and a plentiful supply of water favored population growth, while the need to obtain additional arable land through drainage put a premium on co-operation and social organization. The development of metallurgy encouraged some specialization of labor, and the lack of locally available metal, stone or wood on the alluvial plains necessitated extensive regular trading relations. The increasing complexity of society made necessary a co-ordinating and record-keeping bureaucracy and resulted in the development of writing. The technology upon which the river-valley civilizations were based—an extensive system of drainage and irrigation —was as much social as physical. These irrigation systems were closely associated with centralized states, so much so that a prominent historian developed the concept of "oriental despotism"—a technologically determined political form that he held to be the inevitable result of the need for close co-ordination in societies dependent on irrigation.[11]

Historical evidence seems to indicate that this thesis is overstated both in its application to the Old World and to the empires of Central and South America.[12] But it serves as a useful reminder that, while technology does not completely control politics, it can set limits to them and makes certain practices and institutions more feasible and efficient, and therefore more likely, than others. Man can buy his freedom from the effects of technology, but only at a price, sometimes at a price so high he may be unwilling or unable to pay it.

The civilizations of the ancient Near East reached heights of development that in some respects were not equaled until our own time. Not only were standards of living improved despite vast increases in population and systems of government created that enabled civil peace and settled law to prevail over large areas, but with affluence and peace came a degree of social flexibility and cosmopolitanism that favored the development and circulation of new ideas and even permitted the growth of a certain amount of individualism and secularism.

The civilizations of Greece and Rome, at least at the technological level, represented something of a regression from this earlier period.[13] It is true that science as we know it today had its origins in the speculations and experiments of the Ionian Greeks, and, more fundamentally, it was Greek philosophy that made the crucial distinction between nature—that which is universal—and convention—the ways of particular tribes or races—that laid the groundwork for the very concept of science based on universal laws.[14] But the social system of Greece, resting as it did on slavery, provided little impetus for the development of machines to save labor, and even agricultural technology was allowed to decline as Greek commerce, bolstered by military imperialism, made cheap supplies of grain from abroad available. The antitechnological bias of Hellenic civilization is symbolized by the fact that the famous aeropile —a primitive steam engine invented by Hero of Alexandria[15] —remained a toy. What might subsequent human history have been like had there been the motivation or inclination to put it to practical use? The fact that technology has not been autonomous and all-prevailing throughout history is nowhere better illustrated than by the refusal of the Greeks to put much of their theoretical knowledge to practical use.[16]

The Romans, by contrast, respected technology and were responsible for the development and utilization of many advances, particularly in the field of what might be called civil engineering. Roman roads, bridges and aqueducts are still in use today. Such amenities as central heating and running water were commonplace in Roman cities; it was not until the eighteenth century that any European city again offered such a high standard of comfort and technical proficiency. But Roman technology—in physical matters as well as in their elaborate systems of law and administration—was purely empirical and *ad hoc*, uninformed by any basic scientific principles. Parts of the Greek heritage of speculation and search for universal law were retained, but the Romans did little to extend it.

The causes of the decline of Rome have been a favorite subject for historical debate for generations, but it seems safe to say that social and economic decline led to eventual military and political decline. The growth of slavery and serfdom resulted in lessened agricultural capabilities and forced military dependence on mercenaries. Rome could no longer support the large numbers of armored horsemen needed to defend the Empire against the Germans and the Huns. The Empire, at least in the West, began to crumble, leaving fear and barbarism in its wake. Arts were lost, administrative efficiency declined, cities were gradually abandoned, and darkness seemed to be settling over the earth as men heard wolves howling in forests that in their fathers' generation had been fields.

Yet the extent and duration of the decline during the Dark Ages can easily be exaggerated. European society became decentralized, and many skills were lost. The continuing backwardness of the West relative to the Near and Far East, where technology, the arts and ordered government flourished, was accentuated. But recovery was not long in coming. Spurred in part by the work of the monastic orders, new discoveries were made and new techniques developed, with wood a major material and wind, water and animals as the principal energy sources.

Medieval civilization, despite its otherworldly pretensions, was based on two very mundane technological factors. One was the heavy moldboard plow which, together with the oxen to pull it and the harness that made their use practicable, conquered the dark, moist and extremely fertile soils of the North, making it possible to support a large population with a rising standard of living. This new agricultural technology underwrote the passage of the scepter of military and political power from the lands along the Mediterranean to northwestern Europe. The second pillar of medieval civilization was the stirrup and associated gear, such as horseshoes, apparently taken over from the Ural-Altaic peoples to the east. These made possible a cavalry effective enough to repulse nomadic invaders. Since a relatively large amount of land was needed to support a horse, and since the livery, weapons and time for training in the necessary skills of the new warfare required access to scarce resources, power passed to the hands of a small landed aristocracy. Feudalism was born, and upon the new technological base the edifice of chivalry was erected.

The Coming of Industrial Man

The story of the rise of modern industrial civilization is really the story of how modern man came to be what he is—or at least what he was until just yesterday. It is, accordingly, a more-than-thrice-told tale, and each one who tells it does so in terms of his own special perspective and interests.[17] Our concern here is twofold. First, we wish to discover the role played by science and technology in the shaping of all aspects of the new era—social and cultural as well as economic. Second, we want to isolate those technological elements underlying industrialism that combined have raised the position of technology in civilization to a "critical mass." It is this "critical mass" that presently threatens to explode the civilization created by industrialism so that humanity is left with the choice of creating a new civilization or else living—or perhaps dying—in chaos.

The material roots of industrial civilization reach well back into the Middle Ages. Mining provided both the sinews for the coming revolution and its prototype. Originally highly developed by the Greeks, mining in the Middle Ages depended on the technology of the past and sought the

aid of the renascent sciences. Closely associated throughout history with war and slavery, it presaged the havoc that
industrialism was to bring to the medieval order. Sharp
decline or improvement in the capacity of the mines to
produce precious metals led to economic depression or
growth. The mines provided the weapons and missiles that
destroyed the military basis of chivalry and established the
modern nation-state. And the rationalization and mechanization of work in the mines foreshadowed the labor problems of the Industrial Revolution; indeed, so bad did conditions become in seventeenth-century Scotland that miners
were reduced to literal slavery.[18]

But the real roots of industrial civilization lay in men's
minds, not in their techniques or artifacts. Europe would
not in a few centuries have surpassed the technological
lead of the East and conquered the planet simply through
the piecemeal growth of empirical knowledge and practical
technology based on accident and convenience. The Industrial Revolution was intertwined with an intellectual and
spiritual revolution. Just as the technology of industrial society has provided the jumping-off point for the technology
of postindustrial society, just as industrial man is both the
elder brother and the father of emergent technological man,
so the intellectual foundations of industrial civilization also
provide part of the intellectual underpinnings of technological civilization.

Virtually all living creatures display the kind of behavior that can be labeled "curiosity." Even the humble
amoeba explores its surroundings, and not all of this curiosity can be reduced to the search for food or other ulterior
ends. Most living creatures, especially mammals, engage in
activity that can be called play, doing things simply for
their own sake rather than to fulfill other needs. All living creatures seek power in some sense—if only the power
to protect themselves against their environment and against
the power of others.

Man shares all these attributes and in addition has one of his own: he seeks moral absolutes. Most societies try to justify their actions by references to some being, laws or end outside the acts themselves and usually outside their everyday lives. The foundation of industrial civilization was a fusion of all these drives—curiosity, play, morality, all were merged with the drive for power. Knowledge is power, Francis Bacon said, and, according to Hobbes, power is the goal of all human activity. Industrial civilization is based on the development of science primarily and technology virtually exclusively as instruments to increase man's power over his physical environment and over his fellow humans in order to satisfy his basic animal needs for food, clothing and shelter and his lust for power over things and men.

There is a sense, of course, in which knowledge is power even if it is never used to "do" anything; and in some sense all technologies alter the environment. But knowledge as contemplation has always been valued, and there is a difference between the technology of the bulldozer, which tears down forests, and that of the sailor, who manipulates wind and water to reach his destination, leaving them unchanged in his wake. Industrial man in his purest manifestations—and, of course, few individuals incarnate his spirit this completely—would restrict knowledge and technology to what can be used; for him play is only a preparation for work, and work—effort used to do or make something—is both the exclusive means and the sole end of moral conduct. The intellectual foundations of industrial civilization are to be found in the triumph of the attitude that work is the only proper end of man, and that science, technology and even morality should serve that end alone.[19]

Rivers of ink have been expended on the alleged role of Puritanism in the rise of capitalism, and the whole question of the "Protestant Ethic."[20] Yet not merely Puritanism or Protestantism but Western Christianity itself is at the root of the new manipulative, domineering attitude toward the world that has been the fundamental intellectual precondition of the rise of industrialism.

The dominant religion of the medieval West was radically different from paganism and most Eastern religions in having an historical dimension. The Creation had occurred and, later, the Redemption. The Last Judgment and the end of the world lay in the future. Alone among the major world religions, and in special contrast to those of the East, Christianity postulated that the world was going somewhere, that the future was not simply an unchanging or cyclically repeating replica of the past. The idea of progress—central to the development of science and the modern world—had its roots in Christian eschatology. We need not trace here the process by which, beginning with its reinterpretation by Joachim of Floris (1132–1202), it was progressively secularized—above all by the French Revolution, Comte and Marx—until in our own time it has been remysticized by Teilhard de Chardin.

With a sense of history came a new emphasis on time and its "value"—an essential ingredient of technological civilization. The medieval monks, with their rigid ordering of their workdays in accordance with the hours of their prayer cycle (the "Office"), not only stimulated the development of the clock but could be said to be the first modern men.[21]

Christianity provided a second impetus to the new revolution in ideas because, as Whitehead has noted,[22] the Christian notion of God, as exemplified in the mainstream of medieval Scholasticism, held that the universe and, indeed, God himself were rational, governed by universal laws capable of being grasped by man. Modern science is based on the conviction, in Einstein's words, that "God doesn't play dice with the universe."[23] Though some hostility existed between religion and science from the earliest days—especially because of the worldly motivations behind science and its undermining of certain traditional religious beliefs—the Western religious tradition was clearly more conducive to the development of science than were those of the East, as subsequent history has demonstrated.

Also implicit in Christianity was a basically hostile attitude toward nature. Primitive man was part of nature, and for him nature was holy. Pagan religions were virtually always animistic. Christianity's view of nature, especially in the Middle Ages, was ambivalent. From Judaism it retained the idea of a God outside of and above nature, and the Bible emphasizes the transcendence of the holy. At the same time early Christianity was always torn—between Scripture and natural law, between the transcendence of God and His radical otherness and the belief that God was the creator and that He revealed Himself in His creation. The eventual resolution of this conflict—hardly a neat one even to this day—was the idea that creation was a gift of God to man, to be used by him. Use meant exploitation, and eventually manipulation and even destruction. For nature had no claims against man, man was nature's superior. Though the influence of Greek and other pagan traditions remained strong, and men such as St. Francis of Assisi saw God as immanent as well as transcendent, as time passed Christianity, especially in its Protestant forms, provided a stimulus and a justification for the dethronement of nature and the exaltation of the power strivings of mankind.

The contribution of the early reformers to the assault on nature had several aspects. Calvinism, with its doctrine of predestination, led to the gospel of work, wherein men saw in earthly success a sign that they were spiritually worthy of salvation. Lutheranism led to a radical devaluation of earthly concerns at the same time that it offered no way of escaping them. Protestantism generally, with its emphasis on Scripture and its revulsion against the spirit of the Renaissance, gave the final blow to any possibility that natural law could form the basis of a continuing respect for the

harmony of nature. Nature was to be conquered, not
merely because it was there, but because it was somehow
under Satan's spell, and all natural philosophy was pagan
vanity.

The rise of science and technology was inseparable
from the rise of the modern nation-state, the two drives for
power went hand in hand. With the revival of Roman law
came a renewed interest in rational public administration,
and new technologies of human management came into being side by side with new machines and weapons. Paradoxically, the absolutist state was in some ways more democratic than its predecessors. At the same time that quality
was being reduced to differences in quantity in the speculations of scientists and philosophers, it was realized that
even the humble were a natural resource that could be
put to the service of kingly power. A nascent capitalism
fitted in nicely, since it could provide the masses with a
higher standard of living and the monarchs with the sinews
of national power.

The distinguished economic historian John U. Nef
makes a convincing case for rejecting the chronological
conventions originating with the elder Arnold Toynbee's
famous lectures posthumously published in 1884. He places
the beginnings of the Industrial Revolution in the period
1570–1640[24] since during this era the British economy was
already leaning heavily on industrial production of beer and
tobacco. The emphasis was on producing for the general
population, not merely for a select few, as in the handicraft
era. Both capital investment and technological ingenuity,
Nef holds, was oriented toward "production for the sake of
quantity."[25] Indeed, he writes, "the essense of industrial
civilization is found . . . in a quantitative approach to production and on mathematical considerations as of primary
importance in science."[26]

This new drive to conquer the world, to pry loose its
secrets and use them for political power and economic

growth led first to an increasing regard for science and technology and eventually to deliberate government sponsorship of them in order to promote national power. The Renaissance was initially antiscientific. Men looked to the masters of old for their models rather than to the world itself. But this soon changed. Seeking to paint realistically, the artist was forced to study anatomy; seeking to build in the classical manner, the architect was forced to study physics.

It was soon realized that existing knowledge in these and other areas was inadequate and that many generally held beliefs were simply false. Science had to begin again in a new manner. The new masters of knowledge took the artist as their example (many were also artists themselves) and, in effect, sold their knowledge to patrons bent on power. Leonardo da Vinci was an exception in withholding some ideas—like that for a submarine—lest they lead to social distress.[27] By contrast, the Quaker mathematician Benjamin Robbins (1707–1751) had no compunctions about turning his knowledge to the service of ballistics and war. But this was not enough. Though free-lance scientists could be pressed into the service of the state, the quest for knowledge itself had to be scientifically organized. At the beginning of the industrial era men already had hit on the idea that Alfred North Whitehead held to be the greatest invention of the industrial era, "the invention of invention" itself.[28]

Initially, Elizabethan England, despite what its philosophers and intellectuals might say, was antiscientific and frowned upon technological innovation that threatened to disrupt the planned society of mercantilism. Cardinal Richelieu of France went so far as to have an inventor who kept pestering him with tales of a steam engine jailed as a magician. But gradually this attitude changed. A major breakthrough came when England adopted its first patent law in 1623, an example the United States followed as soon

as it became independent. The Royal Society was founded
in England in 1660, beginning a tradition of gentlemen-
scientists that was carried on in America by such men as
Franklin and Jefferson. Not only to be a scientist but to
dabble in technology was considered one of the marks of
the cultured man in the English-speaking world. This emphasis on amateurism led to decay of the Royal Society,
however, and British science and technology were never
organized to the extent that these endeavors were elsewhere. Great Britain's scientific and industrial head start
masked this failure for centuries; only in the twentieth century have its full consequences become apparent.

Not in Britain, home of the Industrial Revolution, but
in America and the Continent were science and technology
organized in the fashion most characteristic of the industrial era. The attitude of revolutionary France toward science was ambivalent; science represented the Enlightenment, but scientific eminence represented a superior status
that its new egalitarianism could not recognize. "The republic has no need of savants," reputedly said a citizen as
a leading scholar was led to the guillotine.[29]

When Napoleon came to power he leaned heavily on
science and technology, organizing both research and
training so that knowledge of whatever kind, not merely in
the physical sciences but in such fields as geography and
history as well, could be put at the service of the state. The
grandes écoles that stand at the pinnacle of French academic life, especially the École Polytechnique, are monu-
ments to his policy. But political strife and intellectual
conservatism caused France to allow its lead to evaporate.
The political elite that came to power with De Gaulle in
1958—often referred to with some justice as Technocrats—
were in many cases graduates of the Polytechnique or possessed other scientific training, and they struggled with
considerable success to overcome this lag. Technology and
science are heavily subsidized and well organized in con-

temporary France, and much of French economic nationalism stems from a desire to preserve its independent technological apparatus.[30]

It was thus not the nations that were the early leaders
of modern science, but romantic Germany and the plebeian
United States, that organized technology and won the
prize of industrial domination in the early twentieth century. Prussia, a sandy and poor minor dukedom, was transformed into a major European power by the careful organization and utilization of what resources it possessed. As it
extended its control over Germany, the same techniques of
organization—including the organization of knowledge—
were made the basis of the national effort. German industry
was subsidized and protected by the state. Under Bismarck and his successors the factory was looked upon as a
battlefield and the industrialist as a field commander. German industry emphasized organized research, especially in
the increasingly important chemical industries, in contrast
to the situation elsewhere where invention took place on a
haphazard basis, often with little thought about commercial
applications. In due course the professionalism of their technologists and management enabled the Germans to surpass
Britain and France.

The United States only slowly began to organize for
technological mastery. During the nineteenth century, public support for science—governmental or private—was negligible and the tradition of the individualistic tinkerer prevailed, with science and technology going their separate
ways. America did have the advantage of a vast internal
market, so discoveries once made could be exploited more
readily than in smaller states. But perhaps its greatest advantage was the harsh natural environment of the mid-
western and intermountain regions, where settlers had to
adjust to conditions radically different from those of Europe or the more temperate and well-watered eastern states.
As in later assaults on the depths of the oceans and outer

space, the pioneers who tamed the Great Plains or the "Great American Desert" (as much of the West was then aptly called) required organized technology to aid and sustain them, and, despite their individualistic pretensions, farmers, ranchers and miners turned to the government for help. The Department of Agriculture, established in 1862, was in many ways the first modern large-scale research organization. The United States Geological Survey, established in 1879, was the remnant of a plan advanced by the American scientist Wesley Powell for the scientific exploitation of the Rocky Mountain West, a plan thwarted by the political power of land speculators.[31]

But government was not alone for long in the field of organized technology. American private industry (again, as in Germany, the new chemical and electrical industries in particular) placed great emphasis on organized research. Industries and individuals founded such institutions as Carnegie Tech, the Smithsonian and the Massachusetts Institute of Technology, and subsidized science in those older institutions willing to co-operate. The government supported research in "agriculture and the mechanical arts" through a multitude of land-grant colleges. The term "scientist" was coined by William Whewell in England early in the nineteenth century,[32] the term "technology" by the German Johann Beckmann in 1772.[33] But thousands of men—the advance guard of legions of hundreds of thousands—uninterested in the origins of these terms or in the distinction between them, quietly came together, organizing and working.

Contrary to a popular contemporary myth, organized government aid to science in the United States was not simply a product of war, and commercially sponsored research even less so. Yet war was important. American industry had been mobilized for World War I by the War Industries Board, but organized science, represented by the National Research Council, had played only a limited role. Essentially the war was fought with the tools and materials available at its outset. In sharp contrast, World War II saw the creation of a National Defense Research Committee, the Office of Scientific Research and Development, and eventually, of course, the Manhattan project, which created the atomic bomb. World War II also radically affected the outlook of scientists. Whatever their technical skills, our technologists and scientists were new to thinking of their work in terms of military and social power, and their social application of their skills was amateurish. But Hiroshima went a long way toward changing this. Hiroshima is often spoken of as the scientists' equivalent of the apple in the Garden of Eden, the eating of which ends innocence by imparting a knowledge of good and evil. Certainly it gave many scientists a new sense of social responsibility, and in so doing has had an important influence in advancing mankind's increasing awareness of its own powers, an awareness crucial to the advent of technological man.

The Nature of Industrial Society

Civilizations are based on the interaction of technology and human values. We have examined the values that underwrote the rise of industrial civilization—the treatment of nature as simply an object to be exploited for the satisfaction of human desires, the emphasis on quantity as a key to the true and a measure of the good, the valuation placed upon knowledge as a source of power and the conscious organization of the pursuit of knowledge as part of the quest for power. But what kind of technology was associated with these new values, what new powers did it give to man? Only if we understand the ways in which industrial civilization differed from its predecessors as a result of technological change can we hope to understand what technological changes now taking place may be on the way to transforming industrial society into a new civilization and to replacing its central symbolic figure, industrial man, with a new type, technological man.

There is one central feature that distinguished industrial society from all previous societies—its power source. Industrial society was based on the discovery and utilization of new sources of energy found in limited concentrations on the planet that enabled men to do vastly more work than could be done before. This work normally took the form of the production of goods, that is, the alteration of physical substances found in nature to make them useful to man. The concentration of the new energy sources combined with the existing technologies of production gave birth to the twin features of centralization and standardization. Thus, in a typical case, coal found in England would be used to produce energy to drive machines guided by men or women that transformed cotton into cloth, or iron into steel and thence into automobiles. This activity normally took place in a factory, and was called mass production.

Everything else is secondary in delimiting the uniqueness of the industrial system. Men had worked together under direction in workshops before, but without so much power available. New sources of energy made possible incremental improvements in the speed and economy of transportation and communication, but these were secondary. What was basic to the new order was the use of fossil fuels to perform work in factories. When new sources of power are widely utilized or when our present power sources are used primarily for ends other than the production of physical things the industrial system will be on its way out.

Historians differ as to when industrialism was born because it was not an overnight process but took shape within the technology and society of the earlier feudal and agrarian civilizations. One could easily speak of "creeping industrialism." Similarly, many of the factors leading to its radical transformation are already at work within industrial civilization and are sometimes therefore erroneously identified with it.

The mass-production system known as industrialism would have been impossible without earlier revolutions, most notably the agricultural revolution. "It was the turnip, not the spinning jenny, which is the father of the industrial revolution," one economist writes.[34] But though an agricultural surplus large enough to permit the growth of a large population, part of which could be put to work in factories, is a necessary, it is hardly a sufficient, cause for industrialization. So, too, the revolutions in transportation and communication that preceded and accompanied the Industrial Revolution were important factors in its success. After 1789, transportation in England was transformed by the development of a new type of horse-drawn coach, which together with all-weather roads dramatically reduced the time it took to travel from place to place. Canals also played a role. The railroad was vital to the full flowering of industrialization and so was the steamship, but both were dependent on the new energy sources. One could even argue that the institution of Negro slavery helped provide the capital on which the Industrial Revolution was based. But none of these things, taken together or singly, could have produced industrial society without the new sources of energy.

All work requires the expenditure of energy. Before work can be done energy must be available in a form suitable to perform it. Animals and men convert food into energy that can move their muscles and eventually pull plows, lift logs, plant seeds or carve stone. Man for most of his existence has been dependent on the energy available from human and animal sources, derived ultimately from the food they consume. He has seen wind and water move things, and has harnessed their energy through sail and mill, and has even made marginal use of the sun to dry food or other objects. The discovery of fire gave him limited access to the energy locked up in wood and earth and coal, but it was neither efficient nor easy to control. The great breakthrough came when man discovered how to convert heat directly into mechanical energy, to make burning things work for him.

This discovery, as we have seen, was first made in Hellenic Egypt and probably has been made elsewhere in human history. But the basis of industrial civilization was its rediscovery in England and its large-scale commercial utilization in the early eighteenth century. Thomas Newcomen's pump of 1712 and James Watts's steam engine of 1769 mark a new era. First, coal was converted to steam and then into mechanical energy and productive work. Later, coal was converted to steam and then to electrical energy and work; and eventually falling water or the tides were converted into electrical energy and work. Oil, too, notably through the medium of the internal-combustion engine, was used to perform work, especially in moving vehicles. But important as oil and hydroelectric power were eventually to become, the foundation of the Industrial Revolution was coal and steam.

From this circumstance stem virtually all of the major characteristics of industrial civilization—economic, political and cultural. First of all, the new sources of energy were not equally distributed beneath the earth's surface. Coal was found in some countries and not others. Coal could not lead to industrialization without the will and skill to use it, but without coal, modern industry was impossible. As steel replaced wood as a material for making things because of its intrinsic qualities and greater amenability to mass-production processes, iron ranked with coal as a strategic resource, since iron was what one used coal to transform. Iron, like coal, was found in some places and not in others. This meant that nations such as Great Britain and the United States had an early advantage in industrialization. By the time oil and then hydroelectric power became important the pattern of political power was already fixed. Oil emphasized American strength, but it did not make major powers of Venezuela or Saudi Arabia.

Since coal was costly to transport, industry grew up where the coal was—the Midlands, western Pennsylvania, the Ruhr. This led to concentration of industrial activity within, as well as among, nations. Men had to work close to their source of energy so as to utilize it efficiently. This led to a concentration of people at work and, given existing transportation facilities, to residential concentration. Not all urbanization directly reflected industrial activity—many large cities were trading centers rather than centers of primary production—but men and women were drawn from the fields into factories and warehouses and into cities. Coal meant centralization as well as industrialization, centralization nationally and internationally.

Along with centralization of the work process came standardization of the products of industry. Mass production would have been both physically and economically impossible had not the work to be done been broken down into small segments, each of which could be performed by a machine or part of a machine guided or supervised by relatively unskilled labor. How much standardization actually was technologically necessary to industrial society and how much actually took place are complex problems. The assembly line that produced the early Ford automobiles—the symbol of the new era—was more an abstract model of the apotheosis of the new way of work than a typical example of man at work in the new era. A substantial part of the work force remained highly skilled, and machines, often extremely versatile, were available in a bewildering variety. Whole segments of industry were standardized only to a very limited degree; the construction industry to this day remains semichaotic. Many persons held jobs such as driving or maintaining locomotives or trucks that required a substantial degree of autonomy and individual response, and hordes of workers continued to man the service industries.

As time went on, end products became less standardized: today the American automobile industry provides a vast choice of models, colors and accessories to its customers. But it was not without reason that the worker represented by Charlie Chaplin in *Modern Times*—a bewildered man striving to adjust to the discipline of the machine—became an archetypical figure. Standardization may not have been universal or perhaps even technologically essential, but a high degree of it was basic to the new economic way of life.

With standardization came hierarchy. The large amounts of capital needed to compete successfully in mass-production industries and to take advantage of the savings in costs that standardization and centralization brought meant fewer men could be owners of industry, and these owners, of course, exercised their authority in the same ways men of power have always used in dealing with their subordinates or their possessions. But, in addition to this, a standardized work process demanded a high degree of centralized control and co-ordination. Failure to live up to instructions could throw the whole production process out of kilter; human cogs could not be permitted to slip any more than mechanical ones. Even when owners relinquished much of their authority to hired managers, the principle remained that work was directed from the top. Otherwise standardization and mass production would have been impossible.

What was true of economics was also true of politics. In nations where the traditional aristocratic or monarchic distribution of power continued into the industrial era, political life was hierarchical and run from the top down. Medieval Europe, like traditional societies everywhere, had allowed for a great deal of *de facto* decentralization and local autonomy. The rise of the nation-state centralized political power and fitted in neatly with the centralization entailed by industrialization. Nations such as Germany and Japan could industrialize rapidly and without social upheaval under politically unrepresentative systems; the rational organization of economic resources and the rational organization of political resources seemed both consistent and congruent.

The relationship between political and economic centralization was less clear in democratic nations. Here two options were available. One could, in theory at least, opt for a decentralized political system with limited government, based on economic decentralization: a republic of yeomen farmers and small businessmen. Epitomized by Jeffersonian democracy, this ideal has never ceased to haunt modern man, especially in the United States. Alternatively, one could accept the necessity of hierarchical and centralized political control paralleling economic control. One could even argue that such political centralization was necessary if popular sovereignty was to dominate the economic order. Thus in the first years of the twentieth century proponents of strong government such as Herbert Croly could speak of achieving Jeffersonian ends by Hamiltonian means.[35] In such a system the people through the electoral process determined who would head the government; these leaders in turn controlled the government's employees and their activities. But this meant as much centralization and standardization as in nondemocratic governments. For if the bureaucrat in the field exercised any discretion, he was doing something without the approval of the sovereign will of the people. Not discretion but the rule of law had to be the standard, and flexibility had to be outlawed.[36]

The system of common law, medieval in origin, saved the English-speaking countries from the worst rigors of this concept of government, but they, too, generally had to adhere to the basic rule: government in industrial civilization meant hierarchically organized, centrally directed activity. The only difference between democratic and nondemocratic regimes was the fact that in the former those at the top were responsible to the people at large and could be held accountable at more or less regular intervals, just as even the most rigid and centralized corporate management was ultimately responsible to its stockholders.

Modern industrial civilization differed from all its predecessors in another vital aspect. It was both dominant within the societies that constituted it and was world-wide in scope. The dominance of industrialism within the developed nations came about in several ways. In part, it stemmed from the fact that the sheer economic power of modern industry was so great that other aspects of economic life had to be adjusted to it: for instance, the advantage the manufacturer had over the farmer in being able to regulate his production in such a way as to maximize his profits meant the subordination of agrarian interests. Besides, people wanted the products of the factory and would not be denied them if they could afford them; the triumph of the automobile in American life would have been impossible without the development of modern highways, but what government could have refused to build them? Finally, the example of the profits to be made and the assumed benefits to the consuming public of industrialism led to its methods being copied even by those segments of society that did not have to fear its direct competition. Not only did farmers become businessmen to the extent that the vagaries of nature permitted, turning dairy farms into assembly lines or becoming "miners" of the soil, but "business methods" were applied—with dubious success—to government and even to the medieval precincts of academia. Industrial man was the ideal as well as the dominant type in his society.

And his society became the only society. Initially, its

triumph was due to the sheer energy, self-confidence and ruthlessness of European merchants, explorers, missionaries and warriors. But increasingly in the seventeenth and eighteenth centuries the new physical powers given to Europeans and Americans by industrial technology were translated into military terms, and the resistance of other peoples and cultures was physically overborne.

Example played a role as well. At first, non-Western societies sought to copy Western military technology and techniques while maintaining their own social and cultural traditions intact; Ottoman Turkey, Czarist Russia and Japan in its earliest contact with the West are examples. But it soon became obvious that military power rested on industrial power, which meant the wholesale introduction of Western ideas and methods. At the same time, the populations of these countries welcomed the new goods produced by industrialism, foreign or domestic. The result was that mass production, standardization, political centralization and all the concomitants of industrial civilization became world-wide, and with them—though more slowly and less completely even to this day—the attitudes toward work, knowledge, power, and man and nature that were part of the make-up of industrial man. Pockets of resistance still exist in many parts of Asia, Africa and the Near East, just as they do in Sicily, the Scottish Highlands, Appalachia and perhaps the "cultures of poverty" in the large cities of the developed world. But industrial civilization is ubiquitous and world-wide. If the next step in human evolution is to be a fusion of races and cultures into a new culture based on the new technology, industrialism has paved the way by making the world one in fact and in spirit.

What is the picture of industrial man that emerges from this brief sketch of the origins of industrial civilization and its major features? No civilization or culture produces people—even leaving aside sex differences—who all play the same social role or are all the same personality type; nor will all of the features of the dominant types in any society differ from those of the typical man of some other society.[37] But the leaders of industrial civilization, the men who made the important decisions, who were best rewarded by society and most respected even when emulation was out of the question, can be said to have had several characteristics in common. They were rationalists, at least in their work lives. To them knowledge was important but instrumental. Their major interest was in work—performed by themselves or by society. Their major motivations were power and material wealth, and they viewed physical nature, ideas and other men as instruments of that power. They were domineering because they accepted the reality of a competitive struggle for existence in which one dominated or was dominated. Life was a struggle against other men, against nature and in large measure against themselves.

Christianity, especially in its Puritan versions, science and Darwinism combined with elemental animal passions to produce a civilization whose most striking elements were large-scale production and consumption of material goods, alienation from and war against nature, repression of the instincts for play or contemplation or their sublimation into competitive channels, and, above all, competition and war. It was the human type that embodied these characteristics that set the tone of industrial civilization, and if a new civilization is arising—if there is a technological man in the wings—he will of necessity be radically different. There is, however, another possibility: the new powers granted by technology and science to man will not be controlled by technological man but will be acquired by as yet unchanged industrial man. The synthesis of postmodern technology and industrial man could produce a new civilization, or it could mean the end of the human race.

3

The Machine
and Its Critics

Ideas affect the day-to-day lives of men and the destiny of nations and civilizations, and are in turn affected by them. Everyone who wishes to understand the larger outlines of human history is therefore forced to talk at one and the same time about ideas, movements and particular events—the rise of Hellenic civilization and of Christianity, the end of the medieval world and the advent of industrialism, liberalism and democracy. Yet no task holds more pitfalls than that of sorting out the reciprocal and invincibly complex relationship of events, trends and ideas. Were ideas or economic developments primary in the development of capitalism? Was Whiggery in England primarily motivated by religion, economics or politics? Was the American Revolution liberal or conservative, the French Revolution the ancestor of democracy or totalitarianism, or perhaps both? To ask such questions is to remind oneself of the extent to which the movement of events, the philosophical formulations of intellectuals and the attitudes of the common man interlock and overlap but never precisely dovetail.

In this book our central concern is whether, or to what extent, a new technological civilization and a new human type, technological man, is arising out of the womb of contemporary industrial society. But to answer this question we need to know something about the nature of present-day industrial society. Only then can we determine how its underlying technology, its social forms and its cultural norms are being altered, whether we should regard such changes as menacing or beneficent, and what, if anything, we can or should do about them. We have already examined the intellectual preconditions and the technological basis for industrial man, but to understand the full meaning of his existence we must evaluate the effects of industrialism on human life—on man's power, freedom and relations to other men and to nature. What have social critics had to say about the nature and value of industrial civilization? We will find that some of the criticisms leveled against the industrial order are valid for industrial society and possibly for the new technological society as well, while some are not even true of industrial society and are the basis for false hopes or false fears about the coming technological society; still others may be true of industrial society but not of its technological successor.

The problem of sorting out which criticisms are valid and in what contexts is greatly complicated by the fact that most of the critics of industrialism, favorable as well as unfavorable, make little or no distinction between the industrial society of the nineteenth and early twentieth centuries and that of the present. As a result, when they talk of the effects of technology they lump all technology together—coal power and electric power, Gary's steel mills and the Boston area's electronics companies, the railroad and the automobile, dreadnoughts and atomic weapons, the telephone and television—and do not distinguish among their social effects. Also, because the new technology has grown up within the old, arguments tend to go past each other rather than being joined, since one is never sure which technological factors are being condemned or praised for which social and cultural consequences. What is true of the older bases of industrial society need not be true of the new; in fact, the differences may be so great as to make it necessary to speak no longer of industrial society but of something else. The confusion is aggravated because so many critics of industrialism tend to talk in oracular and apocalyptic tones, and are loath to sort out causes and effects with any precision or to qualify their judgments, much less express them in empirically testable or measurable terms.

This difficulty is exemplified by the common tendency of over a century's standing to speak of the present era as the "machine age," a practice that often carries with it the assumption that modern society is as much a machine as those that bottle soft drinks. But metaphors can be dangerous intellectual tools. Is the modern bureaucracy really an assemblage of moving parts in the same fashion as the automobile? For that matter, does it even make sense to speak of the television set as a "machine"? It is far easier for the average person to understand how his automobile engine works than how his television set does, in large part because the latter is not the traditional type of machine which performs work by means of pressure exerted by moving parts.

Similarly it is far easier to think of American government as divided into legislative, executive and judicial branches than to understand how it really works. To visualize electronic and political processes requires a difficult, perhaps impossible, exercise of the imagination akin to imagining biological processes at work. One can see levers exerting force on gears more easily than a child's growth or than video tubes selecting waves from the air and converting them into pictures. Increasingly, mechanical action is being replaced by electronic or physiochemical processes in a variety of ways and at all levels, yet the popular imagination and that of many critics fails to take this change into account; the evaluations of the "machine age" are too often based on inadequate and inaccurate metaphors.

A further difficulty in trying to understand the human meaning of industrial or technological society stems from the fact that technology has not been a central consideration in social thought. Everyone today is aware of the fact of industrialism and of the impact of technology upon the daily lives of men throughout the world. Yet technology is accepted more or less as a given, and its results are regarded as accidental and largely uncontrollable. All of the basic ideologies that are influential in the world today—liberalism, conservatism, capitalism, socialism, romantic conservatism and romantic adherence to revolution—all directly or by implication have something to say about the meaning of technology for man's social existence, but save for a few short-lived sects such as the Technocrats none have made it a central issue. In this respect, the triumph of modern industrialism well deserves the title of the "accidental" revolution.[1] Thus we gain little valid insight into the social meaning of technology from examining the major intellectual-political movements of our day. Indeed, one reason why political philosophy is presently in such disrepair and disrepute is its failure so far to come to grips with the issues posed by the new technology and the advent of technological man.

One major political strain, romantic conservatism—hardly represented in America because of our lack of a single established church or a widespread landed aristocracy—has in many instances sought to control technology and to admit only those aspects that would not disturb the *status quo*. Save for a few remote nations, such as Yemen and Tibet, this approach has not survived even into the early twentieth century as a significant force, and today even in its strongholds it is on the wane.

Another intellectual stance toward technology is what might be called moderate conservatism. Many of its adherents deplore the results of change but can do nothing about it because of their prior commitment to the rights of private property and the dominance of the market. By seeking to maintain old forms of government and social relations while accepting the validity of privately promoted technological change, they (like their hero, the businessman who is committed to expansion and progress but wants to retain limited government and old patterns of social deference) reveal their intellectual irrelevance in the contemporary world.

Liberals—and here I use the word in its modern American sense—seem ready to accept technological change as a natural outgrowth of intellectual freedom and as benefiting society by providing a rising standard of living for all; but they seek to mitigate what they perceive as its antisocial side effects by *ad hoc*, piecemeal, palliative measures. Mrs. Johnson's highway-beautification program is typical, almost to the point of caricature, of this approach.

Socialists are increasingly ambivalent about technology. Marxists view technological change as leading to a socialization of the production process, which must in turn lead to socialization of ownership, thereby making possible an affluence that will both eliminate scarcity and free the individual from many social controls. Yet more and more they find themselves facing the problem of "bureaucracy," with socialized economies just as oppressive of the workers as privately owned systems of production.

Today in many parts of the world a new inchoate ideology is arising, especially among the young, that rejects traditional Marxism and its exemplars. Romantic revolutionism looks to men such as Castro, Mao, Ho Chi Minh and especially the late Che Guevara as its heroes. In part, this new creed stems from an unwillingness to accept the compromises that socialist states and movements have made with the functional necessities of industrial civilization, and, especially as influenced by men such as Herbert Marcuse,[2] involves a condemnation of industrialism itself. Yet this rejection exists largely on the rhetorical level; no

apostles of the new revolutionary movement are clear on
how they would prevent the abuses they deplore in capitalist and socialist society alike.

Thus all of the major extant political ideologies fail to
deal adequately with technology, since they either do not
make it a central factor in their calculations, or, in the case
of socialism, do not resolve the problems it poses. Social
critics who do view the technological aspect of society as
of major significance are therefore forced to abandon the
dominant ideologies and to strike out on their own. Most of
them have through logical necessity chosen one of two directions. Some have embraced what might be styled "technological Messianism." They believe that technological
advance will solve all human problems: affluence will
eliminate class conflict and eventually international conflict as well. Thus Alvin M. Weinberg speaks of the "technological fix" that will provide short cuts to solving most
basic domestic and international problems.[3]

Some foresee, as a result of our common technology,
the social and political systems of East and West moving
closer together, so that ultimately the lion will lie down
with the lamb in a world of human fulfillment. An opposing
school of thought holds that technology is instead the fount
of most of the evils in the contemporary world, but that it is
nonetheless bound to triumph at the societal level—only
through what can be called "cultural withdrawal" can individuals and small groups hope to escape its constraints
and consequences. At its extreme this position is exemplified by Timothy Leary's injunction to "turn on, tune in,
and drop out."

The Indictment of Industrial Civilization

The anxiety of modern man has deep historical roots.
The distaste for industrial society and advanced technology
and the fear of the future, which in our own time have
found classic expression in such works as Aldous Huxley's

Brave New World and George Orwell's *1984* are only the latest manifestations of a long tradition of dismay that goes back almost to the beginnings of industrial civilization.

From the outset the attack came from many quarters, had many particular targets, used various weapons, and chose to do battle on different kinds of terrain. Traditional moralists, both Catholic and Protestant, resisted many of the practices of early capitalism, holding, for instance, that the taking of interest was usury, forbidden by the Scriptures and Aristotle and the traditions of all Western religions. Others objected to the growth of the market system with its disruption of feudal relations. Those who had a stake in the inequalities of the old order resisted any move toward democracy, insisting that most human beings are inherently inferior to their betters and so are incapable of self-rule. Democracy was looked upon as the cause of the lowering of particular value standards, rather than as one of the effects of a deeper revolution in values, in which the qualitative was giving place to the quantitative.

Yet from beneath the fog of controversy over capitalism, democracy and related phenomena, the fundamental issue posed by modernity began to emerge. The real problem was the place of man in nature. Men, and society as a whole, were not only embracing the machine as a device to gain power and wealth undreamt of by earlier civilizations; in the process they were allegedly becoming more like machines themselves. The traditional philosophical dualist necessarily saw this as a subjugation of spirit to matter, and he centered his fire on "materialism." The humanist, increasingly important among the enemies of "progress" and "enlightenment" (a reversal of his earlier role), became a Romantic, who found in untouched nature the standard of beauty and value, and who attacked the new civilization not for being sensual and worldly but for not being sensual and worldly enough, and for turning man into an abstract, lifeless, inorganic object.

Among practicing politicians, Edmund Burke was one

of the few to give intellectual expression to his misgivings. He attacked those who were assimilating the political community to the market place and who looked upon the state as "nothing better than a partnership agreement in a trade of pepper and coffee . . . or some other such low concern,"[4] and he bitterly opposed Jacobins and nascent capitalists alike. But he could do little to stem the tide. For most men were absorbed in such "low concerns," not excluding the men of power. Besides, capitalism was based on the established law and property relationships that Burke's own philosophy defended as "natural," the result of prescription and organic growth. This makes Burke the forerunner of a flock of philosophical conservatives who have been politically meaningless because of their failure to realize that neither organized government nor the masses as such but the business community has been the fountainhead of social and cultural innovation. In its search for profits it has been the leading promoter of technological change, and therefore the greatest enemy of the moral, aesthetic and political values that the philosophical conservative and the "conservative" businessman both profess to cherish.

The laboring masses originally joined in the revulsion against the new way of life. From 1811 to 1816 England was the scene of the Luddite campaign of smashing the new machines, which were blamed for unemployment and low wages. The movement, like so much of the political unrest in England during the period, was readily suppressed. Though many skilled workers continued to adopt restrictive practices in their own workplaces ("featherbedding" after all remains a commonplace to this day), the lower classes soon became convinced that industrial progress was all for the best and benefited them in the long run, and opposition to change became the province of particularly or locally disadvantaged interests and of the intellectuals.

But the intellectual opposition to industrialism did not

easily give up hope of finding a popular base for its struggle. Some Romantics, attacking the new order on the grounds of aesthetics and the debasement of the common man as he had supposedly existed in the preindustrial era, recognized, unlike the Burkeans, that the real enemy was the *bourgeoisie*. William Cobbett was the founder of what might be called the left-wing aesthetic critique of industrial society. An admirer of pre-Reformation, precapitalist Merrie England, he attacked Jacobin, capitalist, Protestant and state socialist alike, and advocated a kind of guild socialism in which the common people would run their own economic affairs. In his social thought the emphasis was on local control and traditional craftsmanship with a concomitant opposition to centralization and mass production.[5] The schemes of many modern reformers of industrial society, from Ralph Borsodi to Erich Fromm and Paul Goodman, are not essentially different from those Cobbett proposed in the early part of the last century.

William Morris with justice can be said to be the founder of the "artsy-craftsy" critique of industrial society. Thousands of persons, especially in the United States, living in demipoverty and making ceramic jewelry and psychedelic posters between peace marches are his spiritual descendants. Unlike Cobbett, Morris came to politics and socialism late in life, as a means to ends that were essentially aesthetic, the only way to preserve art and poetry from the desecrations of the machine age. In *News from Nowhere* Morris provides a more systematic utopia that did Cobbett; one focused on the future, rather than the past. But the essence of his critique of capitalism was embodied in what he envisioned would be the motto of the workers, once freed from capitalist clutches, "Now at last we will produce no more for profit but for *use*, for *happiness*, for LIFE."[6]

Life, that was the issue. Central to the attack on the new civilization was the belief that men themselves were being turned into lifeless machines, laborers and capitalists alike. The poet Robert Southey wrote of manufacturers who used their laborers as "bodily machines for producing wealth" and ended by becoming intellectual machines themselves.[7] Thomas Carlyle lamented that he and his contemporaries lived in "the Age of Machinery, in every inward and outward sense of that word."[8] Matthew Arnold spoke of a "whole civilization" which was "mechanical and external,"[9] while Samuel Butler's influential utopia *Erewhon* (1872) celebrated a civilization in which man had liberated himself from the slavery of the machine. Not only the machine but science itself came under increasing attack. For novelist George Gissing science was "a remorseless enemy of mankind, which would destroy 'all simplicity and gentleness of life,'" all beauty, and in time would "restore barbarism under the guise of civilization" and "plunge the world . . . into blood-drenched chaos."[10]

But though horrendous the indictment and bitter the attack, it was of no immediate political consequence. Ruskin spoke of "anarchy and competition" as the "laws of death."[11] Morris was even more direct. For him nothing should be made that "was not worth making," and ugliness, commercialism and capitalism were intertwined; "the cause of Art," he wrote, "is the cause of the people."[12] But if revolution and beauty went together, it was only in the sense that as ugliness increased revolutionary ferment abated. The English worker accepted industrialism as his real income rose in the latter part of the century. When the economy began to go sour after World War I he turned not to anti-industrialism but toward state management of the industrial economy. Guild socialism, distributism and their cousins remained crank causes with little more political relevance than Theosophy or nudism.[13] The literary protest of course continued. But when T. S. Eliot sought to promote the revival of a Christian monarchy based on measure and order[14] his arguments were regarded as source material for literary criticism rather than as serious political messages. D. H. Lawrence, less explicitly political, was in a way more successful. His rejection of modern rationality and his exaltation of the animal drives of mankind as part of a conscious rejection of industrial civilization met with a positive response at least at the personal level.[15]

But the basic outcome of over a century of anti-industrial polemics in England was clear. No one was listening save the critics themselves. In despair, some of the Romantic opponents of the machine turned to fascism of various kinds. Others drifted into a vague, apolitical socialism, socially relevant only in forming part of the general climate of rejection of bourgeois society that is sometimes labeled the "anti-capitalist mentality."[16]

In the United States, which by the turn of the century was clearly destined to be the heartland of the new industrial civilization, the situation was only superficially different. The American republic had a strong and lasting agrarian tradition based not on feudalism but on the yeoman farmer, and it was a tradition to which most American thinkers related. "The pastoral ideal has been used to define the meaning of America since the age of discovery; and it has not yet lost its hold on the native imagination," Leo Marx could write in our own time.[17] Moreover the farmers retained political and economic power long after their numbers dwindled, which meant that their suspicions of industrialism and the city continued to be political and socially relevant. Suburbia is in part the ghost of the earlier ideal. Yet even in America the anti-industrial cause was doomed to failure.

For along with its agrarianism the new nation was imbued with liberalism, Whig to the bone. Neither throne nor altar, nor, above all, reverence for the past existed as barriers to the new leveling forces unleashed by industrial technology.

The political turning point was the defeat of the South

in the Civil War, which ended forever any possibility of a nation based on agrarian values—and, indeed, destroyed forever the possibility of a conservatism that was anything other than intellectual preciousness or a shield for particular business interests. Bryan's constituents in the crucial election of 1896 were small farmer capitalists who were resentful of their disadvantaged position within the system rather than of industrial processes as such. When in the 1930's a group of southern writers responded to the American economic crisis and the attendant cultural crisis of industrial capitalism with their manifesto *I'll Take My Stand*, looking to agrarianism and rejecting both socialism and industrial capitalism in favor of small property, they found little resonance. Dixieland reacted to the Depression by standing in the vanguard of those supporting the state capitalism of the New Deal.

Literary protest against the new order was as futile as it was widespread. Mark Twain could present an essentially pessimistic view of technological change in his *A Connecticut Yankee in King Arthur's Court* and entitle one of his final essays "Man a Machine?," but his increasing bitterness was little recognized in his own time, and today he is popularly remembered as a writer of romances for children.

Agrarianism was defeated; socialism gained only a short-lived, halfhearted hearing; and the qualms of intellectuals were without effect. For the social thinking of America was dominated by a liberalism and a so-called conservatism, both of which had the same basic attitudes toward private property and the rights of the capitalist. Invention and change were good if they led to an increase in material power or comfort, and democracy was not only no barrier to change but spurred it on. In *Babbitt* Sinclair Lewis gave Americans a classic portrait of their dominant type, to whom bigger axiomatically meant better. When Calvin Coolidge said that "the business of America is business," he spoke for almost all of his countrymen.

But while the criticism of industrial civilization in the English-speaking world was an intellectual exercise that was politically futile, and the triumph of bourgeois values, materialist and quantitative, was as complete as the triumph of the assembly line and the stock exchange, this triumph was not world-wide. Some parts of the world still lagged behind in the acceptance of industrial technology; more important, they adopted some of the technology but not the values that made it possible, workable and endurable.

Russia had never experienced either Renaissance or Reformation. She knew the Englightenment only by rumor, and the French Revolution had meant alien invasion. Czarist Russia was an Asiatic autocracy which only in 1861 abolished serfdom. Yet the Russian ruling elite, or at least the dominant group, knew that in order to preserve her independence Russia had to adopt some of the economic and military technology of the West; Peter the Great had taught them that. What would result from the amalgam of new technological powers and archaic social forms? The nineteenth-century Russian liberal thinker Alexander Herzen feared the worst. Technological advance in Russia, he predicted, would produce "Genghis Khan with a telegraph."[18] Paradoxically, his predictions were fulfilled by the Russian Revolution. Spawn of the Enlightenment, and imbued with the ends of Western humanism, it adopted the terrorist means appropriate to overthrowing Czarist tyranny and was absorbed by the Asiatic despotism underlying Russian political culture. Technology plus Russia equaled Stalinism, forced industrialization under the aegis of a ubiquitous police state.

The island empire of Japan had throughout history shown considerable ability to adopt those features of its stronger neighbors' cultures that it deemed useful or necessary to survival. Nineteenth-century technology made America and Europe its neighbors, as it was forced to

realize when Commodore Perry knocked loudly on its door.
Japan proceeded to take over the technology of the Industrial Revolution while at the same time making the most
minimal and superficial changes in its political, social and
cultural life. The synthesis proved unstable, and the result
was an aggressive militarism that set eastern Asia and the
whole Pacific aflame. Twentieth-century military technology plus Shinto values produced the kamikaze pilot seeking to incarnate the Divine Wind of Japanese mythology
in rubber and steel.

But the most spectacular and significant example of
the perils of mixing the technology of the Industrial Revolution with an incompatible culture was provided by Germany. Germany, by the turn of the century, had become
one of the world's leading industrial powers, and its science
and scholarship were models for the world. Yet Germany
had repulsed the Renaissance with the savage pieties of
Lutheranism; it had been the homeland of romantic conservatism's counterattack on the Enlightenment, and following the fiasco of 1848 Germany had shown that it was
not ripe for democratic revolution. Authoritarianism, Romanticism and racism were the cornerstones of German
political culture. When the breakdown of world capitalism
gave the last blow to the Weimar Republic, unloved child
of military defeat, political power passed into the hands of
men who exalted "blood" over reason and preached a deliberate atavism, a return to primitive norms and styles of
conduct. In the long run this creed caused Germany a decrease in technological efficiency, especially insofar as it
meant the loss of its Jewish technicians and scientists. But
German technology was already so far advanced that it became a formidable weapon with which the Nazi band of
primitivist adventurers, supported by a population that had
accepted industrialization and its fruits without altering
their basic outlook on life, terrorized and almost conquered
the world.

The German experience was important not only in terms of actual political and military events, however. It had tremendous intellectual consequences. How could it have happened that Germany, leader in science and industry, had been converted into a political nightmare threatening the world? This was a question that troubled thoughtful men in the thirties, forties and beyond, not least of all the many distinguished German social thinkers who had been forced to flee their native land. Most developed explanations that made industrialization itself the key element in the collapse of democracy and humane values in Germany, and it was easy to extend the diagnosis from Germany to advanced industrial states elsewhere, including the United States. These explanations of the rise of Nazi primitivism in technologized German society were synthesized with the general critique of industrialism that had been made by conservative thinkers. The result was the practically influential and intellectually challenging theory of mass society.

The Theory of Mass Society

As in the case of all broad categories of social analysis —revolution, stability, liberalism, totalitarianism, for instance—mass society has many definitions, depending in part on whether the person using the concept is interested in origins or consequences—in politics, economics or culture. The notion of mass society is basically political, since it was created in an attempt to explain political developments such as the German experience, but its underlying premises are sociological, and it has its counterparts in such usages as "mass leisure," "mass culture" and the like. For our purposes, William Kornhauser's definition of mass society as "a social system in which elites are readily accessible to influence by non-elites and non-elites are readily available for mobilization by elites"[19] is as good as any. This definition highlights the lack of differentiation and pluralism, and the lack of protection of the individual against the pressures of society, that supporters of the mass-society theory hold to be the hallmark and inevitable consequence of industrialism.

If the "mass society" critics are correct, then one of two things will be true of the new technological age. Either technological advance will simply reinforce the effects of industrialism so that technological man will be not a new human type but only industrial man writ large, and a bad situation will become worse. Or, alternatively, new technological factors may alleviate the situation and lead to the demise of mass society. In this latter case technological man could be a truly new type and technological civilization really different—and different for the better—from industrial civilization.

If instead one concludes that the theorists of mass society are wrong, it may be because, given the overlap of events and influences that makes it so difficult to divide history into neat periods, the new liberating forces inherent in technology have been at work almost from the beginning of industrialism, offering resistance to mass trends that actually stemmed from earlier social attitudes and institutions.

In any event, whether mass-society theory is valid or not, it has brought into focus important questions—the problem of freedom and the problem of identity—questions that will be basic for any future society, no matter how different from industrial man technological man turns out to be. For these reasons it is both useful and important for us to attend to what the theorists of mass society have to say.

Mass-society theory owes its long prominence as a mode of analysis and a subject for debate both to the trauma that Nazism constituted for many intellectuals and to the general hostility toward industrial capitalism that became part of the intellectual baggage of most literary men and social thinkers by the turn of the century. But it has deeper roots as well. They lie in the at first startling fact that the mainstream of sociological thought is essentially conservative, however liberal most sociologists may be in their own personal and political opinions, and however much the discipline of sociology may be viewed as a disruptive force by political conservatives and fundamentalist preachers.

What we know as sociology today is the descendant of a tradition that goes back to the Romantic reaction of the nineteenth century, to such men as Chateaubriand and De Maistre, who were fighting a rear-guard action against the French Revolution. They held that man was made to live in a structured community, not as an anonymous atom in a fragmented society. The breakdown of community became the major theme of sociological thought. Ferdinand Tönnies contrasted *"Gesellschaft,"* the modern situation in which impersonal commercial relations prevail, unfavorably with *"Gemeinschaft,"* a society based on close face-to-face personal ties. For Émile Durkheim the contrast was between the "egoism" and *"anomie"* of the industrialized, urbanized masses of the late nineteenth century and the satisfactions available to men in situations of greater social cohesion and less rapid change. Auguste Comte, despite his embrace of industrial technology, sought to re-create a status system similar to that of the Middle Ages. Even Marx and Engels added to the chorus their accounts (most noteworthily in the *Communist Manifesto* itself) of the destruction of the quality of life occasioned by the rise of industrial capitalism and by so doing championed the mystique of the happy peasant as opposed to the unhappy worker, thus becoming the unlikely allies of Cobbett, Morris and their followers.

As the cult of scientific objectivity became dominant among social theorists, outright condemnation of the impersonality of industrial civilization was muted. But the categories of description used by theorists and researchers and the problems they chose to investigate betrayed their point of view: man had fallen from a happier state.

Max Weber was a leading figure in proclaiming moral detachment as a duty of the social scientist, but it is impossible to read his writings, especially his pioneering work on bureaucracy, without becoming aware of his underlying preference for "communal" as opposed to "associative" bonds and his haunting distrust of "rational" as against "traditional" authority.[20] In the United States this sociological heritage was reinforced by the fact that many American sociologists came from rural backgrounds; they regarded urban life as inherently pathological and reflected this view in their analyses and choice of problems.[21] It was inevitable, therefore, that into the twentieth century such dichotomies as Robert Redfield's folk-urban classification[22] (in which the first term implies harmony and social cohesion and the latter conflict and *anomie*) have deeply colored the thinking of both sociologists and political scientists.

Rationalized urban industrial society robs man of his humanity; this is the message these social theorists convey, however heavily shrouded in qualifying language. In recent years this same message has been the stock in trade of the purveyors of the theory of mass culture.

In pre-Hitler Germany a curious marriage had taken place between Marxism and Freudianism. Its offspring (pre-eminently, the Frankfurt Institut für Sozialforschung, which became attached to Columbia University) were forced to migrate to the United States, where they became extremely influential. Their major tenet (here grossly oversimplified) was that the instinctual drives of man, repressed by industrialism, are manipulated by the capitalists who control the economy and the cultural media in the interests of their own private profit and in order to maintain their political and economic domination. It was largely out of the work of these men that the theory of *mass culture* took shape.

This cultural counterpart of the mass-society theory had the not-so-incidental advantage of explaining why the rise of the masses had not led to the liberating social revolution Marx had predicted. This theory was especially congenial to intellectuals and to the professional class generally. Forced by the conditions of their work and training to be status-conscious, believing strongly in the superior value of some ideas and ways of doing things over others, usually individualistic in their personal attitudes, they were at the same time often vaguely liberal or socialist in their political leanings. The theory of mass culture provided them with a weapon for attacking a democratic industrial society that was forcing them into bureaucratic bondage and degrading their cultural norms without making them give up their belief in the goodness and wisdom of the common man.[28] The common man was not really himself; his intellect had been deceived and his instincts perverted by the manipulations of a few selfish political or economic leaders.

Mass society was evil for two reasons: it threatened man's freedom and his identity. Freedom was conceived of primarily as autonomy, as self-direction, in terms that, despite their differing philosophies, Hobbes, Locke and Jefferson would have understood. Even Marxists, when they spoke of freedom in industrial society, seemed to ignore the definition of freedom as the conscious acceptance of natural or community norms, and collaboration with them derived from Rousseau, Hegel and Marx himself. It seemed obvious that industrial capitalism, with its concentration of economic activities under centralized, hierarchical direction, deprived the worker—and increasingly the manager as well—of freedom in the productive sphere of life. The political concomitant of this economic concentration was centralized government, which, whether formally democratic or not, made the individual citizen a mere subject, enslaved to party or government bureaucracy, at the same time that party leaders and bureaucrats themselves were

mere cogs in a machine. Culturally, the individual had no
option but to accept the mass-produced products of the
media, which ground out the self-expression of the thinker
and artist at the same time that they destroyed folk culture
and autonomous activities among the masses.

Identity was discussed primarily in terms of its opposite, alienation. For Marx, man is alienated because he
has no control over what he produces; he can not decide
what he wishes to make and is himself simply an object, a
thing, in the production process. Actually, the concept of
alienation is rooted in Romanticism. Alienation is man's
divorce from nature, from a postulated real self. For the
early Marx, as for Feuerbach, it is primarily sexual, the
repression of instinct.[24] The idea of alienation, in short, is
based on the belief that there is, in effect, a real essence of
each individual, consisting of his basic instinctual make-up
and perhaps the accidental and individual aspects of his
childhood experience, and that he is forced to deny this in
order to conform to the demands placed upon him as
worker, consumer or even voter. As an actor in these roles
he goes through the motions, but the "real" person is not
involved. He is forced to wear a mask to conceal his true
self. Sometimes the strain becomes too great and results
either in individual psychological breakdown or in social
conflict or, more likely, simply in the pseudo identity re-
placing the real one, the mask becoming the face. The problem of identity, the psychologist Erik Erikson has written,
is central to our times.[25] Certainly the huge literature on
the subject bears witness to the fact that identity and its
opposite, alienation, are a major theme of concern among
sensitive men in Western society.[26]

The indictment of industrial society is a sweeping one
that assumes that loss of freedom and loss of identity are
exactly parallel, and indeed constitute the same phenomenon. From popular writers we hear of organization men
and status seekers.[27] A political scientist warns that we are

already subject to "bureaucratic infeudation."[28] A psychologist tells us that the "process of self-alienation has penetrated into consumption" and "man becomes a mass-product,"[29] while an influential neo-Marxist social philosopher asserts that the reason man appears happy is that "the people recognize themselves in their commodities," they identify with their chains.[30] "Society becomes an anthill," a leading economist writes: "contemporary industrial society tends to be totalitarian," and "no self-identity is possible."[31] Not merely is man enslaved to the work process or its products, not merely has he lost all possibility of freedom or self-identity as worker or consumer, but his whole culture is being destroyed as well through being "homogenized,"[32] through the creation of a "flat cultural mass."[33] Like the other losses, the destruction of culture is the result of technological factors: "Modern technology is the necessary and sufficient condition of mass culture."[34]

Beyond all the differences of emphasis among its attackers, despite the different levels of abstraction and the conflicting motives, premises and types of evidence offered by the critics of industrial society, a common image emerges. The essence of industrialism is mass production by means of the machine. A machine is a device that performs work through the use of moving parts that exert physical force upon one another in a rigidly organized and regular fashion so as to produce a standardized product. Society itself has become such a machine, an assemblage of standardized moving parts acting on each other by force so as to produce standardized products that in turn become parts of the machine. Man is a cog in the machine, or a product produced by it, or both. He is subject to forces beyond his control, just as are his fellows to whom he has become identical. Gone is freedom, gone is identity. Man is simply a machine, in a society of machines, in a physical environment of machines.

How does one respond to such an indictment? One

can accept it, in which case one's alternatives are revolt, withdrawal or despair. Or one can reject it by denying that the facts are as stated, or that they lend themselves to the interpretations given them by critics of mass society. But perhaps one need neither deny nor accept the indictment in the terms in which it is presented. It is possible instead to hold that the quarrel over whether or not industrialism has created a mass society threatening human freedom has been rendered meaningless by the continuing development of technology itself, that the industrial era is already in the process of being superseded by a new phase in human history and that industrial man, whatever his characteristics, is evolving into something different and superior—technological man.

4

The Prophets
of the New

Who is technological man? What is technological civilization? What changes are taking place in human society that presage the end of industrial civilization and its replacement by something else? What changes are taking place in man's relationship to his environment that are about to alter radically his existential situation and to initiate a new phase in human evolution? Before we try to assess the extent to which basic changes in the human condition are taking place in fact, let us first attempt to discover what the adherents of the concept of technological society and technological man say is taking place.

The proponents of the idea that industrial civilization is coming to an end can be divided into two groups: those who are primarily concerned with the quotidian details of life as it exists today and will develop over the next several generations, and those who anticipate basic changes in man's relation to his own being and the natural universe, many of whom devote as much effort to advocacy as to explication. Though by no means all of those in the former category are sociologists, it is nevertheless convenient and

not implausible to call them the sociological prophets and
to refer to those who speak in more vatic tones as existential prophets.

The Sociological Prophets

Within both groups there is disagreement about what
is happening and what should happen, but the sociological
prophets are more likely to agree about more things than
are the existential prophets. The sociological prophets differ
in terminology, emphasis and sometimes in important par-
ticulars. But while each would object to being taxed with
the sins or errors of any of his fellows, they have borrowed
liberally from one another in language, specifics and tone.
Many are associates in the futurist movement among American academics, others are involved in practical planning
for the future. Although it would be cumbersome, it would
not be impossible to construct a detailed chart of their
agreements and disagreements; this is unnecessary, however. All are united in holding that technological factors
are radically altering the shape of modern society to create
a new civilization different in many fundamental respects
from the industrial civilization we have known.

Some of the sociological prophets have devised their
own names for the new society. Ellul calls it "technological
society."[1] For Marshall McLuhan the "mechanized" environment of the industrial age has been replaced by the
"totally new environment" of the "electronic age."[2] Bertram
Gross talks of the "mobiletic revolution."[3] Brzezinski writes
of the "technetronic era"; Amitai Etzioni of the "postmodern period."[4] Others eschew such neat or provocative
labels and simply speak of the vast changes that will take
place in "the next generation," "tomorrow" or by the "year
2000." But though terminology differs and minor disagreements are legion, most of the sociological prophets are in
substantial agreement about the fundamental nature of the

changes that modern industrial society, especially that found in the United States, is undergoing.

The key to these changes (though none of them puts it in quite these terms) lies in the fact that communications in the broadest sense of that term is replacing work as the foundation of the technological system. Energy is still utilized, but increasingly it is used to affect states of consciousness rather than to move physical objects. Though machines abound, there is a sense, not clearly grasped by all the prophets of the new, that the age of mechanization is over. Not levers and pulleys exerting force but sounds in the air, lights flashing on the dial of the computer, are the archetypal symbols of the new era, and electronics rather than mechanical physics is supreme. The overshadowing of the blast furnace and the assembly line and the bulldozer by the laser and the transistor and the chip is not merely a change in the appearance or incidental aspects of technology, it is basic. For the instruments of the new technology are like the human body in having few rigid moving parts; as in the biological organism, what is most important is not forces but process. Hobbes, who thought of the total universe, including the brain itself, as consisting of matter in motion, would find the new world, though still composed of things called "bodies," far less material and far more difficult to understand.

The shift of economic activity from production and work to communication and interaction is, according to the sociological prophets, witnessed to by several developments. The most significant indicator is that the United States by 1956 had allegedly already moved from being primarily a blue-collar to being primarily a white-collar society.[5] This is held to be a revolution as important as the movement from agrarian to industrial, rural to urban. Another way of putting it is that the United States is now primarily a service economy, with fewer and fewer people engaged in primary, secondary or even tertiary economic activities.[6] Alternatively, one can note the rise of the knowledge industry to a position of prominence in—some would even say to virtual dominance of—the American economy.[7] These are technological changes, politically permitted or perhaps even politically generated, that have consequences for the economic, social, political and cultural aspects of civilization. Some see these changes as creating a new kind of property in licenses, jobs, services, franchises, pension rights, etc., as important as that in land and factories of old.[8] And one can even think of education as a form of capital, increasingly the dominant form of capital in our society.

Many futurists believe that the decreasing importance of physical production and old-style property rights will lead to more attention being paid to technical expertise in social decision-making, perhaps even to the domination of our society by a scientific elite in place of the present political or business elites. Increase in the importance and status of professionals, government employees and those in non-profit activities is assumed. Many anticipate an era of mass leisure and/or unemployment, created by automation and marked by affluence, for the developed nations at least. Some see the revolution leading to decentralization and a new foundation for human dignity; others fear the unblinking stare of Big Brother. Though they differ on what this development will mean politically, virtually all see the world being drawn closer together into a more intense and denser pattern of interaction.

Many sociological prophets foresee a political revolution following upon the heels of the economic one created by the new technology. Some see politics disappearing as technology becomes completely autonomous, and technicians make decisions on purely rational-technical grounds.[9] Others envision the possibility of the politicization of all of life, with politics becoming more ubiquitous and unstable as planning becomes more extensive, and "style" or cultural questions increasingly supersede today's more mundane issues as the principal subject matter of politics. The rise of "image" politics in America and Great Britain due to the growth of TV is viewed as a harbinger of the future; image politics, to use McLuhan's terms, is "cool" and "non-linear." It is assumed that culture, like politics, follows technology. Traditional religion will decline, so will the family. Sex mores will be more permissive and the cultural differences between the sexes will gradually disappear as they lose their economic and much of their biological function. Mankind, bored by affluence and leisure in a technologized, rationalized world, will turn to various kinds of hedonistic indulgence. Society will become consumption oriented and "sensate."

These prophecies, even after the contradictory elements have been factored out, together constitute a formidable, far-reaching and basic set of social changes. It is not unfair to speak of a society based upon these new circumstances as a new society and, insofar as they are technologically conditioned, as a technological society. If one focuses on what these trends will mean to individual character structure, social roles and personal values, one could also speak loosely of the coming into being of a new human type, technological man. But while technological man so conceived might differ from bourgeois man almost as much as bourgeois man does from the man of the Middle Ages, his emergence would hardly constitute a change in the basic nature of the human animal. Technological man would be simply another social type. Something more is necessary before we can speak of an existential revolution. And this something more is already coming into existence.

All the futurists predict rapid and fundamental changes in man's relationship to his own and exterior nature: steps toward man's conquest of the universe, toward control of his own biological and mental processes, toward symbiosis with machines or other animals. Yet the tendency of the sociological prophets is to regard these as isolated and almost epiphenomenal events and potentialities, to recognize their importance and novelty in and of themselves but to look upon them as simply new and startling elements in the technological and cultural landscape, rather than as possibly being the integrating elements that could give it its meaning. They may be right; the new civilization may turn out to be eclectic to a degree unparalleled in human history, without any integrating forces. It may be that technological man will never fully come into being in an existential sense, whatever discoveries or social changes occur.

The Utopians

But another group of prophets say no, this is not possible. Man cannot come into possession of the new powers that all see on the horizon without crossing an evolutionary threshold. The existential prophets proclaim—often with stars in their eyes—that man has embarked on a new destiny made possible by technology, that he is taking a step of the same magnitude as that which took his ancestors out of the sea, that the new man being created by technology is a transitional stage toward the replacement of man by a new species of being.

Chiliasm is as old as Christianity, and millenarianism has haunted the human race since the beginning of the modern era. Belief in the imminence of Parousia was sidetracked after the Church came to terms with the Roman Empire following the conversion of Constantine, but once human energies revived after the Dark Ages, millenarianism revived, too, the only difference being increasing secularization of the idea of the Second Coming. Modern belief in the creation of a new race is the culmination of a tradition that goes back to Joachim of Floris in the twelfth century. The idea that rebirth shall come about through man's own efforts—now through the medium of science and technology—has roots as old as Pelagius.

The history of utopianism is one possible way of describing the history of human thought during the period from the Renaissance to the late nineteenth century.[10] While conservatism always existed as a counterpoint to millenarianism, especially in traditional religious circles, it was only with the full flowering of industrialism in the mid-nineteenth century that antiutopianism began seriously to contest the field among the intellectual elite, and that utopianism began to appear more and more *outré* and cranky. But utopian speculation continued. Renan, in his *Dialogues et fragments philosophiques* (1876), predicted the coming of technological man when he envisioned a world in which men created new types of men and became as gods themselves. Much later, Olaf Stapledon was to go him one better by creating a world in which men not only had achieved all their goals in the present but could also influence the past.[11]

Auguste Comte foresaw a new society that would be run by an elite of industrial managers and scientists. Comte's Positivism had much influence in Europe and Latin America, at the levels of both philosophy and practice, and many subsequent thinkers and movements are in his often unacknowledged debt. But the Positivist utopia, while it envisioned many changes in the institutions and beliefs of society, did not contemplate a basic change in human nature. It lived in the glow of the Enlightenment and was still essentially humanist. Science and technology would provide men with more and more of the kinds of benefits they had always desired. The good life would be achieved on earth, but the good life need not be redefined.

The relationship of Marxism to the utopian tradition is more complex. The brutalities of Stalinist Russia and the idiosyncracies of Maoist China have led some observers to regard Marxism as simply a variant of an antihumanist philosophy called totalitarianism. But, even leaving aside these phenomena as essentially historical accidents that would be deplored by Marx, the problem remains: does

Marxism represent another way of achieving the goals of classical humanism, or does it seek to set man on the path to something beyond humanity, something inhuman?

Marx and his major interpreters down to our own day have placed Marxism in the context of humanism, treating it as a philosophy born of the Enlightenment, with roots going back as far as Democritus. Man was part of nature. His transformation would come about when socialism had so unleashed the scientific and productive powers of society as to give man power over nature and thus end the alienation that was not a result of capitalism but was inherent in man's subjugation to the brute forces of nature. Here Marx is thrown back upon his youthful Hegelianism, for, though he denies man's spirituality, man for Marx is still different from brute nature. Dualism remains. In man, nature somehow transcends itself through becoming self-conscious, and the Marxist is asked to conquer and to use nature in a manner not dissimilar to the exploitativeness engendered by Christianity. Yet the end of this conquest of nature is essentially modest, in tune with the classical and humanistic culture in which Marx and his followers were steeped (even the ruthless Lenin read Tolstoy in his spare moments during the dark days of the civil war). For most Marxists the aim of the scientific conquest of nature was building "Parks of Rest and Culture" for the masses, and was epitomized by Khrushchev's statement in Budapest that Communism consisted of "goulash and ballet."

But Marxist socialism contained the same inherent tensions as Christianity. Just as Christian millenarianism sought to destroy the sinful part of man, identified usually with his animal nature, so did Marxism. Trotsky writes that "through the machine, man in Socialist society will command nature in its entirety."[12] For a time "the passive enjoyment of nature" will disappear from art, then, later, technique and nature will be reintegrated in a higher synthesis.[13] But man will dominate himself as well as nature.

"The human species . . . will once more enter into a state of radical transformation."[14] After all, Trotsky writes, humanity has not given up "crawling on all fours" before God, kings and capitalists only to "submit humbly before the dark laws of heredity and a blind sexual selection."[15] Man's ultimate goal under socialism will be "to create a higher social biologic type, or, if you please, a superman."[16] A superman. Then Marxism, too, may seek to lead man across the next evolutionary threshold.

But Marx failed to provide his followers with a blueprint for the future.[17] While certain lines of speculation have been inhibited because they have seemed obviously antimaterialistic and idealistic, with time there has flourished in Marxist circles especially in the Soviet Union, an eclectic utopianism. The popularity of science fiction has inspired Soviet publicists and scientists to spend much time and energy on flying saucers, extraterrestrial visitations (the great Siberian meteorite crater is frequently attributed to such an event) and the like. Paradoxically, the study of telepathy and other forms of extrasensory perception is much more respectable in the Soviet Union than in the West, and the potentiality seems to exist for something resembling a Marxist theosophy. What are we to make of the statement of a Soviet scientist that the population explosion has a hidden meaning: since man cannot conquer space with only three billion humans, nature is at work preparing mankind for this next step?[18]

The future of Marxism is in doubt. Many Marxists seek to return to what they regard as the essential humanism of Marx, at least the younger Marx. This line of reasoning can lead to a criticism of industrialism and technological society remarkably similar to that of Western thinkers; the essential shared component is the use of the concept of alienation, combined with the assumption that socialization of property rights means only the beginning of the conquest of alienation, not its elimination.[19] Much of this neohuman-

ism is, of course, politically tendentious, a means of using
the safety of the words of the enshrined prophet as a cover
for criticism of Communist society, but much of it has a
deeper meaning. The major lesson it conveys is that within
the socialist part of the world the issue of man's future is as
clouded as in capitalist lands. For if, so far, Marxism has
not completely committed itself to technological Messianism, and humanists are fighting an intellectual rear-guard
action, nonetheless Marxism yet has to find within itself the
basis for resisting the day-to-day, pragmatic pressures toward allowing technology to become an independent
force capable of radically altering human existence.

   Though utopianism declined as an intellectual influence among literary men in the nineteenth century, it continued to reign unchallenged among practical men. People
were convinced, on what seemed to be the direct evidence
of their senses, that everyday life and the world in general
were getting better and better. People had more to eat in
quantity and variety, more to wear and better houses.
Travel and communications were faster and cheaper. Education and, as compared with the past, popular government flourished. The energy revolution introduced by the
industrial revolution had been a boon to mankind. So widespread was this belief, so much a part of common sense,
that it needed to be affirmed only in reply to those who
denied it. In our own era the scientist-litterateur C. P.
Snow has been bitter about those intellectuals who have
failed to acknowledge the extent to which science has en-
riched human life and made the world a better place, a
failure that he attributes to their lack of scientific knowledge (the fruit of the dichotomy between the "two cultures") and their callousness to the sufferings of the masses
in past eras.[20]

   Within the Western world technological Messianism
does not take an organized form, either politically or intellectually. But there is no question that the rising tide of

technological change, which is lapping at the existential foundations of human existence, is welcomed by many. Some who prophesy great changes taking place, such as Ellul, are fundamentally hostile to them; others, such as Marshall McLuhan, while welcoming the new, implicitly restrict their welcome to changes in certain aspects of life. The precise views of both Ellul and McLuhan are difficult to pin down, since both look upon the syllogistic forms of reasoning, which have prevailed in the West since the time of Aristotle, as outmoded and proclaim the new era in a disconcerting new style of argument. But whatever reservations they may have about technological Messianism, their influence has given credence to the idea that fundamental change is at hand and is both necessary and desirable.

The French scholar Jacques Ellul is essentially a conservative Christian in his values. But though he seeks more to warn than to welcome, he is so convinced of the dangers that threaten man in an era when everything will be technological and technology will become a completely autonomous force that he becomes an agent of his own enemy. By exaggerating the situation, he creates a despair so profound as to render resistance hopeless, leaving many who accept what he has to say with the conviction that the only dignified thing left to do is to await the end, savoring one's knowledge of its inevitability, like a figure in a Greek tragedy. Perhaps something can be done, Ellul admits, but he gives scant hope and no clues.

Marshall McLuhan proselytizes on behalf of the new era with all the fervor of the convert. Originally a romantic-conservative critic of modern mass industrial civilization,[21] he has become an exponent of contemporary culture who now regards with favor the new electronic environment that he sees as the essential fact of modern life, determining all others.[22] Uninhibited by any significant amount of learning in any of the social sciences, he has become very much à la mode as a prophet to the communications industry, telling them and the world that they are the shapers of a new and better life. But McLuhan has a wide following among serious thinkers as well, which cannot be attributed simply to his modishness. He is basically correct in his assessment of the nature of the communications revolution and its importance, though like all monist social theorists he is wrong in attributing all social change to the influence of this one factor; his enthusiasm for the changes he sees and foresees blinds him to real problems that we must ourselves look at in due course. The cultural critic Gerald Sykes draws upon both Ellul and McLuhan to predict a world in which the "Aztech," the barbarous man of action, will dominate the more humane and thoughtful "Toltech," but his only advice to the latter is to "cherish your obscurity," thus combining McLuhan's diagnosis and Ellul's despair.[23]

The Existential Prophets

But the new era also has prophets who proclaim it with neither doubt nor qualification. Two of these, B. F. Skinner and Arthur C. Clarke, though they are widely read, have fathered no movements; a third, Richard Landers, is an intellectually obscure engineer; a fourth, the paleontologist Teilhard de Chardin, is the focus of an intellectual cult and has already achieved the status of a culture hero, as evidenced by the fact that he is widely discussed by so many who have never read him. Others could have been chosen, but what is important to us is not how representative they are of current intellectual trends but their usefulness in showing us some of the existential alternatives facing man in the late twentieth century. All of them say, in one fashion or another, that postindustrial man is coming —welcome him and throw off your nostalgia for the humanity and the world you have lost.

Most modest in his prophecy of possible changes is

B. F. Skinner, the distinguished Harvard psychologist who is primarily concerned with technologies of social control through psychological conditioning. Yet he raises important issues about the nature of man in any society in which man is capable of controlling his own mental states, whether through nonmaterial psychological techniques or by pharmacological methods. What Skinner asks in his widely read and widely criticized utopian novel, *Walden Two*, and in his other writings, is what does man really lose by determining his actions himself? Freedom, Skinner argues, is an illusion anyway. Men are conditioned by their childhood and their environment, by their biological nature and by random and unstructured social events, sometimes with results that we generally regard as bad. Why not condition men to such ends as social survival, benevolence and pleasure, ends that he assumes are obviously and axiomatically preferable to their contraries?[24]

Attacks on Skinner have focused on defense of the classical notion of free will against his assumption of universal determinism, on the pragmatic argument that one cannot trust those who would do the conditioning, on the contention that the uniformity that would result from his methods is bad because boring and, perhaps most trenchantly, on the argument that evolutionary progress demands a variety that would be eliminated in his ideal world.

But what is most interesting about Skinner is the implication of his central thesis, which cannot be denied: it is now theoretically possible, given a certain investment of resources and access to the persons involved, to control human personal and social development in a systematic way. Whether one has regarded previous situations as freedom or bondage to blind fate, as preferable or not, is beside the point. The point is that now a choice can and must be made. No longer does ignorance or impotence offer us an escape from the possibility of control by means of social technology. The power exists. It may or may not be

used or abused, but it is there. To say that Skinner is wrong
and technological man should not convert himself into any
particular model personality is one thing. But to rail at
Skinner as a monster is irrelevant, since the choice he places
before us is a real one, and insofar as it exists technological
man exists.

Richard Landers is an industrial engineer long associated with the Thompson Ramo-Wooldridge Corporation, a
firm whose peculiar history tells volumes about the changing shape of American civilization.[25] Like Skinner he both
predicts and advocates. He looks with anticipation to a
new environment for man called the dybosphere (from the
Hebrew "dybbuk," unassigned spirit). In the new era men
and machines will converge and become indistinguishable.
(Landers himself is at work on a self-reproducing machine.) Landers is prescient in recognizing that the mechanization of men and the humanization of machines is
possible precisely because at the same time that we are
gaining a more exact understanding of human life as a
physiochemical process we are also becoming more aware
of the subtleties of the physical universe. The traditional
dichotomy between man and machine is breaking down because the old crude concepts of mechanism and materialism are breaking down. Men and machines both operate in
terms of process. Not only have heart transplants and the
use of artificial organs heralded the new symbiosis but so
has the intellectual revolution that is now underway.

For Landers, the astronaut is the prototype of the new
man. "What is true for him today will be true for the rest of
us tomorrow."[26] He lives as we will in a "machine oriented"
rather than a "biologically-oriented world," one in which
machines will be dominant, and like the inhabitants of any
conquered nation men will have to learn to think and act
like their conquerors.[27] Landers is in favor of eliminating
or reversing the age-old distinction between the natural
and the artificial, and is inspired by an almost pathological

rejection of nature. Artificial lawns—green concrete—are better than real ones and a person "can live and flourish in an asphalt jungle as well as a tree-filled jungle."[28] He is fascinated by the idea of combining men and machines to form new systems or even to form individual creatures physically superior to human beings.

Why should man accept this new environment? It is good in that machines are "morally pure," without the guile, avarice and other faults of human beings,[29] a somewhat inconsistent point given his equation of men and machines. The new world will be more comfortable with "wondrous new products,"—fewer diseases, less strenuous work and more free time.[30] But, anyway, the new era is inevitable. Like Ellul, Landers believes technology is irresistible. Men must change to fit it "as we find it."[31] Man creates technology, but inevitably so. He ends his argument with a stern warning to those who might not wish to become a new species. Those who will be most comfortable in the "mechanistic" future are those who are most enthusiastic about its coming: "Darwin's theory of the survival of the fittest is as valid in the dybosphere as it was in the biosphere."[32]

It would be even easier to caricature and attack Landers' ideas than Skinner's, but equally fruitless. Regardless of his values, he has neither overstated nor distorted the problem. Man is entering into a new symbiosis with the machine in part because of an increasing understanding of the essential unity of process in organic and inorganic objects. At present he is doing so under the spell, which Landers reflects, of the power and ease to be gained by allowing the machine to take control. But to what extent the symbiosis is inevitable and which element is to be dominant are as yet unanswered questions. Knowledge of the affinities of man and machine cannot be suppressed practically, but use of artificial organs or computers can be. How new organs and computers are used can be regulated. But it is clear that just as man must choose how much and to what ends he wishes to condition his personality, so he soon must choose how he shall use his new powers of combining with the machine.

Both Skinner and Landers are concerned with particular aspects of man's destiny, though the acceptance of the utopia of either—a psychologically conditioned world or a mechanistic one—would involve fundamental alterations in man's nature. But other prophets have an even broader vision. Technology is accepted by many religious thinkers as revolutionizing man's relations with nature and God, while some scientifically oriented persons look upon technology itself as fulfilling the function of religion in orienting man to the universe, indeed, as fulfilling the function of God in specifying man's nature and determining his destiny.

Harvey Cox is representative of a number of theologians in celebrating man's breach with nature and his embrace of technology. Cox regards with approval "technopolitan" man living in a world from which God has withdrawn, leaving man, finally adult, to his own devices,[33] a position not dissimilar from that of "death of God" theologian Thomas Altizer, who sees atheism as a Christian imperative.[34] Teilhard de Chardin reaches much the same destination by an essentially different road.

Teilhard's current prominence is the result of many factors. It is due partly to the need of religious believers to forge an alliance between science and religion; in part it may be attributable to the affinity of some scientists for mysticism or to their pleasure that a religious figure should look to science for basic philosophical norms. Partly it is sheer modishness for its own sake. And the fact that Teilhard was a Jesuit has given him a built-in publicist apparatus of some significance. But the basic reason is far more deeply rooted in the cultural currents of the times. Dualism, whatever its attractions, is inherently an uncomfortable and unstable position. Thus in the past philosophers and theologians such as Thomas Aquinas have sought to create syntheses in which science was the junior partner, while other thinkers have reversed the process, making philosophy and theology dependent on science. In the twentieth century religiously motivated persons have increasingly rejected the supernatural as a separate realm and have looked to the world as the arena of significant choice and activity, while secular thinkers are increasingly unsure as to whether the sciences are capable of providing an adequate answer to basic questions about man and the universe.

The philosophy of Teilhard was essentially one of those ideas whose time had come. Evolution was more than Christianized, it was made the essence of Christianity. The dualism was broken—matter was spirit and spirit worked through matter. Not only was there no incompatibility between science and religion, between the natural and the supernatural, but they were the same. Morality was identified with evolution, and cultural and physical evolution were combined. Here was a new faith that could inspire the religious mystic, the scientific worker, the political activist. Man's unity had been restored.

Teilhard represents a synthesis of dominant trends and a point of departure for their extrapolation.[35] In his evolutionary theories, not only is the distinction between matter and spirit eliminated, but, equally important, salvation becomes collective rather than individual, and evolution, now cultural rather than merely biological, becomes the pathway to collective redemption. He quotes with approval his friend Julian Huxley's dictum that man is "nothing else than evolution becoming conscious of itself."[36] Man's evolution is now social rather than biological, however; his culture is part of him, "organically inseparable."[37] Modern man differs radically from his ancestors; the difference between a man of the first century and one of today is greater than that between an adolescent and an adult. Mankind's history from the Neolithic age onward has been leading up to the great turning point of the present, for "in our time Mankind seems to be approaching its critical point of social organization."[38] "Our species," he writes, "is entering its phase of socialization."[39] Interacting mankind now covers the earth. Communications theorists who follow McLuhan (whose ideas converge with those of Teilhard at many points) speak of tribal society, of all human beings being simultaneously present to each other as a result of electronic communications, but for Teilhard the union is metaphysically real.

Teilhard's thesis is that the development of mankind has eventuated in a superorganism, a collective being, which he calls the Noosphere. The Noosphere is "a domain of interwoven consciousness,"[40] but it is more than simply a term for individuals in communication, it is a collective being, a "single, hyper-conscious arch molecule,"[41] a "stupendous thinking machine."[42]

Some religious thinkers, such as Romano Guardini, have anticipated the new world of technological man with fear and foreboding, but for Teilhard and his followers the appearance of postmodern man is welcomed as a step toward the collective redemption of mankind. For progress is the natural end of man, an endless striving toward a higher form of life. The supreme purpose of humanity is science, knowledge and power—"pursuing even further, to the very end, the forces of life."[43] In this perspective the discovery of the atom bomb is a step forward, the explosions herald the coming of the new spirit that will dominate mankind, the "Spirit of the Earth."[44] We are about to cross an evolutionary threshold, that of the "superhuman."[45] Teilhard does not refer to his new creature as technological man, he prefers to call him progressive man, "the man to whom the terrestrial future means more than the mere present,"[46] but technological man is who he really is.

Teilhard sets the new man off against his predecessor,

bourgeois man, whom he excoriates with the fervor of the revolutionist attacking existing society. Progressive man does not seek a life of ease, that would be to yield to the bourgeois spirit; Teilhard is as hostile to pleasure and play as any Puritan deacon.[47] Marxism and Christianity are on the same side in the confrontation with bourgeois man, both of them positive evolutionary factors moving in the same direction, as indicated by his most famous phrase, "Everything that rises must converge."[48] There are really only two forces in the world today, the "bourgeois spirit," which seeks only to make the world a "more comfortable dwellingplace," and the spirit of the true "toilers of the earth," who will one day "simply by biological predominance . . . constitute the human race."[49] Like the engineer Landers with his paean in favor of man-machine symbiosis, Teilhard is bitter in his condemnation of those who prefer to be mere men and resist the great leap forward. All these will be the "cast-offs."[50] Individuals can resist progress, the race as a whole cannot. "Absolutely nothing" can halt the progress of man toward "ever greater interdependence and cohesion."[51]

Teilhard is especially bitter toward the critics of industrial civilization. He speaks disparagingly of "the nightmare of brutalization and mechanization which are conjured up to terrify us and prevent our advance,"[52] and he is particularly wroth that so many of his fellow Christians are to be found in the camp of those who hang back from progress. Yet in what does this progress consist? It adds up to nothing less than the destruction of the human individuality that humanist and Christian traditions alike have seen as man's special glory, and which many biologists have viewed as the goal of the evolutionary process. Life, Teilhard writes, "shows signs . . . of requiring us by very virtue of its movement toward a state of higher Being, to sacrifice our individuality."[53] We are part of nature, he avers, rejecting dualism, but our nobility consists not in ac-

cepting nature as it is, finding our place in it and conform-
ing to its rhythms, but "in serving, like intelligent atoms, the
work proceeding in the universe,"[54] in becoming part of a
progressive nature. The development of the individual is
not the end of evolution; indeed, individualism robs us of
those "ineffable joys of union and conscious loss of self in
that which is greater than self."[55] He applauds the col-
lectivization inherent in modern society, the rise of the
masses, economic integration, "totalization of political
regimes," closer physical contact of men and nations and,
above all, "the increasing impossibility of being or acting or
thinking *alone*—in short, the rise, in every form, of the
Other around us."[56]

Critics of Teilhard de Chardin have pointed to his
praise for totalitarian regimes, which he held to be "in line
with the essential trend of 'cosmic' movement,"[57] and the
wooliness of his qualification that unanimity should be the
fruit not of coercion but love. Actually, his remarks are
simply an indication of his general lack of serious interest
in social questions, though, paradoxically, many modern
Christian social revolutionaries look to his ideas and rheto-
ric for inspiration. What is most significant about Teilhard's
thought is not any particular political or social idiosyncracies, but his overarching impatience with the messiness of
ordinary human life, the real mark of the true totalitarian.
Teilhard is not concerned with individuals or individual
desires, hopes, fears or needs, but only with the race as a
whole. Thus he can speak of "boredom" as "Public Enemy
No.1" in a world still beset by hunger, disease and a host
of unsolved or perhaps insoluble personal problems.[58] Lone-
liness and death not of the individual but of the race are
his interests. To seriously contemplate the idea that mankind might come to an end would "paralyze all the vital
forces of the earth," he says,[59] thus necessarily rejecting
the Shakespearean "ripeness is all" as the weakness of one
seduced by an unprogressive Nature. Yet unlike many

prophets of infinite human progress, he does not see space travel as the answer; he is skeptical about its very possibility and about man's ability to live on other worlds.[60]

Teilhard is only partially aware of the existential revolution. He knows that man through science, including genetics, is now the master of his fate, and uses the metaphor of a card game in which humanity has now "become aware that . . . we are the players as well as the cards and the stakes."[61] Yet for Teilhard the game is fixed, there is nowhere to go but forward, and no goal but redemption. Man necessarily must find salvation in the cosmic Christ, the omega point of the universe. But he reaches this omega point through the evolution of the material world: "It is in intelligent alliance with the rising tide of matter that we shall draw closer to the spirit."[62] In the last analysis Teilhard's world view dissolves into a materialist mysticism in which the outline of technolgical man becomes blurred by a kaleidoscope of strobe lights and votive candles combining to obscure rather than illuminate.

Teilhard de Chardin is neither original nor unique in his view of the universe as simultaneously physical and spiritual or in his belief that a common system of explanation must be found both for accepted physical phenomena and for events or alleged events usually denominated as spiritual or mystic in nature. Some of the earliest proponents of evolution as a scientific doctrine looked forward to man's next step as a heightening of "spiritual" powers, which they saw as the product of physical causes.[63] In more recent times, serious scientists have hypothesized that telepathy and clairvoyance not only exist but can be studied by the techniques of physical science, while pseudo scientists have even sought means of photographing the soul. Many Marxists, as we have seen, are tantalized by the extrasensory and parapsychological despite their repudiation of "idealism" and allegiance to dialectical materialism. Julian Huxley, an important influence on Teilhard,

saw in evolution a means toward the spiritual fulfillment
of the race, and thought such Eastern religious practices as
Yoga a step toward human self-discovery, an attitude that
was not shared by Teilhard, who despised non-Western
men and their ways.

Perhaps the furthest steps in the direction of both proclaiming man's untapped spiritual powers and assimilating
them to matter, however, have been taken by Arthur C.
Clarke, whose views, while possibly no more extreme than
those of Teilhard, are more wide-ranging and above all
more specific.

Though a science-fiction writer and popularizer of science (he is the coauthor of the widely heralded motion
picture *2001*), Clarke enjoys a well-deserved reputation as
a prognosticator who has forecast with precision and in
detail such developments as unmanned contact with the
moon and manned extraterrestrial flight. Even in professional scientific quarters he enjoys an increasing vogue as a
savant.[64]

Clarke's major prophecies are summarized in his *Profiles of the Future*, which is noteworthy not only for dealing
with the future development of the accepted sciences but
for discussing in a matter-of-fact manner such questions as
extrasensory perception, invisibility and the interpenetration of matter. Clarke, like Landers and, in a way, Mc-
Luhan, is concerned with the machine-man symbiosis in
which artificial sensors will make it possible for man to feel
he is actually present wherever his creations are. The ultimate would be a human brain without a body which could
be "present" anywhere in the universe. Such a creation has
long been envisioned by writers of science fiction; Clarke's
contribution has been to point out that such a being eventually can be created and would constitute a form of immortality that might be regarded as normal maturity for individuals of the human species. But if the individual can be
immortal, the race need not be. Clarke accepts the end of

mankind with more equanimity than Teilhard because he visualizes it as coming to an end not in catastrophe but in obsolescence, through evolving into something higher, the man-machine symbiosis, the Cyborg.

But evolving into man-machines is not the only way in which humanity might come to an end. In Clarke's best novel, *Childhood's End*, contact with an alien race, higher in ability than man but arrested in its own development, provides the catalyst that enables newborn human infants to achieve a breakthrough in mental ability that permits them to manipulate the universe directly through intellectual power. The final outcome is a Götterdämmerung in which individual human bodies disappear and mind and matter merge in an identity toward which the universe has been evolving throughout its history, as if the world spirit of Hegel had finally become fully conscious of itself and immanent spirit had consumed its material base in order to create a new consummate entity.

What is the significance of the prophets of technological millenarianism? Some of them, such as Skinner and Landers, call attention to the radical changes in human existence that are already within mankind's grasp. All of them remind us that what is at stake is not merely the new society that the sociological prophets foresee but a radically new definition of man. The fact that men as intellectually significant and influential as Teilhard and Clarke can regard with equanimity, indeed, with eager anticipation, the end of humanity as it has existed since the Neolithic age is a sign that the existential revolution could take a form in which technological man would be the last stage in the progress of mankind toward its own extinction.

5

The Existential Revolution

Mankind, it is alleged by the prophets of the new man, is on the threshold of a new age. He has, so they tell us, within or almost within his grasp new powers over himself and his environment that will radically transform the whole character and meaning of human existence. But before we can affirm or deny the reality or extent of this existential revolution we need to be more specific about the changes technology is making possible that threaten the persistence of civilization as we have known it or that herald the coming of the new technological man.

Trying to understand what is happening to man today is difficult for several reasons. Many of the new scientific and technological breakthroughs, like the development of the atomic bomb or the circumnavigation of the earth by astronauts, are or appear to be isolated events. It is not at once apparent what effect they are having on man's social life and self-image; most of us go about our daily business as if they had never occurred. We may once have thought of building a fallout shelter or we may have stayed at home to watch the first manned rocket launchings on television, but soon we are once again caught up in the daily routine of bills, promotions, vacations and lawns to mow. Other triumphs of science, like the successful transplantation of the human heart, strike us as novel and possibly important to a few humans with medical problems, but they seem like more of the same thing: further steps in a long upward spiral of medical progress, added conveniences like faster cars and color TV. Isn't it wonderful, we say, and then belie our words by going on about our business.

Still other additions to man's power over nature, such as the synthesis of DNA, involve such esoteric scientific problems that to most of us (though not necessarily to our more alert offspring) they are largely meaningless. Not understanding the scientific issues involved, we soon lose interest (though we may feel guilty about this if we are middle class and college trained, for today not being interested in science is not unlike admitting to being bored by classical music). Having no philosophical or scientific context within which to place these discoveries, we soon forget about them.

Finally there are a great number of possibilities that never enter our consciousness at all simply because through lack of background knowledge and interest we never hear about them or, if we do, we unconsciously dismiss them as mere speculation or even fantasy. Gene banks and artificial brains, extrasensory perception and the ability to derive atomic energy from ordinary rocks many crop up in the headlines of our newspapers, but they become a kind of background noise to the stock-market reports and the war news, filtered out like the television program our children are watching in the next room. If we do notice these items, we may simply suppress them, as many of us do with information relating to the dangers of nuclear war or a world population that will more than double in the next generation. The power of the ordinary to reclaim our attention is enormous, and is in part a necessary condition of our san-ity. It also may represent a healthy acceptance of fate. An early modern saint is famous for his reply to a question about what he would do if he knew that God was going to bring his life to an end within the hour. His reply was that he would go on playing billiards. But his faith in the state of his soul and the beneficence of the Almighty may not be an appropriate response for those whose civilization is threatened by developments all of which might not be beneficent (in part because the present civilization is not as morally healthy as it might be), developments that it still has some power to affect.

There exists today a sizable literature about the foreseeable future (the period from today until the era of our great-grandchildren) in which the leading experts in various fields set forth their views as to what technological developments are likely to occur. Ability to predict technological change is far from absolute, but usually the unanticipated event occurs in addition to the anticipated rather than as a substitute for it, so most of what is predicted probably will occur. Many predictions necessarily rest on assumptions about how much effort will go into certain lines of research as well as about what appears to be intrinsically possible, but increasingly the prophets take this complication into account. Some predictions are to a certain extent mutually incompatible, in practice even if not in theory. Thus improvements in communications technology might lead to a slackening of efforts to improve transportation or vice versa, or an increased ability to convert ordinary substances such as sand and rock into scarce minerals might make interplanetary mining uneconomic; but this does not negate the possibility of any of the alternatives or the need to take cognizance of them.

While not all futurists agree on details—and today every competent scientist, businessman, military leader or government official is continually involved in predicting the future through sheer necessity to plan ahead in his own activity—there is considerable consensus on basic trends in technological development.[1] (In part, of course, this may be due to common orientations or to the fact that there is developing a futurist Establishment that dominates most studies and conferences.) Most disagreements are about probabilities rather than possibilities and about timing. When one realizes the magnitude and probable impact of the events forecast, one is struck by the wide measure of agreement rather than by the minor disagreements. If only a small fraction of the developments predicted take place, the existential revolution will present humanity with psychological shocks and practical problems on a scale unknown to recorded history.

The Extension of Environment

Because of its remoteness from ordinary human life, progress in the conquest of space presents perhaps the fewest immediately disturbing elements for contemporary civilization to assimilate. We are already getting used to the intercontinental missile and its cousin, the satellite that can observe or destroy any part of the earth's surface unless prevented from doing so. Mechanical contact with or electronic observation of the surface of the moon and Venus is already a reality. What does the future hold? Some predictions are so certain that a consensus exists as to the actual date of their probable occurrence—a permanent lunar base by 1975, permanent manned stations on some planets by 1990—given certain assumptions about budgetary commitments on the part of the governments concerned.

There is nothing very startling about these predictions. Less expected by most of us, however, is the probable discovery of an antigravity drive on a principle other than rocket propulsion, which one panel of experts expects soon after the year 2020.[2] Such an event would open the door to travel beyond the solar system, in addition to being a contribution toward nullifying the force of gravity (rather than merely overcoming it) here on earth. Some predictions such as competition for the raw materials of other planets and extraterrestrial farming by about the same time would have important economic and psychological effects if fulfilled.[3] But even if they came to pass they would simply mean that man's conquest of the solar system was essentially Europe's conquest of the earth in the colonial era writ large: colonies, bases, plantations, economic exploitation.

More significant are those technological developments associated with the conquest of space that have direct implications for the nature of man himself. Journeys into outer space—especially beyond the solar system—would take vast amounts of time with any immediate foreseeable techniques. Scientists therefore predict placing voyagers in a state of coma from which they would automatically recover at a set time. An even more significant alternative would be multigeneration missions in which those who arrived at their destination would be the descendants of the original crew. Should this occur, man would really have left earth behind, scattering his seed far into the universe. Those born and reared in space would be in a sense a different kind of man. They might never be able to communicate with the planet that sent them forth. But the impact of their going on the consciousness of those who remained behind would still be immense.

The difficulties of operating in and adjusting to the physical conditions of outer space and strange planets have led to speculation that the astronauts of the future would be Cyborgs, men who would have many artificial organs and thus would be better able to cope with harsh and novel surroundings. An alternative or supplementary means of exploration (at least within shorter distances where something like real-time communication was possible) would be a kind of machine-man symbiosis, in which there would be direct electromagnetic connection between the human nervous system and equipment that was receiving transmissions from sensors elsewhere in space. Those humans involved would control the exploring machines and receive impressions (muted, if necessary) as if they were actually physically experiencing the exploration themselves. Space would thus become part of the human environment, since even those not in the direct symbiotic relationship would be part of a culture that knew the sights and sounds of the expanses of space firsthand.[4]

Not only in space but also on earth itself is the environment about to be radically extended. The oceans will in a generation or two become part of the human habitat.[5] They will not merely be crossed by travelers, fishermen or the world's navies, or explored by a few aquanauts for scientific, military or recreational purposes; they will become as domesticated as the land surface of the planet. Men will farm the waters, breed and herd fish, and mine the bottom of the high seas. The conquest of the 70 per cent of the earth's surface that is under water will mean changes in man, society and nature. Permanent undersea colonies will be established; individuals and even whole families may eventually spend most of their lives under water. Cetaceans, many of whom exhibit a high level of natural intelligence, will be bred and trained as helpers; already the U.S. Navy is using dolphins in undersea recovery work.[6] Man himself will learn to breathe water through medical alteration of his lungs or other means; the U.S. Navy's leading expert's target for the creation of "gillmen" is 1972.[7] Extensive research in breathing water impregnated with compressed gas is currently underway at Duke University under the direction of Dr. Johannes Klystra. Whether or not any particular developments now foreseen actually will take place, man's over-all relation to the oceans is about to change inexorably and irrevocably. Just as we soon will no longer see the moon primarily as an aid to romance but rather as a revolving mining camp or military base, our children standing on the shores of the Pacific will see not a vastness of untamed water stretching far beyond the horizon to Cathay, but a pond full of derricks, mines, ranches and perhaps even suburbs.

What of man's economic life? Some predict that the race between technological progress and population growth will be won by the former. How likely this is we must judge in due course. Certainly there seems to be increasing consensus among scientists that new weapons will soon be available for the war on hunger and scarcity. Most startling and important, it is even hoped that the alchemist's ancient dream of transmuting base metals into precious ones will be fully realized at last. Man already can create new sources of energy and new elements through his mastery of the atom. But this ability is so far restricted by the need to use naturally unstable radioactive minerals as a point of departure. If man can unlock the energy in ordinary iron or hydrogen and use it to turn the common elements of the land and seas into mechanical or electrical energy or into other elements, scarcity would lose most of its meaning. Some predict that the world's need for fresh water soon could be remedied by economically feasible desalination using radioactive materials; if ordinary minerals could be substituted this would remove all obstacles to unlimited water supplies. It is already technically possible to create synthetic protein from petroleum; once we are able to do this on a large scale no one need ever go hungry or suffer the physical or mental defects caused by lack of protein; for petroleum itself can probably be made available without limit through chemical alchemy. In time man should be able to use any part of the earth's surface or interior for any purpose he wishes; through recycling he could use it over and over again.

Today natural forces still get in the way of man's productive activities, especially in agriculture. This, too, will soon be a thing of the past. Completely accurate prediction of the weather over the globe is almost unanimously expected in a relatively short time; many foresee control of the most significant aspects of the weather within a generation.[8]

The single factor that most distinguishes the coming civilization, whatever one chooses to call it, is the substitution of "communication" processes for traditional "work" as man's primary activity. That automation in one form or another will be the basis of the new civilization is generally held by futurists. Teaching machines will become the norm, and in time information will be directly transmitted to the human brain electronically. Use of the computer will lead to what, in effect, will be a universal language for some purposes, based on the computer's needs. By 1990, many confidently predict, computers will be available with the equivalent of IQ's of 150 in terms of their ability to respond to directions, understand their environment and initiate activity. Routine labor will be taken over by robot household servants (though many see as an alternative the breeding of intelligent animals, particularly primates, for low-grade routine labor on the land as well as in the sea). The climax of this process will come when machine-man symbiosis begins to play its role on earth; a median date predicted for its large-scale practicability is 2010.[9]

The progress of technology will increase vastly the means available to men to control other men. New biological and pharmacological weapons will be available that will coerce without destroying men or property, largely through their direct effect on the will. Electronics will increase greatly the means of centralized surveillance available to ruling groups (a national data bank is already a subject of controversy in Washington, and it could be instituted tomorrow, Congress permitting).[10]

The Impact of Biology

But neither the extensions of man's effective environment into the depths of space or the oceans, nor the vision of automated affluence, nor even the greater social controls that are predicted for the near future most radically affect man's existential situation. He has always sought knowledge, ease and power over his fellows. The coming of the new man is foreshadowed most by the contemporary revolution in the biological sciences.[11] We have noted already the extent to which man's biological integrity could be affected by various kinds of symbiosis with the machine, whether through increased use of artificial organs or by being literally plugged into a computer. But increasing understanding of the processes underlying biological activity will also make it possible to subject organic processes to human control. Drugs may become widespread not only as means of social control but as accepted means of self-realization. General and permanent immunization against most diseases is considered increasingly feasible. Physical and chemical treatment for psychological and psychotic states may soon relegate the Freudian analyst to the role of witch doctor that many scientists feel is only appropriate. New contraceptive techniques are constantly being developed to bring fecundity under control, and increasingly the aspiration of researchers is something (a capsule implanted in the body that permanently inhibits formation of appropriate cells unless neutralized, for instance) that would make breeding, rather than prevention, require a special medical act. New medical discoveries lead researchers to expect the lengthening of the human life span fifty years, which in their view would only be a return to the normal. It is already virtually certain that even the brain can be rejuvenated by injections of DNA, thus making it possible to maintain memory and problem-solving ability unimpaired into old age.[12]

However, it is not the curing of disease but the control of genetic processes and the shape of man that most excites speculation. Man's physical shape will be alterable by new and radical forms of medical cosmetology; the nose job and

the paraffin-inflated breasts of today will be succeeded by
a variety of techniques to alter color of hair, skin or eyes or
to change contours or even sex, with only the basic skeletal
structure constituting any limitation. Mental states will be
alterable as well: intelligence and character affected by
chemical means, dreams stimulated or even preprogramed.
Biochemical processes may make possible the growing of
new organs to replace old ones; the year 2007 is predicted
by some as the date for this breakthrough.

But at best the human mind and body, once formed,
present a difficult problem for the biologist. Far better to
"adjust" them beforehand. The breaking of the genetic
code will in the reasonably near future make it possible to
predetermine not only sex but other characteristics. Genetic
defects could be countered by excision or addition of
genes in embryo; if suitable artificial wombs being worked
on at present are perfected, "foetal therapy" is well on the
way. New knowledge of the mechanisms of heredity, stor-
age of genetic materials and artificial insemination will
make it possible for women to order the kind of child they
wish as they would order a new car. For parents with
higher self-esteem, techniques are being developed that will
make it possible to produce exact duplicates of the father or
mother by substituting the cell nuclei of the desired parent
for that in the fertilized human egg. This has already been
done with frogs.[13] Alternatively, society could breed sub-
types of men as it now does dogs for various roles and
functions. Biologist Bentley Glass predicts artificial production of children "will probably be realized by the end
of the 20th century."[14]

What do all these discoveries in biology and the increasing symbiosis of man and machine, even if only on the
social and intellectual rather than on the physical plane,
add up to? Physicist Herman Kahn, in these respects more
conservative than other futurists, perhaps because he is not
a biologist, lists two "far-out" predictions that, he holds,

nevertheless deserve serious consideration. One is the almost complete genetic control of man, wherein he still remains, however, *Homo sapiens*; the other is the end of
Homo sapiens and the creation of a new species by man's
own actions.[15] If in time, as some predict, man is able to
create new species of plants and animals directly in the
laboratory rather than through the more time-consuming
process of selective breeding, just as he already can create
live viruses from inanimate matter, why not a new species
built up from human genetic materials? But whatever the
specifics, man is about to enter upon a new plane of existence. "The logical climax of evolution can be said to have
occurred when, as is now imminent, a sentient species deliberately and directly assumes control of its own evolution," is the way a leading medical researcher describes
man's new status in the cosmos.[16]

Probably not all of these things will come to pass.
Many of them will take longer than predicted; the conservatism of scientists in the past is being replaced rapidly by
a euphoria in the present, which many would justify by
claiming that the speed of change seems to be increasing
exponentially. But the central core of these predictions will
become technologically feasible within the next seventy-
five years—advances in space travel, exploitation of the
oceans, new sources of energy and new resources, increased substitution of communication for physical labor, a
great increase in the technological means of social control,
and above all the ability of man to affect his own biological
and mental composition and that of his descendants. Together these changes constitute an existential revolution
that poses a new challenge for mankind. If man can do or
be whatever he wishes, how shall be choose? What should
be his criteria of choice? In the past, nature and ignorance
set limits to man's freedom and his follies, now they need
no longer stand in his way, and technological man will be
free even to destroy the possibility of freedom itself.

The Population Explosion

But these scientific advances do not tell the whole story. For while man through science and technology has been extending his power over the universe and himself, another force has been at work that alone would have brought modern civilization to the brink of existential revolution—the population explosion. Here is a case where increase in quantity has clearly resulted in a change in quality; the population explosion has meant that man while gaining more power over nature and himself has also largely overwhelmed nature and is forced to live cheek by jowl with his fellow man. Teilhard de Chardin and others are certainly correct in holding that the new civilization—call it Noosphere or technological civilization or what you will—would have been impossible as a result of advance in communication or other technologies alone. Increased human interaction is a function of human density as well as of the technical means for interaction. As a sober demographic periodical states: "These next twenty-five years form part of a process which began 200,000 years ago and which is about to culminate in man's full possession of the earth."[17]

The human population increase in recent centuries has been both a result of technological advance and a cause of it. New sources of wealth have made it possible to support more people, new medical techniques have kept many from dying young. At the same time large population densities have provided the "critical mass" necessary for economic, political and scientific development. The result has been a radical change in the human environment and a new challenge to human technology and wisdom.

It is almost impossible to understand the magnitude of the population problem without a cursory look at its origins. Demographers estimate that there were five million human beings alive at the time of the invention of agriculture, two

hundred million at the birth of Christ. By 1650 there were
five hundred million, by 1800 some nine hundred million.
By the beginning of the twentieth century the number had
risen to one and a half billion and in the last seventy years
has more than doubled so that there are more than
three and a half billion humans today.[18] In short, the first
great population explosion followed the invention of agriculture. Then there was a leveling off until the Industrial
Revolution, at which time another explosion ensued, which
is still going on, with population increasing not arithmetic-
ally but geometrically according to the laws of compound
interest. Some even predict a world population of fifteen
billion, more than four times the present number, by the
end of this century, some three decades from now.[19] Technological man must find some way of causing population
to at the least start leveling off again, a feat of large-scale
rational social control unparalleled in human history. Individual societies have brought death, birth and resources
into balance by various means throughout history, but
never has the race as a whole faced this task.[20]

For whatever the possibility of increased resources becoming available through technological advance, this will
not solve the population crisis. Even if the rise in population does not itself inhibit technological advance through
competition for the resources, the seed money, necessary to
finance new technologies, the problem is increasingly not
one of food or even shelter but of simple living space. At
present rates of increase there would literally be standing
room only in time, with the world like a culture of bacteria
in a laboratory ready to burst out of its receptacle. Space
travel, of course, provides no solution; even if habitable
planets were available, the cost of planetary colonization
would be too high in any foreseeable future; even here on
earth migration has proved only a temporary palliative to
population pressures.

The problems posed by the population explosion can

be put in perspective by a consideration of urbanization. As late as 1800, only fifty cities in the whole world could boast a population of more than 100,000, but urban concentration increased until there are today more than 1400 such cities, and over 140 metropolitan areas with at least a million inhabitants which contain 11 per cent of all the world's population.[21]

One can argue that a totally urbanized world (however much one might or might not like to live in it), making full use of the resources of the seas and the polar regions, to say nothing of resources drawn from other planets, is conceivable, and that such a world could support many times the world's current population, with food and other needs all produced artificially through the transmutation of elements and the synthesis of organic molecules. Therefore even if the earth's carrying capacity is limited, why not go to fifty billion before stopping?

Such an argument, of course, assumes that the new technologies needed to provide for such masses can be developed before world famine engulfs us. But it also neglects that fact that the new technologies themselves consume resources; the modern American with his house or apartment, automobile, food, office, schools and so on consumes and wastes an increasing amount of resources and requires a large amount of living space. Technological advance itself crowds the very men it sets out to save. Everything humanity needs might be created by science—even air and water could be depolluted and reused forever if enough energy were available—but space cannot be created. Only some inconceivable breakthrough into another dimension—the discovery of a coexistent universe in which, in effect, two or more systems of interacting energy could occupy the same space, analogously to the way frequency modulation permits a single radio wave or laser transmission or telephone wire to carry many messages simultaneously—could make it possible for human procreation to go on unchecked indefinitely.

In any event, the kind of civilization capable of supporting a significantly larger number of men through technological advance would necessarily have to be a new civilization, one based completely on rational calculation, maximum social discipline, recycling of resources and so on. Its institutions and culture would be utterly at variance with the blind procreative urges that have led to the population explosion as well as with most of man's customs and attributes as they have hitherto existed. Whether world population is stabilized at the present or a higher figure, the population explosion has already set the precondition for existential revolution by populating the earth to an extent where man cannot forgo using his new powers.

Power over man and nature, power that both limits human freedom and gives it new meaning, coexists with a density of interaction and interdependence among men that also both limits freedom and gives it new meaning. The existential revolutions caused by technology and population, though different in their origin and history, lead to the same climax at the level of the species. Beneath the surface of twentieth-century civilization the rumbling can be heard clearly and the earth is already starting to move.

6

Technological Change
and Economic Inertia

"The Bourbons forget nothing and they learn nothing."
With this epigram, history has sought to explain why the
downfall of this once great house was inevitable.

Man is an animal incapable of forgetting. The persistence of behavior patterns that were functional for a
small band in a vast forest today increasingly threaten human survival. But is man also incapable of learning? Can
he not at least superimpose upon his basic drives the wisdom to channel or overcome them?[1]

The question of whether technological man is myth or
reality turns on the question of the extent to which the
existential revolution that is altering man's very place in the
order of nature is also reflected in human society and in
man's ideas of himself. Even if he does not grasp what is
happening to him, the past and the man of the past is gone
forever. But what will succeed the past may not be a new
civilization but a new Dark Age in which animal blood-lust
and greed will have at their disposal means for mischief
and self-destruction inconceivable in the Dark Ages of old.

It has been the explicit contention of the sociological prophets, and the implicit assumption of the existential ones, that contemporary society is changing radically in response to technological change, and that these changes are evident in society's economic, political and social institutions, and in the cultural values that reflect or underlie these institutions. Though the point is rarely made explicitly, such change is often looked upon as a hopeful sign (though not, of course, by such as Ellul and his followers). In a sense, the contention that things are changing is irrefutable; technology is bound to condition other aspects of society. But this is quite different from saying that technology is providing the basis for a wholly new society, that it will become the integrating element in a new civilization. The effects of technological change instead may be dislocation, disjunction between ideas and reality, uncertainty, confusion and a disintegrated society.

Some social scientists would contend that the latter is impossible, that societies, whatever their size or complexity, always intermesh, are always interrelated wholes. In a sense this, too, is true; but it tells us nothing. A burning garbage dump is, from the point of view of physics, an interrelated system in some sort of equilibrium, with exchanges of energy interlocking and relating to each other; anything else would cause an explosion, leading abruptly to a new order.

Western Europe in the Dark Ages, China during the reign of the war lords in the early twentieth century and the recent experience of the Congo show under what confused conditions human beings can continue to feed, love, breed and die. It is not necessary to postulate some spirit of social integration as a *deus ex machina* hovering in the wings waiting to construct a new society out of the ruins of the old. The human animal, whatever its defects, is a tough and adaptable species.

The Myth of a Changing Economy

What effect, then, is technology having on society? The obvious first place to look for the impact of technology is the economic order. Material things form the physical basis of human life, and throughout history technology has set the limiting conditions for civilizations, first, by making possible advances in agricultural production and, in recent centuries, in laying the groundwork for industrialization and the rise of bourgeois man. The utilization of new technologies is typically expensive, and therefore their existence presupposes an economy that can support them and which in turn will be affected by them. Thus when the sociological prophets speak of changes in the nature of our society, they talk in terms of the rise of technicians and managers at the expense of production workers, the increasing importance of pure science to the economy and the movement from primary production to the service industries. These changes in the basic structure of the economy are in turn assumed or alleged to lead to changes in the class system and eventually in the political and cultural aspects of civilization. The net result will be technological civilization, the dominant figure in which will be a new man with a new economic base, new lifeways and new attitudes—the creature we have chosen to call technological man.

Is all this in fact taking place? Is the economy changing in the wake of technological development, and are these changes leading to the basic social changes alleged? The answer is both yes and no. Significant alterations are under way, but they have not gone as far as claimed nor is there any guarantee that they will continue indefinitely. Most importantly, they may not have the extraeconomic consequences predicted. A quick overview of what actually is taking place is necessary if we are to discover to what extent technological man is emerging in the economic order of civilization. It also should give us some clues as to what is happening to modern man politically and culturally. Many social critics have viewed industrial and technological civilization as the same phenomenon, and have ascribed certain characteristics to them jointly: enslavement or liberation, spiritual impoverishment or enrichment, a more equal or more stratified society. An analysis of what economic life is like today and how it is changing can shed light on all of the questions regarding the meaning of the "machine age" for man.

Throughout this and the following chapters we shall, except when otherwise specified, be dealing with conditions and trends in the United States. It is assumed that to some extent these are due not to national peculiarities but to the fact that its wealth has made the United States the prototype of the new civilization and the American the prototype of the new man, that what is going on in many parts of the world can better be called "modernization" than "Americanization," and that in time all the world will follow the model of man as made in the U.S.[2]

These assumptions, it must be recognized, can be challenged on several grounds. Some may claim that other nations will respond to technological change in accordance with their own histories and civilizations; so Chinese man in the twenty-first century will be very different from American man. Others might argue that only the United States and perhaps one or two other nations have the wealth and power to reach the plateau of the new civilization, and that most of the world's population will continue to be members of the old breed for an indefinite future— living fossils in the history of human evolution. Both of these positions will be touched on later when we examine the future international order. For our present purposes it is sufficient to realize that once a certain number of creatures change their characteristics and breed true to the change, a new species has come into being, regardless of what happens to the genetic pool from which it emerged.

Before one can understand the drift of contemporary history, one must recognize that by no means all of the controversy about where we are heading is the result of simple ignorance, stupidity or deception on the part of individual social commentators who differ on what is happening. The problem lies in the intrinsic difficulty of interpreting the data. In the long run, the only source of confirmation for hypotheses about changes in economic and social structure is the basic empirical data, ultimately expressed in statistical form. But statistics taken from different sources, especially statistical samples, do not necessarily agree.

The most basic data for the United States is that collected by the Census Bureau, but though sampling is done at regular intervals for specific purposes, the total universe, all the people at once, is questioned only every ten years. A further complication of enormous magnitude is the fact that some six million Americans apparently were missed by the last census, in 1960, if sample studies are any indication. These people are to be found largely at the bottom of the social ladder and are epitomized by the young unemployed Negro male school dropout living in a large city. People without jobs, families or permanent residence, possibly with reasons to avoid contact with the authorities, are not likely to be around when the census taker arrives. Not all or perhaps even a majority of those missed by the census have all the characteristics described, but most seem to have most of them and census data has to be weighted to take this into account.[3]

But problems of simple accuracy are not the only or even necessarily the most difficult ones that confront anyone who uses statistics as a means to get hard answers to the rather grandiose questions that we have posed. Problems of interpretation loom even larger. A substantial portion of the American labor force (34 per cent in 1964) and of labor forces elsewhere are not men but women. When one talks of a shift from blue- to white-collar jobs, from profit to nonprofit undertakings, does one speak of the total labor force or of men only? Clearly men's jobs are still more important in defining the character of a society, but how much more so? There is no scientific way of answering this question. And what do the categories themselves mean? No statistical category can deal with more than one characteristic of the thing counted (we can make cross tabulations, but while this is sometimes helpful we still have to choose which two or three things we count together).

Thus simple statistics may be misleading. H. L. Hunt, one of the two or three richest men in the world, is in the same statistical category as to type of occupation ("self-employed") as the corner candy-store owner, while most Hollywood stars with salaries in six figures can be counted as employees, along with persons barely eking out a living.[4] A road crew moving dirt may be government employees and so in the service industries, or they may be working for a private contractor and considered part of the basic construction industry. For certain statistical purposes an army private, well fed and sheltered by the military so that he is free to spend what money he earns on women, cars and liquor, is considered to be a member of the poor, while a teacher struggling to raise six children on his somewhat higher salary is considered middle class. As the controversy over the "war" on poverty especially has pointed up, statistics, like the Bible, can be quoted to many effects.

It is possible, therefore, to take refuge in placing the burden of proof upon those who hold that drastic changes with putatively drastic consequences are taking place in the shape of the American economy. Given the fact that statistics are subject to interpretation and qualification, unless something is so grossly obvious as to defeat reinterpretation or cavil, it must be regarded as still dubious. Certain things, of course, are beyond question. The farming population of the United States has shrunk to a small fraction of what it once was, absolutely as well as relatively. The overwhelming majority of American homes have television sets, and it can be presumed that they are used. The proportion of the population that receives its paychecks from a governmental agency at some level has increased spectacularly in recent decades. In these and other instances, both the unequivocalness of the definition—one has a TV or not at any given moment—and the sheer magnitude of the change—from no TV sets in 1930 to sets in 92 per cent of households in 1964,[5]—render the statements unassailable.

In this light, certain key contentions of the prophets of sociological revolution deserve consideration. It is widely alleged that Americans are turning from primary production to the service industries, that the role of technicians is increasing, that theoretical knowledge rather than business principles is setting the tone of society and that science is playing an increasing role in industrial and administrative processes. As a concomitant but not a necessary consequence, it is alleged that the class structure is becoming more egalitarian and open and that technicians rank high on the less rigid class scale that results. Other sociological prophets predict that automation will replace workers both blue and white collar and lead to a society with technicians on top and largely unemployed workers on the bottom, thus climaxing a movement toward a leisure society long under way. What work will remain in society will become more technical and therefore more dignified, with less hierarchical direction and centralization as a result both of the communications revolution and the increasing importance of the expertise of one's subordinates. Automation is thus simply one step toward a more affluent society in which most of the problems of scarcity have been solved and the main problem is how to use leisure.

Some of these contentions, not all of which, of course,

are made by the same people, are false. Some are true
but misleading. Some that are true do not add up to fundamental change, and the fact that they do not, given the
essential underlying conditions of modern life (the increasing power available to man through science and the rise in
the size and concentration of human population), means a
build-up of the dangerous combination of existential revolution and social inertia.

What of the contention, advanced by writers such as
Daniel Bell and Victor Fuchs, that the United States has become the world's first "service economy"? Bell places the
transition point at 1956, citing as evidence the fact that in
this year white-collar workers first began to outnumber
blue-collar workers.[6] Fuchs calculates that America is the
first nation in which more than half of those employed are
"not involved in the production of food, clothing, houses,
automobiles or other tangible goods."[7] Both these statements
may be true, but what do they signify? First of all it must
be noted that, as Bell admits, the figures are for the total
work force of both sexes. How important is it that more women now act as professional baby-sitters (350,000 re-
ported in the 1960 census, probably an understatement)
rather than amateur ones, for instance, when at the same
time "blue-collar" workers increased from 49 to 50 per cent
of the total male work force during the decade 1950–60?[8]
Actually, it is a good guess that automation, first affecting
unskilled labor, will relatively affect white-collar workers
even more.

Most men still work in the traditional sense. Indeed, it
should be noted how meaningless are such statements as
"not involved in production." Salesmen, truck drivers and
gas-station attendants may be "involved" in distribution
rather than production, but they are the creatures of industrial production and most may work with their hands and
get dirty. Mixing categories of activity (lawyer or manual

worker) and source of employment (private industry or government) results in almost insurmountable confusion. Lawyers may work for steel companies or the Department of Justice, drivers may deliver milk to supermarkets or collect garbage for the city government. What is incontrovertible is that unskilled labor is continuing to decline in significance and that government at all levels, but especially below the federal level, is more and more significant as an employer.

The Myth of a Technical Elite

What of the subsidiary contention that the economy is coming more and more to be dominated by a technical and scientific elite? The number of persons classified as professional and technical has increased steadily and rapidly over the past several decades so that it now constitutes in excess of 10 per cent of the total male working force. To it must be added some of the approximately equal number of managers, officials and proprietors. But by no means all, since the managerial category includes not only a Robert McNamara but department-store buyers, corner grocers and peanut vendors. Nor should it be forgotten that the category "professional and technical" includes clergymen, photographers and umpires.

But the professional-managerial class, however constituted, is still a minority of the population, and by no means all professionals and managers have had higher education or, more importantly for their power, are in the top fifth of the population in the amount of money they earn.[9] Thus the idea that the nation is coming under the control of a group of highly educated, well-paid technical experts must be severely qualified. Even insofar as they exist and play important roles, their standards do not predominate. Their economic position is controlled by the continuing dominance of the mores and laws of bourgeois man. Salaries of scientists, or managers for that matter, are taxed higher than rents and dividends. The way to get rich is not by being recompensed for technical work according to bureaucratic norms but through patents and stock options, or through saving one's salary or fees and speculating in real estate or the stock market. Being self-employed helps, but not much, and since back-yard nuclear reactors are unfeasible, the scientist who wants to beat a bourgeois tax system must set himself up as a consultant and deduct the rent of his home study as a business expense.

How can such a minority become dominant? At this point, prophets of change may argue that numbers are not what is important anyway. After all, most of the members of industrial society were not businessmen, yet businessmen and business values called the tune. Bourgeois man was a minority, but a dominant one. In the new society it is alleged that technical values will be dominant. This is how Ellul would view all aspects of life regardless of statistical quibbles. Bell explicitly says that "production and business decisions will be subordinated to . . . other forces in society. . . . The crucial decisions regarding the growth of the economy and its balance will come from government [and] will have an increasingly technical character."[10]

Is there any evidence that this is taking place? When one says that decisions regarding the economy will have an "increasingly technical character," one presumably means that some objective standard, subject to scientific verification, will be the basis for allocation of resources, that technical rationality will not simply determine the means used to get what is desired, but that technical considerations will provide the goals of action. But this Bell himself contends is impossible. Citing a noted economist's demonstration that the value preferences of the public cannot be combined into a single structure of priorities, Bell holds that increasing technical sophistication about the choices involved in public policy will lead to more, rather than less, political struggle,

that planning will stimulate rather than reduce controversy.[11] Seeing no way in which science can provide objective standards of value to guide policy making, he foresees
it as sharpening our perceptions of wherein we differ rather
than eliminating disagreement. Thus in the future, as today, the politician will dominate the technician.[12]

What America produces, or communicates, is determined by what the market will accept; it is a function of
popular demand conditioned by advertising, and of government expenditures determined by politics. Highly technical considerations enter into such matters as fiscal policy, for instance, but the inability of economists, to say
nothing of Congress and the Executive, the Treasury Department and the Federal Reserve Board, to agree on such
questions is notorious. Shall balance of payments be eased
by a travel tax or by taking GI's out of Germany? This is
surely a political decision in which no amount of technical
considerations can do more than define the perimeters of
the problem. Government economic policy still reflects the
political ability of business and labor to raise prices and
wages and to combine to promote the interests of particular
industries at the expense of the consumer's pocketbook and
safety.

Where then do we derive the widespread assumption
that technological society is increasingly exemplified in the
American economy? One factor is the decreasing visibility
of the blue-collar worker, symbol of the industry of old. He
drives to work and changes clothes when he gets to a factory that those who talk and read of technological man may
never see. The communications media do not make him the
hero of their situation comedies, and only a few general
magazines are aimed at him. He is gradually coming to
realize and resent his being shunted aside, and men such
as George Wallace shrewdly sought to make political capital
of this fact.

The other side of the coin is the high visibility of the

supposed new elite due to their extreme concentration in a few areas. The industries in which the scientists and technicians play the greatest role are the highly publicized and politically salient defense and space industries, located in the fastest-growing and most glamorized sections of the nation. As Bell has noted, the emphasis on scientific and technological innovation is concentrated in one segment of the economy—the war industry; what President Eisenhower called the "military-industrial complex," and what is more euphemistically referred to as "defense and aerospace."[13] This is the home of the new elite, if it exists at all. As President John Kennedy noted in his 1963 economic report: "The defense, space and atomic energy activities of the country absorb about two-thirds of the trained people available for exploring our scientific and technological frontiers."[14] This is where the physicists are, where the ratio of Ph.D.'s to production-line workers is so fantastically high, where the new technological class has its own enclaves and culture in Los Alamos, White Sands, Huntsville, and Livermore.

But how typical is the "defense-aerospace" industry of the American economy? To what extent is it setting the tone for the future? Economists may argue about the degree to which the American economy is dependent upon expenditures for war and defense, but what is more relevant to our concern is the extent to which the methods, characteristics and ethos of the new industries is spreading throughout the economy. Actually, the two questions are difficult to separate. Industrial engineer Seymour Melman has even argued that America is falling behind Europe in consumer technology because of our concentration of technical talent in war industries.[15] In any event, it would appear that the role of science and technology in the defense industries has yet to revolutionize the American economy.

To begin with, the very existence of these industries is

hardly the result of scientific rationality. Many scientists have been highly critical of the whole defense-aerospace enterprise; even NASA activities are far from the product of a consensus of the scientific community.[16] Though the pseudo science of the war-gamers and other military-scientific seers has been used to expand, explicate and justify our recent defense and space programs, the basic decisions have been made by generals, admirals, Presidents and congressmen, backed by a largely passive public opinion.[17] The fact that both Congress and the public are less and less enthusiastic about space exploration and the program is threatened with serious curtailment not only indicates the extent to which not a technological elite but a lay power structure calls the tune, but also suggests that the glamour industries may play a less significant role in the future American economy than they do at present.

Severe disagreement exists among both scientists and economists as to the extent to which defense and space activities have led to the acquisition of knowledge and techniques of direct benefit to the American economy generally.[18] Nor is there any indication that the methods of management developed by them can be applied to other aspects of the economy or to the solution of social problems. Systems analysis and PPBS (planning, programing, budgeting systems) are still touted as panaceas for economic and social problems but with less and less conviction.[19] Aerospace firms are moving into oceanography with much success (the problems and goals are not dissimilar), but their experience with urban problems, job-corps training programs and related projects has been less than happy. The technical revolutionizing of education that many electronic and related firms hoped to spearhead has not taken place. The diversity and decentralization of lower-school systems and the increasing unwillingness of taxpayers to spend money have combined with the teachers' fear of innovations to stymie change, while at the university level a system that still relies on the lecture method half a millennium after the invention of movable type is unlikely to allow itself to be pushed rapidly into the world of automation.

Paradoxically, it is war itself—which initially opened the way for so many victories of the technical and managerial class—that has spurred the increasing resistance to their power. Vietnam has proved the grave of many of the hopes that human behavior could be predicted and rationalized; it has, in addition, turned many of the young against the technical class and its assumptions and way of life. Even at the Pentagon, citadel of the new elite, disillusion has set in. After McNamara left, his successor told Congress that he made his decisions sometimes by "intuition." The managerial faith, as columnist Joseph Kraft observed, seems in retreat even in the Vatican of the new church of military science.[20]

Thus despite the attention given in the media to the defense-aerospace complex, American industry on the whole still plods along its accustomed ways. Such scientists as it employs are engaged in deciding what kind of plastic to use in hula hoops or in creating milk shakes that contain no dairy products. Businessmen and the consumer decide what will be produced and how much. Bourgeois man is still firmly in the saddle.

Patterns of education and recruitment into the labor force cast further doubt on the notion that a technical-scientific elite is taking over. Despite post-Sputnik hysteria, students are not flocking to science courses in high schools. Science is still often viewed as nasty and hard. Teachers are frequently ill prepared; most of those who might be teaching science are working on warheads. Only 30 per cent of the students enrolled in higher education are majoring in science or engineering,[21] and many of these are premeds or men who will wind up as salesmen. Business administration is generally holding its own, save perhaps in the caliber of its students. Throughout the world—except in some Communist countries and perhaps in France—science does not dominate the elite-generating educational institutions, and the impact of scientific training in the Soviet Union is muted by misallocation of scientists. In the United States, scientific training is now a useful means of getting on the ladder to top management, but a scientific degree, like a law degree, is a supplement rather than a substitute for entrepreneurial skills, and on the job the scientist qua scientist is not his own master.[22]

Automation, Unemployment and Affluence

Some prophets base their belief that the economy is coming under the domination of a technical elite on their conviction that the routine aspects of industrial production are being automated away and that the level of skills and status of the remaining workers will be such that they will have to be considered technicians rather than labor in the traditional sense. But there is little justification for the contention that skill levels are on the rise and we are passing from an era of mass production with unskilled or semiskilled labor to one in which skilled labor predominates in the work force.

To begin with, skilled labor was never entirely replaced by the "man on the assembly line," even during the first industrial revolution, and many skills used today are virtually identical with those developed in the preindustrial past. At the same time, vast new areas are opening up for the use of semiskilled labor. Mechanization of agriculture combined with increased stress on preprocessed foods leads to demands for people to work on the assembly lines in canneries and food-freezing plants. Despite the stubborn resistance of organized labor, the construction industry, even in home building, is moving toward rationalization, and in time prefabrication and assembly on the scene will provide many more semiskilled jobs. The service industries

provide a vast and growing reservoir of jobs for those with
few marketable skills (motel maids and those who serve
roadside hamburgers can hardly be considered even semiskilled).

Thus semiskilled and unskilled labor still play a large
part in the American economy and will probably continue
to do so. Prophets of change allege that this can be only
temporary, that the march of automation will cause mass
unemployment of workers while upgrading the skills of
those who remain and is increasing its pace to the point
where we must give serious consideration to providing economic support for the unemployable—perhaps a majority
of the population—and amusement for their empty hours as
well. But there seems little to indicate that these prophecies
are accurate and that we are about to be faced with a combination of affluence, unemployment and domination by a
technical elite.

One can, of course, argue that the American economy
is in the position of a person who has fallen from the top of
the Empire State Building, and as he passes the tenth floor
cries out, "Everything all right so far." But no evidence that
our movement is so unidirectional exists. Certainly automation continues to increase, but so does the labor force. In
part this is because there is more to do. It has been estimated that if automated telephone switching were eliminated a substantial portion of all American women would
have to be employed by the telephone companies as
operators. Those who have feared unemployment seem to
believe that there is a fixed amount of work to be done.
This is perhaps in part a reflection of a basically Puritan attitude that divides life into luxuries and necessities, useful and time-wasting activities. Whatever may be said for
this position, our population no longer shares it, and work
to be done continues to increase. Employment statistics do
not indicate any incipient mass unemployment caused by
the spread of automation.

Such figures may be faulty, of course, since only those actively looking for work are counted as unemployed, and it is likely that the population groups missed by the 1960 census are among the many Americans who have left the employment market because of lack of salable skills or of hope itself. But most of the uncounted unemployed probably have never been part of the active work force, so this is irrelevant. If automation is causing unemployment, this should show up in a positive decrease in the number of Americans employed, and this is simply not the case; quite the contrary.

One can argue that the major reason that the unemployment rate has been low in recent years is the war in Vietnam, which has both stimulated production and removed young men from the job market. But American society, if it wished, could easily find substitutes for Vietnam as an economic stimulant. If it were politically feasible, a real war on poverty, not only at home but abroad, would provide work for all Americans for several generations despite any foreseeable level of automation. So would the educational enrichment of the lives of our population from infancy through adulthood. Much of what we produce may be junk, much of what we do may be silly, as Paul Goodman has argued,[23] but this is true of nonautomated activities as well as automated and is a cultural rather than a strictly economic problem. And, to anticipate, should we make a serious assault on air pollution and similar problems there would be work for all for a century; for instance, it has been calculated that the cost of merely easing the problem of water pollution near American cities by the year 2017 would be something in the vicinity of two hundred billion dollars.[24]

Is automation creating a new leisure society for the average worker (every futurist seems to take for granted that the professional and leadership classes will continue to work sixty-hour weeks—even if these do include three-hour

business lunches)? This is a myth, at least as far as the
next generation is concerned. Employment figures, including those from western Europe, simply do not show mass
unemployment resulting from technological change. Many
American industries can never be efficiently or economically automated; one economist has calculated that the total
cost of automating the American manufacturing industry today would be two and a half trillion dollars, a sum not
likely to be forthcoming.[25]

Like epidemic unemployment, leisure, too, may be a
myth. Sebastian de Grazia has studied the question of leisure in modern society with as much scientific precision as
the matter allows, and he concludes that we have less free
time, to say nothing of leisure in the classic Greek sense,
than our ancestors.[26] Consider the time spent commuting,
working out one's income tax, taking the family car to the
garage for repairs or trying to find a replacement part for
last year's appliance, to say nothing of time spent moon-
lighting. As members of the working class move up into the
middle classes they simply add P.-T.A. committee meetings, cub scout meetings and car pools to dancing classes
to the household maintenance chores. Leisure still belongs
primarily to the wealthy and the unattached. Shorter work
hours would mean a limited increase in free time for the
workers directly affected (providing they did not take on a
second job, which, judging from the way in which police-
men, firemen and teachers use their "free time," many of
them would); at the same time it would mean more work
for the people who sell hot dogs, gasoline or theater tickets.
These functions can, of course, be automated, but only to a
point. Loading and checking and repairing vending machines and maintaining recreational facilities generally, including removing beer cans from highways and parks, require some human labor.

All these considerations about leisure point to an apparent inconsistency in many people's views of the future.

For along with an increase in the scientific and professional classes—which is occurring, but not fast enough to meet today's demand for physicians, social workers, teachers and so on, to say nothing of what the demand would be in a really egalitarian affluent society—there is postulated an increase in service workers. There is no question but that the number of service workers is increasing and the proportion of workers engaged primarily in production is going down, but this has some paradoxical consequences. Productivity in the service industries cannot increase as fast as in primary production, thus the more the service industries come to dominate the economy the slower a nation's economic growth and the less the increase in affluence.

Next year one worker may be able to make two television sets in the time it takes to make one today, but barbers can be only marginally more efficient at cutting hair or dentists at filling teeth. Some futurists have argued that even the service industries can be automated, using teaching machines as an example. But teaching machines probably will mean only additional programmers, counselors and administrators, with little change in student-teacher ratios; the students may learn more, but probably more rather than fewer people will be involved in the process of educating them. Similarly, machines can take over much routine work of a clerical nature, but someone will have to talk to relief clients, parolees, mental patients and taxpayers, unless they are to become even more disaffected than they are at present. Machines can do virtually anything, but they are likely to remain uneconomic for many uses. Dust-free, self-sterilizing motel rooms are possible, but even disposable bed sheets will have to be replaced, and any Rube Goldberg type of mechanism for doing so would almost certainly be more costly than human help. Use of trained animals with artificially raised intelligence for some of these menial tasks is possible, but even here some human supervision would be necessary.

The whole question of productivity and cost break-throughs is basic to the vision of an affluent society with a class of supertechnicians on top and a mass of semiemployed workers below. It is also intimately tied up with the question of resources. Evidence seems to indicate that productivity in primary production, as opposed to service industries, maintenance, etc., is increasing. Also, more unexpectedly, resources are not vanishing but are becoming cheaper, even domestically, through more efficient extraction[27] (the cost of resources drawn by major powers from other nations is, of course, often a function of political or military power, of imperialism or neocolonialism, rather than economics). Thus the law of diminishing returns, a major prop of the scarcity economics of Ricardo's day, seems no longer to hold, refuting neo- as well as paleo-Malthusians. But what none of this takes into account is the rising problem of offset costs, that is, of costs incurred in making primary activities possible. Suppose, it has been suggested, that the cost of a can of beer is raised sufficiently to cover disposing of the empty can, say, after a teen-ager throws it onto the road from a moving car? Would it not double? One might ask who *should* bear the costs—the manufacturer, the buyer, the citizens in general? But the problem of who pays for offset costs is a political question, albeit one of the most important facing modern society. From the economic point of view, it does not matter.

What is important in the present context is the fact that air and water pollution (whether by physical products or through thermal pollution), problems of waste disposal generally, increased inconvenience caused by crowding (a function of both population increase and increased resources available to people through affluence—a two-car family may use the streets as much as two one-car families), are becoming major economic factors, when in the past they could be ignored. Regardless of who bears what share of particular costs, the total social costs are becoming an increasing burden to the economy as a whole. Theoretically, socialism or a more aggressively expansionist fiscal policy on the part of government might mobilize all available resources to the point where all of the costs of producing goods, providing welfare and services and maintaining a livable environment could be taken care of easily, but at present such a policy seems highly unlikely.

Today in some demisocialist welfare states the movement is toward belt tightening—Uruguay and Great Britain are examples; elsewhere, as in Scandinavia, voters have rejected socialist governments, apparently preferring less welfare and less inflation to more of both. In the United States a reaction against taxes on the part of the middle class has led not only to a retreat in the "war on poverty" but also to increasing trouble even for the hitherto sacred public-education system. Even relatively well-off parents find it increasingly difficult to finance the college costs of their children, and college students are forced to take time off from studies to work so they can remain in school. Whatever may be fundamentally possible and ultimately likely, Western man in the twentieth century is not acting as if the era of affluence and enforced leisure is at hand.[28]

Communication and Centralization

Centralization and hierarchical domination of the work process and the worker were prominent aspects of the Industrial Revolution. To what extent has the new electronic technology altered this state of affairs? There is no question that the decision-making process in industry is more decentralized than it was at the height of the Industrial Revolution. But this is due less to technological than to directly economic factors. Decentralization of decision-making in industry reflects the fact that once competition, product differentiation and frequent model changes became a major factor, consumer-buying patterns became increasingly unstable and some flexibility was necessary to respond to consumer preferences. This consumer freedom may be illusory, as men such as Galbraith hold;[29] advertising does much to condition attitudes, as do the simple facts of life—one cannot choose to ride a bicycle on a freeway. But the consumer does have some choice among products, and does express it. In order to cope with this situation large corporations often break up their operations and, like some automobile firms, compete with themselves. Also, many corporations are engaged in diversifying their product line for security against fluctuations in demand, acquiring smaller firms in related or even unrelated activities.

More and more ties are financial rather than techno-logical. If a meat-packing firm acquires an aerospace divi-sion or an aircraft company does research on race relations it simply makes no sense for the chief executives of the parent company to try to tell their subordinates what to do. Thus management theorists who describe modern control systems as a circular process, a kind of continuous confer-ence of equals rather than the hierarchy of the past are right; specialization, diversification and the need for on-the-spot decisions have radically altered old patterns.[30]

But the process of decentralization of decision-making has not gone as far as might be expected. Electronic tech-nology has had an ambiguous effect on administration. The telephone and computer make it possible for the "home office" to maintain minute controls over operations, especi-ally at the budgetary level. While the instant communica-tion made possible by electronics means that traditional centers of control, the great political and financial capi-tals, can be replaced by new ones and that it is now pos-sible to run things from anywhere, it also means that authority can be centralized more effectively at whatever point in space this may be. Some students of international affairs have long deplored the effects on traditional diplo-macy of the airplane and the radiotelephone, which made ambassadors increasingly messenger boys and allegedly centralized decisions at the summit. Military commanders have bemoaned the extent to which Washington has controlled minute decisions about targeting and similar matters during the Vietnamese war. Evidence indicates that, with the rise of the computer, business firms, too, have centralized rather than decentralized.[31]

The dream of a decentralized world in which the availability of cheap and flexible electric or atomic power and the simultaneity of communications would destroy the dominance of the great cities within nations and the world is still just that. Gottmann's study of megalopolis indicates what anyone's impressions reveal: leaders like to congregate with people of similar achievements and interests.[32] In the United States, New York remains a center of finance and of the communications industry, Washington of political life, and Detroit, Pittsburgh and Houston are control centers of industries, even when actual production is decentralized. Newer and smaller centers exist to supplement or compete with older central cities, and decisions are made in technological or intellectual centers such as Redstone (Alabama), the Jet Propulsion Laboratory at Pasadena, Los Alamos, the National Institutes of Health in Bethesda and in major university cities. But while there are more nodal points of social decision-making around the nation, centralization per se is not decreasing. Every activity in society is dominated by a few centers where decisions are made, even if these are outside the large cities.

The Myth of a Classless Society

Consideration of the production processes of the new society leads inevitably to a consideration of the class system of the contemporary world. The assumption that technological change is turning routine work over to the machine, bringing into existence a new dominant class of technicians and elevating the population generally can be tested at the level of incomes and social interaction as well as by consideration of the physical processes of production. Viewed from this angle, the assumption that we are entering a radically new era seems somewhat premature. Inequality of income distribution in the United States and the Western world generally has not been affected by any technological change in the mid-twentieth century and is not being so affected. The class system of the industrial era remains dominant.[33] The fundamental fact is that legal and political considerations ensure that the technical elite remains secondary to the business elite. As we have seen, the way to become rich is as a speculator or investor, not as a scientist, since wages and salaries are taxed more heavily, certainly and regularly than profits and rents. The notion that an income revolution in the direction of equality is taking place is simply a myth.

It is possible to think of the American income pyramid as a five-class structure. The top 20 per cent receive something over 46 per cent of the income, while the bottom 20 per cent get only one-tenth that much, or 4.6 per cent of the income.[34] Such movement as has occurred since the Depression has been largely in the direction of leveling out the very top incomes toward a more average figure for the economic elite; no changes in the tax system since 1932 have made any basic difference in the distribution of income in America. Indeed, changes since 1960 have made taxes at the national level more rather than less regressive.[35]

In Great Britain, France, Germany and other industrialized Western nations the class structure is similar to that of the United States. If anything, income differentials are sharper and property ownership even more concentrated in the hands of the upper class. Even in the Soviet Union, where legal ownership of industry is in the hands of the state or other social bodies, widespread disparities in income are the norm, though the pattern tends to fluctuate more than in the nonsocialist states.[36] Also it seems likely that most available data underestimate differences in income and hence differences in class position: part of the income and perquisites of the upper classes never appear at net income on tax returns, and the millions missed by the census are probably mostly quite poor. In addition, some families have relatively high incomes only because more than one person works, which means that the family income is not necessarily a true index of class status.

Nor does the class system as defined by differences in income levels disappear when we take into account the impact of taxation and the provision of welfare services. The effect of taxation on class differentials is highly debatable —cost-benefit analysis is an especially difficult facet of economics—but it would appear that not only is the tax system regressive, but so is the incidence of the benefits supported by taxation. The poor may be on relief or use public hospitals more than the middle or upper classes, but their schools get the poorest teachers and the fewest repairs, they use the highways and airports less, and benefit little if at all from hidden and not-so-hidden government subsidies to industry such as the oil depletion allowance.

It is true that there is a sense in which it is impossible to directly correlate individual life-style with income. But common observation would indicate that various life-styles exist within the United States based largely upon income differentials. Certain cultural and political aspects of class will be dealt with later in our discussion of social change, but some relate directly to the work life of the individual. It has been said that while the worker may dress and live in a house like the man of the middle class because he has a similar income, he still "works like a worker."[37] Sanitation workers may be ashamed of how they look or smell when they come home in a way bank clerks are not. There is a subtle difference between "calling in sick" and having it taken out of your sick leave, and telling your immediate superior or your secretary that you will not be able to get back to the office and never having it become a matter of bureaucratic record.

Automation has seemingly done little to reduce the drudgery of work. Where the assembly line exists, it is still irksome. The "myth of the happy worker" (to use Harvey Swados' phrase) is still just that.[38] Where the old centralized rigid processes have been automated with machines taking over routine tasks, working conditions, especially psychological ones, have not improved. Such evidence as exists indicates that the watcher of dials—the checkers and maintainers—are likely to be lonely, bored and alienated, often feeling less the machine's master than its servant.[39] Dealing with computers can be as frustrating for the worker as for the client-consumer, with data on a print-out even more difficult to check and rectify than that in human accounts or reports.[40] Evidence indicates that what is true of the United States is true throughout Western society. Members of the lower classes feel that, regardless of their income and consumption patterns, at least while on the job they are members of a different class from those in the front office.[41] Though patterns are not absolutely clear-cut, members of different classes tend to live differently off the job as well. They reside in different neighborhoods, are educated differently and reflect class differences in subtle and not-so-subtle patterns of consumption and recreation.

Given all the complicated questions about American class structure, one can be sure only that general living standards are on the rise, but that class differences continue to be important. Technological change has not eliminated or even revolutionized the basic class pattern set by industrial society. Rich and poor, gold coast and slum remain.

But even if economic classes persist, is it not true that the character of the upper class is changing, especially its ethos? Are we not entering a bureaucratized society led by technicians? Is not organization man[42] the forerunner of technological man? Whether organization man exists as a personality type off the job will be discussed later, but on the job he seems to be a myth. There have always been men who adhered to bureaucratic norms and preferred rules to initiative, and bureaucratic power and prestige to wealth. Many of these exist today, in government services especially—education and social welfare as well as politics and taxation. For several generations this type has been important in business, especially in monopolistic non-product-oriented enterprises: the railroads, the telephone company, insurance and so on. But the evidence again indicates that organization man is in a minority among managers as far as business in the United States is concerned (although Great Britain and Europe, traditionally more cartelized and less competitive, present slightly different pictures).[43] The average American executive is almost bitterly competitive. He fights for opportunities to show his special skills, in order to gain power and prestige—and money as well.[44] The economic man of Ricardo is as alive today as he ever was. Methods of competition are more subtle sometimes in large organizations, whether business, nonprofit or governmental, but they still exist.

What is true of the capitalist nations is in part true of so-called socialist and Communist nations as well, at least those with a Western background. Differences exist, as they do between Japanese and American business structures and mores, but essentials are much the same. In the Soviet Union and Communist Europe there are class differences, in attitude as well as income, between ordinary workers and the "new class" of bureaucrats.[45] The latter are increasingly openly competitive with one another, oriented toward monetary income as much as their system permits, and motivated more by economic than by technological considerations. Their concept of efficiency is that of bourgeois man: produce or do as much as possible as cheaply as possible, provided the consumer (individual or government agency) eventually picks up the bill.

Population Patterns and the Myth of Suburbia

Just as the individualistic striver of the bourgeois era has not been shouldered aside by the organization man, so the population boom and the resulting increase in urbanization that were the product of the Industrial Revolution are both continuing. The rate of growth of the world population is difficult to ascertain; estimates range from Harrison Brown's horrendous fifteen billion by the year 2000 to Donald Bogue's belief that world population will soon level off at a figure not far in excess of the present total.[46] But world figures are somewhat beside the point, since they are in large part a reflection of the high growth rates of the nonindustrialized nations. What concerns us is whether or not patterns of population growth in postindustrial society will differ from those of the bourgeois era in the advanced countries. At present no marked changes are evident.

There has been a tendency in recent years for the birth rates of some countries to fall to a point where the rapid growth of the early industrial era is no longer the norm, but how long range this trend may be is still in doubt, and absolute growth in populations remains the rule. Decisions as to the size of families are still made primarily on an individual rather than a social basis, the operative question being not how many children can my society as a whole adequately care for, but how many can I as an individual support? Insofar as any social factors are taken into consideration at all, there remains a lingering if sometimes unconscious adherence to the belief that an expanding population means prosperity through the creation of larger markets and a growing working force. But in general individualism reigns supreme, and even among the wealthy and well educated who recognize the need for population control for the poor and undeveloped, personal predilections remain the basis for decisions about procreation.

New technological developments have had a more direct effect on the spatial distribution of the population over the earth's surface than on its size. The newer sources of power have permitted greater decentralization of industry, and changes in transportation based primarily on the internal-combustion engine have made the worker more mobile. Given the fact that most Americans prefer rural to city life[47] and seek to make their cities as much like small towns as possible (Philadelphia has three trees for every inhabitant)—to the despair of certain intellectuals—the outcome has been an erosion of the dominance of the central city in urbanized areas.

But the result has not been the suburbanization of the nation, as some allege. The picture of an America in which the typical individual is a white middle-class person living in a house in the suburbs complete with crabgrass, barbecue pit and perhaps swimming pool, and commuting to work in the central city, is essentially mythical. So, too, is the belief in economic, cultural and political homogeneity often associated with it. Certainly the central cities are less and less significant or even necessary in American life. More and more, the important people, whether technicians or managers, live and also work in outlying areas—near the Pentagon in Virginia, around Massachusetts' Route 128, on the San Francisco peninsula, near the space center at Houston, and so on, and only banking and finance continue to congregate "downtown." Reviving the city forms of the first industrial revolution is as romantic a notion as that of reviving the medieval village, since modern society does not find this kind of city useful.[48]

But the new urban pattern is not the suburbia of legend but megalopolis. So-called suburbs are now difficult to distinguish from satellite cities, since they are the site of industry and commerce as well as residential areas. They differ from one another, and, within themselves, in income levels, culture and politics. What is emerging is a number of very large complexes, some stretching for hundreds of miles, within which a variety of land uses are interrelated, separated by areas of much lower and in some cases falling population density. The megalopolises will have their nodal points where leaders of various activities—government, communications, particular industries—may congregate, but few points of concentration will coincide with each other. The new urban areas will manifest a pattern of mixed land usage and relatively high population density, combining open spaces, high-rise apartments, industry, shopping centers, single-family dwellings, cultural centers, recreation areas and even some high-yield farm land, a sprawling, almost centerless, chaos held together by a variety of transportation devices. Greater Los Angeles today provides a glimpse of the Western world tomorrow.

In sum, therefore, the new technology has not at all affected any of the fundamental aspects of the capitalist-industrial system. Science is more and more used as a tool, and persons with scientific training form a larger and larger proportion of the economic elite. But control of production is still highly centralized; what is produced is determined by considerations of private profit and the highest economic rewards go to those skilled at measuring economic activity in terms of profit. The class system of industrial society continues largely as before, though living standards are on the rise. Population continues to increase on the basis of individual decisions based on the assumption that the over-all size of population is no problem, and while there are more nodal points within the megalopolises the process of urbanization continues. Government is more active in the economy just as the knowledge industry is more important, but they supplement rather than supplant old-style private productive industry. What is emerging is a pluralism of competing interests, a neofeudalism in which all seek their private economic or bureaucratic ends, with no over-all direction. Contemporary man is essentially bourgeois man with new tools and toys.

Private Capitalism and the Existential Revolution

What will be the consequence when the existential revolution makes its full impact upon this neofeudal, neo-corporativist economy still motivated primarily by private profit? The space race already provides some clues. Despite the fact that NASA is technically a civilian government agency, the space race is primarily military in motivation. Its larger purposes are defined as public purposes, as in war. But the means for fulfilling them—services as well as hardware—are procured from private agencies interested in turning a profit. What results is a riskless, state-subsidized capitalism. Space exploitation and military uses of space are not, as of now, intrinsically profitable in economic terms, but when they do produce by-products that can be privately exploited, these are turned over to private industry; the communications satellite is a case in point. The basic research is paid for by the taxpayer, while any profitable results go to the shareholders.

If past performance is any index we can expect that eventual mining of the planets, if it occurs, will be undertaken in terms of the economic interests of private corporations operating under government sponsorship and the rubric of national strategic interests. Control over details of policy guidance will be the object of a constant struggle between financier and bureaucrat; in the case of any Soviet activity bureaucrats alone will be involved, but each will seek his own agency's interests. Many decisions of the most far-reaching social consequences may be made in almost offhand fashion in response to the dictates of capitalist economics. It would be ironic if the first Cyborgs were not explorers on a public mission but miners working for a private corporation. Men today accept high risks to health and safety in hazardous jobs on earth; why should they not do so in space? Thus man-machine symbiosis or any other evolutionary step beyond man may come about not because of any decision on the part of the human race as a whole, or even of any individual political community within it, but in response to the economic needs of private interests.

Given the model of the communications satellite, it is not inconceivable that private industry could take over weather forecasting and weather-control services, just as it might well take over interplanetary transportation whenever it becomes commercially feasible. The airline industry already enjoys sizable government assistance in the form of development costs, subsidized airports and weather forecasting services; why not a space-travel industry based on previous public research and the provision of public launching facilities? After all, the pattern is as old as the technical services of the Department of Agriculture; indeed, as old as public roads or the United States Post Office. What is new is simply that the few private interests subsidized are more readily identifiable than the many small businesses, farmers, commercial and industrial interests helped in the past.

One thing is certain: as long as equipment is privately produced, those who manufacture it will continue to push their own products, and thus particular strategies for exploration and use of space, just as they do within a military context today. The struggles over the manned bomber and the TFX fighter, involving as they did corporate giants of the aircraft industry, will be repeated when it comes time for space travel and exploitation. At the very least, the fact that equipment for the space race is privately produced means that a built-in lobby exists for more activity in space. Man's conquest of space will be spurred by particular interests, just as it was in the case of European colonization of the earth.

A similar pattern is emerging in the conquest of the oceans. Here much of the basic research is already being done by private industry, especially in mining and fisheries. As in the case of agriculture, government subsidy is sought for further research to permit profitable exploitation, and the land-prant college act of 1862 has its successor in what is loosely called the sea-grant college act of 1966, designed to spur oceanography. Private firms have been urging the United States government to make classified data gathered by the military publicly available, holding that exploitation of the ocean's resources by American business is the best guarantee of national security and of undersea power. Man's use of the oceans presents even more international complications than his space explorations, but the current tendency is for decisions about how the seas will be used— for fishing, mining, recreation or whatever—to be made in terms of private profit. Here again the extension of man into a new environment does not reflect considerations derived from the existential significance of that extension, but is apparently to be based on piecemeal and particularistic factors. No one speaks for mankind with regard to the use of the oceans, just as no one will speak out for him in regard to the use of space.

As we have already seen, virtually every possible extension of man's powers over nature and himself almost certainly will be made or not made, shaped in one direction or another, not by considerations of what is good for man but what is good for some men; problems that are basically scientific and ethical will be decided in economic terms. Shall the use of a myriad of drugs become more widespread? The drug companies will in large measure decide through pressure on government (administrative and legislative) and through advertising. Rumor even suggests that some tobacco and liquor interests, feeling themselves threatened by competition from the illegal drug industry, may seek to alter public policy so as to be able themselves to enter this lucrative field.[49] The pattern of cancer-producing cigarettes being urged on the public over the "public airwaves" for private profit may be repeated with various drugs in the future. The American entrepreneurial system is geared to this kind of activity and shows no signs of changing.

Whether and to what extent computers are built and how they are to be used is another decision of vital importance to society that continues to be subject only to private controls. Since the onset of industrialism, private firms have, in effect, decided when and where new cities would be built and old ones abandoned;[50] now the continued existence of certain occupations and perhaps the continued economic utility of certain segments of the population rest in their hands.

Perhaps the most startling disjunction between old motivations and old centers of control and the new possibilities for human existence lies in the area of medicine and genetics. The availability of high-class medical care has always been a function of the class system.[51] Who will survive has always been a question decided partly on economic grounds, especially where new and expensive techniques or equipment has been involved. Organ transplants and use of artificial organs will probably follow the pattern of accessibility of iron lungs, kidney machines and the like in being most available to those of high income or status. The more that man can do and the more expensive it is to do it, the more the differential between classes in life experiences. Black markets in scarce, especially newly discovered, medicines have always cropped up; a black market in human organs could result from the conflict between scarcity and economic pressure on the one hand and ethical norms relating to equality of treatment on the other.

In the area of genetics the problem is even more striking. If supermen can be bred, whose children shall they be? Who will have their genetic defects corrected in embryo?

Genotyping to detect defects is extremely costly; to what extent and on whose offspring should it be used? Will artificial insemination with supposedly superior stock be an option available on an equal basis to all, or will parents have to qualify as they now do to adopt children? Advances in pediatrics and preschool education have been more readily available to the upper than to the lower classes because of economic factors. May not advances in genetics be simply another factor in making the rich richer and the poor poorer?

Mankind, from primitive times onward, has permitted or encouraged physical deformation of the bodies of individuals or groups for the sake of custom, economic or military utility, athletic prowess or beauty. But these acquired characteristics—the athlete's enlarged heart, the galley slave's overdeveloped back muscles, the African tribal woman's artificially enlarged lower lip or the Chinese woman's tiny feet—could not be passed on to succeeding generations. Now modern genetic research opens up the possibility of breeding specialized men with special characteristics for particular tasks, new subspecies who can breed true. Shall the economic market for new "skills" be allowed to decide the limits of permissible changes, or shall this be subject to conscious social decision?

In the area of urbanization, profit considerations have long determined land usage, despite attempts at zoning. As increasing population and the increasing density of interaction in the megalopolitan world make land usage a more urgent problem, continuance of this pattern could promote inefficiency as well as rampant ugliness. Instead of a tolerable metropolitan world emerging, advanced nations could become vast "slurbs."

Finally, in the recent past, population size has been determined in the West by private considerations; above all, by the direct income available to parents to support children and the cost of preventing unwanted children. Tax

credits, availability of welfare programs (including public
schools) and even subsidization of birth-control measures
have already affected the free market in children. How
much further should the community go to meet the existential challenge posed by the ongoing population explosion?
Should it regulate family size directly or continue to work
through economic measures designed to condition individual choice? One economist has even suggested that population control could be combined with certain features of
the free market by giving each human being at birth the
right to one heir; couples could then pool their rights, or
they could sell them to others or buy more from couples
not choosing to use theirs.[52] Whatever device is used, it
seems possible that some mechanism for making population
size responsive to other than private economic considerations may be introduced in the future, since here as in
other economic areas the results of private choices affect
the total society.

How shall mankind respond to the new dangers and
difficulties presented by the existential revolution? Suppose
one grants that the "invisible hand" of the classical economists cannot bring about a good society any more than
unaided it can bring about general economic well-being?
Suppose one assumes that new developments in man's control over nature must be directed by holistic action by and
on behalf of the species rather than be determined by the
aggregation of individual decisions, how in practice can the
new powers be brought under effective social control? For
the problem is not simply one of removing decisions about
the use of space and the oceans, drugs and computers, and
biological knowledge from the vagaries of the market place
and the whims of private interests. There is a built-in bias
for change and growth in the whole method and institutional structure of industrial civilization. Expansion as such
is considered good because it brings profits to someone;

towns therefore must grow larger, industry must be attracted, more must be produced and bought. This attitude is not a function of private capitalism alone. Socialist systems, too, are subject to this bias. Socialism per se can do nothing to prevent technology from changing the conditions of human life for the worse as long as it shares this attitude toward change and expansion. In the Soviet Union, despite public protest, lakes are being polluted by government agencies almost as rapidly as in the United States; red tape and a productionist bias lead to the same results as does the pursuit of individual private gain.[53] Despite government policy, cities continue to grow, and to grow in a disorderly fashion.[54] Russia is well into, indeed perhaps ahead in, the space race without private industrial promoters being involved, and its fishing practices on the high seas would put even a nineteenth-century American robber baron to shame.

What is at fault is not ideology at the level of the trivial question of who owns what, but basic attitudes. The most that any government can do is to provide the tools—the administrative and legal technology if one will—to deal with the situation on a co-ordinated basis. Are these tools being made available? We have seen that technological man is largely a myth as far as the economic order is concerned. But what of the political order? Perhaps here the problems of social inertia are not as great, and a new man is emerging conscious of and prepared to confront effectively the problems posed by the existential revolution.

7

Technology and the Rediscovery of Politics

Throughout human history technology has greatly influenced the political life of mankind. In part this influence has been indirect: by affecting the economy, technology has affected the class structure and thus the political system. Poverty stemming from technological backwardness has usually led to the development of oligarchic societies, while the Industrial Revolution provided the basis for mass democracy or at least for political systems in which the masses participated, if only as the objects of propaganda and political organization. The direct effects of technology upon politics have been equally important. Military technology determined who could coerce whom; communications technology, who could convince whom. Predictions about man's future, therefore, necessarily reflect judgments about current or foreseen technological developments and their presumed effect on political institutions and behavior.

Predicting the Political Future

Some political prophets look for a continuation and intensification of what they consider to be the characteristics of the present. Those who accept the mass-society thesis, who contend that industrialism has led to a loss of freedom for the common man and to the control of his cultural and political behavior by an elite of capitalists and militarists, foresee a future in which freedom will be eroded to the vanishing point, an era that will differ from the present mainly in the degree to which scientific and technical skills will be the criteria for membership in the ruling elite. Finally even the elite will be bound by the chains they have forged for humanity. Thus Ben Seligman argues that even the archons who run the new state will not know freedom.[1] All will be dominated by technology, which will make its own laws.

This is also the point of view of Jacques Ellul and his followers. Despair about the political future is a basic ingredient in their general fear of the future, for if politics retains its independence it could control technological change, and therefore technology would not be the autonomous force whose existence is the touchstone of their analysis. Ellul seems to believe (although his style tends to obscure his position) that politics and the role of the politician will be eliminated in the coming new world. Technology (which, it should be remembered, he confusingly identifies with all "technique," all means to ends) will set all social goals and will provide the answers to all questions of social policy, and the only role left for the politician will be to use the techniques of organization and persuasion to elicit popular co-operation with the plans made by the experts. The increasing role of technology will lead to government by a technological meritocracy and eventually to totalitarianism. Political structure and political theory alike are subordinate to technique. "The state and technique," writes Ellul, "increasingly interrelated, are becoming the most important forces in the modern world; they buttress and reinforce each other in their aim to produce an apparently indestructible, total civilization."[2]

Many of those who venture predictions about the political future have a less highly developed theoretical framework, but they, too, begin with the same basic assumption of an inevitable loss of freedom. "The higher the state of technological development," a noted political scientist writes, "the greater the concentration of political power."[3] Technology means planning, rationalization and centralization, and, it is assumed, as a natural consequence, the loss of individual freedom to a faceless bureaucracy. Propaganda makes men manipulable; drugs and weapons make him controllable. Man is destined to be ruled by a scientific elite. Technology will bring politics to an end.

Most of the sociological prophets of the future are more optimistic, however, since they represent a growing reaction against the "mass society" description of industrial civilization. It is their contention that technological developments such as automation can help create a more egalitarian and leisured society at the same time that modern communications can create a more flexible and democratic one. A leading exponent of this latter view is Marshall McLuhan. Having begun his intellectual career as a conservative critic of industrialism, he has now determined to his own satisfaction that industrialism is currently transforming itself into something new and better. Though not especially interested in politics per se, he argues that electronics destroys the centralization characteristic of the industrial era in all fields. The telephone may have restricted the freedom of diplomats and other subordinates and temporarily centralized power, he admits, but now "circuitry brings people into relation with each other in total involvement which creates the possibility of dialogue and discovery on an enormous scale."[4] Instead of a hierarchical, mechanical power structure, politics is now becoming a total process in which the foci of power are everywhere and nowhere.

Not all the sociological prophets of the future would go all the way with McLuhan—even insofar as it is possible to ascertain exactly where he is or where he is going—but they do tend to be optimistic. Even when they foresee new and difficult days ahead, the difficulties stem not from rigidity but from greater flexibility, and are a sign that the days when an industrially based mass society could constitute a major threat to humanity are over, and that the notion of domination by a scientific elite is only a bad dream. Thus while Daniel Bell believes that certain constraints will be placed upon political decision-makers in the future by the exigencies of foreign policy, the importance of technical considerations and the general future-orientation of society, he sees man still essentially in control of his fate, with the basic choices remaining open. Scientists will become a more important force in the political process, he holds, but hardly a decisive one.[5]

Even on issues where their predictions diverge, most futurists view the alternatives with equanimity rather than alarm. Some see growing federal power,[6] others a process of governmental decentralization. But the issue can be viewed calmly because of a shared belief that the classical theories of bureaucracy and planning were wrong, and that so much flexibility and diversity and responsiveness are possible within the planning process and the operations of bureaucracies that the older question of centralization versus decentralization has become formalistic and meaningless. Decision-making is viewed as a continuous ongoing process, and institutional labels as having little meaning.

Sharper divergence exists on the issue of citizen participation in politics. Most sociological prophets would probably accept the contention of the philosopher Hannah Arendt that industrial society itself is the culmination of a long process in which the political sphere, central to the men of Greece and Rome, has receded before the economic, while human beings have become more and more privatized.[7] However, not all would share her distress over this state of affairs. There is no question that her diagnosis is essentially sound, regardless of her implicit value premises. Not the state but the individual is the center of our concern today in democratic nations. Karl Deutsch, however, sees a reversal of this trend, with the spread of leisure and education leading to greater popular involvement in politics. On the other hand, Herman Kahn, reflecting a belief in the emergence of a politically powerful technical elite, thinks that citizens, regarding political decisions as too complicated to understand and lapsing even further into apathy, will seek the individual good life instead.[8] This, in milder form, is also the view of political scientist Robert E. Lane, who sees such a situation already taking place, with affluence leading, if not to apathy, at least to consensus based on a growing belief that political conflicts are not really very important.[9]

But Bell and others would argue that regardless of what citizen reaction turns out to be—greater involvement or greater withdrawal—in a technologized society issues are not eliminated by being translated into questions of technique, as Ellul holds, of mere technical means to ends; rather political issues are further acerbated by the fact that the impact of the goals chosen and the means used are so much more apparent to those affected. Bell argues that planning leads to conflict rather than eliminates it, since it rationalizes and sharpens the available choices without providing standards by which to make them.[10] Once we are able to determine precisely what proportion of the education budget proposed by a school board benefits middle-class white children as compared with poor black children, we are confronted with the necessity for making basic value choices. Once we are able to determine precisely who and what are causing the pollution of our rivers and how this pollution can be prevented, we are faced with the problem of who is going to bear the cost of keeping our waters clean.

In a similar vein, Peter Drucker contends that the emphasis on economics throughout American history was a

means for arriving at consensus by subordinating or mask-
ing other issues, but that economic blocs are eroding and
the reality of hard value choices about race, civil liberties,
foreign policy and similar matters which are essentially
ideological cannot be suppressed forever. President Johnson's "Great Society" program, he holds, was a last attempt
to solve some of these problems without really talking
about them, of acting as if consensus existed before it was
generally realized that it did not.[11]

If Bell and Drucker are correct, then what we must
look forward to is not the technologizing of politics but increasing dispute over values—indeed, over the nature of
justice itself. Television has been credited or faulted for
making style more important than content and for stressing
the image of the politician rather than his views, but,
paradoxically, perhaps images and style are what politics
will be all about in a technological society. The computers
will solve the simple problems, leaving only the gut issues
for the citizenry.

The Myth of a Mass Political Society

Predictions about the political future are in large
measure extrapolations from beliefs about how contemporary politics is affected by technology. So before we
can come to any conclusions about what is to come and
how well future political institutions and patterns of behavior will be able to deal with the problems presented by the
existential revolution, it is important to understand the nature of our contemporary political system.

In surveying the economic order we determined that
the belief that technological change was radically affecting
the dominance of bourgeois man was essentially false, and
that the economic order was still basically that of industrial
capitalism as forged during the past several centuries. Assessing the political order and how it is being affected by

technology is a somewhat more complex task, however, since one's predictions about what is happening are greatly affected by one's diagnosis of what has happened already, and there is serious disagreement about the effect of technology on contemporary politics. If the theory of mass society is valid, then many of the most gloomy predictions about the future are probably true as well; if it is false, we may still face difficulties, but difficulties that do not stem from government's overwhelming power over the individual but rather from its lack of power.

Belief in the existence of mass society rests upon several pillars, all of them sand. Central to the mass-society theorists' concept of the political order is the premise that modern industrial civilization has destroyed the intermediate structure of groups that protected the elite from being overwhelmed by the mob, and the masses from being manipulated by the elite. In the picture of politics painted by these theorists the individual confronts the massive power of the state naked and alone.

Such a description runs almost completely counter to the facts. Industrial technology and the attitudes of rationality that are associated with it do in fact lead to the end of status and privilege based on nonfunctional criteria, on what are called "ascriptive" factors, such as family background or membership in a priestly caste. But even here the transformation has not been complete, the society still gives respect and status to those specially marked by descent and ordination. What has happened, however, is that special estates based on ascription, although not supplanted, have been augmented by those based on achievement and social function. The press has long been spoken of as the fourth estate, taking its place as a power alongside the aristocracy, clergy and commoners. Don K. Price writes of the "scientific estate" as another in the modern democratic realm.[12]

But modern society knows not four or five but a myriad

of estates. It is a commonplace of social analysis that technological development leads, or at any rate has so far led, to specialization. People with the same occupations have interests and often attitudes in common. This promotes the formation of interest groups, which are the hallmark of modernization. The more industrialized a nation, the greater the role technology plays in its life, the less alike people are and the more organized and unorganized groups appear on the scene. A mob of peasants or unskilled workers may be a mass, but masses cannot exist in a modern society.

Totalitarian rule is sometimes alleged to have been based on the mass society created by modern industrialism, but every totalitarian ruler has so far fought in vain to stem the tide of differentiation. Hitler was unable to destroy completely the network of associations and special interests found in the Germany he took over despite a reign of terror unparalleled in modern history. Stalin was faced with the paradox that as Russia industrialized under his lash, the social breakdown, approximating a mass society, created by the revolutionary era was replaced, against his will, by new and strong social differentiations. The army and navy, the scientific and professional elite, managers of heavy industry and managers of light industry, the party and the secret police, every possible social group began to take form and to try to act in its own interests. Stalinist terror could not stem the tide, and, though treatment of open dissidence has varied somewhat, Stalin's successors have been forced to recognize that in the house of communism, like that of democracy, there must be many mansions. The cultural revolution and associated turmoil in Communist China are the results of Mao's attempts to prevent a new class system and new forms of social, economic and political differentiation from rending the seamless garment of the Chinese revolution.

If totalitarian states, despite the use of mobilized terror, have been virtually helpless before the tendency toward group formation, group identification and group action among their populations—the inevitable concomitant of economic and technological modernization—in the tolerant climate provided by the social *laissez faire* of political liberalism groups and group activity have flourished. The belief that the political process in democratic societies is simply the outcome of the struggle among conflicting interest groups is waning among political scientists, but there is no denying that organized interest groups play a major role in politics and society.

Can anyone seriously hold that the American Farm Bureau Federation, the American Bar Association, the American Medical Association, the Air Force Association, the American Jewish Committee, General Motors, the Catholic Church, the sanitation workers' union, the National Rifle Association, the state of Alabama, the Daley machine in Chicago and the thousands of groups from local civic associations to the Senate "Establishment" are helpless, undifferentiated elements in a homogeneous social and political system? The danger is not that industrialism has destroyed the intermediate group in modern democratic society, but that the group is so strong that the individual, instead of finding freedom in the interstices created by group competition, may be crushed between the contending parties, or that, instead of a dominant total government riding roughshod over an inert society, public purposes will be lost sight of in the feudalistic struggle of competing special interests.[13]

The Myth of Omnipotent Government

But does not contemporary technology make it possible for the government, if it desired to alter this situation abruptly—to seize power and, while retaining the shells of substructures if necessary, to use coercion and propaganda to work its own will? Do not the newest discoveries in weaponry, drugs and motivational techniques make total government possible?

The record so far would seem to indicate that though such dangers exist they are hardly insurmountable. To date at least, totalitarian states, though possessing what some students have described as technologically conditioned monopolies of means of communication and control, have not been able to keep everyone in line.[14] Nazi Germany lurched to defeat in disorganization and disarray; the dissident officers' plot against Hitler failed but was not forestalled. The Soviet Union and its satellites are hotbeds of dissension, among young people and intellectuals especially, and China is in a state of endemic civil war. Widespread acceptance of a totalitarian regime's symbols and party line may be achieved, especially outwardly, but teaching human beings to hate scapegoats, mouth cant or rally to a renascent nation is something different from inducing humans to forget self-interest, to agree on positive policies or to refuse to accept the evidence of their senses about the nature of reality.[15]

Just how effectively a modern state could use coercion against a majority or even a substantial minority of its citizens is a moot question. In part it is a question of what losses a nation is willing to sustain. Atomic bombs can destroy a city and its inhabitants, but can they be used effectively to put down riots in Newark or Detroit? There is little difficulty in suppressing political rebellion when it is only the work of a small minority, since, by definition, at least the passive co-operation of most citizens is available, and the problem is analogous to that of catching ordinary bank robbers and thugs. If it becomes a larger political problem then the co-operation of citizens and the loyalty of the armed forces themselves come into question. Defection was what made the temporary success of the Hungarian revolution of 1956 possible. The sympathy of many whites has played a major role in such success as the black revolution in America has had to date.

Thus, regardless of what weaponry is used, the crucial factor is the degree of support for political dissidence, which is no different from what the situation has been throughout history. It is theoretically possible to create a small elite guard psychically isolated from the general populace, a kind of Janissary secret police, and to use them to terrorize a nation to which they are strangers, but should such bodies come into existence it would not be a reflection of technological change, but of the willingness or helplessness of the citizenry that permitted them to be created in the first place, and their power would be the effect, not the cause, of a loss of freedom.

But the amount of political dissidence is not the sole factor in determining the effectiveness of coercion in present society or any more highly technologized successor. The very centralization made possible by technology, which many look upon as automatically bolstering the power of the state, may have contrary effects. The more complex an organism, the more vulnerable; a single skillful blow of the hand can kill a human being, while dinosaurs and amoebas require a broader attack. A minute and skillful band of saboteurs could paralyze any modern industrial society by striking at its water supplies, transportation terminals and, above all, its communications network. The great Northeast blackout of 1965 illustrated how vulnerable the United States would be to co-ordinated rebellion by a small group.

Force alone is not enough to secure compliance to a central will. Some degree of acquiescence on the part of the oppressed is necessary, whether this is conditioned by propaganda, surveillance or simply despair. Prisons could not operate without the usual compliance of their inmates, and studies of concentration camps have indicated the extent to which a symbiotic relationship between prisoners and guards was an element in their continued functioning.[16] Simple physical coercion has its limits; if men are desperate enough they will die rather than submit to force (the Indians in the Caribbean, for instance, chose extinction in preference to slavery). One must persuade one's prisoners in order to control them, even if only by not completely destroying the hope of ultimate escape.

But does not modern technology, however, place increased powers of persuasion and surveillance in the hands of the community at large sufficient to make total control possible? Here also the picture is not clear-cut. Surveillance, like coercion, is radically affected by the amount of popular support for dissidence. It is theoretically possible by means of electronics to maintain absolute surveillance of every human being at every moment of his life. Two-way television in every room, electronic eavesdropping on conversations in open fields, computerized checks on everyone's actions and location similar to those used to handle railroad cars on modern railroads or suggested for controlling freeway traffic can be designed and built easily enough. Members of Congress and others have been exercised, with good reason, over the proposals for a national data bank that would contain all information about Americans possessed by government agencies: school grades, military record, fingerprints, police record, income-tax data, etc. The potential for abuse of such a system is obvious, but recording the past is quite different from watching the present.[17]

A system of total surveillance would be a clumsy monster. Unless each two-way TV was directly and continuously monitored by a human controller—something that would require a fantastic amount of personnel (and the monitors, too, would have to be monitored)—the computer would have to be taught what to watch for and how to listen as well. Computers are already used, albeit with as yet limited success, for translation purposes, and it has been suggested that computers could be set up to alert human monitors to such words as "assassinate," "rebel," and so forth, when used by citizens. But potential defectors could resort easily to Aesopian language as the young, criminals and dissidents in authoritarian structures always have, or could find other means of hiding their meaning. For such a system to work, everyone would have to learn and be willing to limit their speech to computer language, to simple grammatical sentences without irony or inflection, for as Norbert Wiener points out the very "fuzziness" of human thinking is something the computer cannot manage.[18]

The machine also would have to learn to read facial expressions as well as listen. Endless human time would have to be spent on deciding whether failure of a "bugging" device was the result of normal breakdown or sabotage, whether what appeared to be mechanical error or static really meant something untoward was happening, and so forth. Information retrieval already presents difficulties for programmers and designers and, more generally, "communications overload" is a problem for machines as well as for humans. But the master computer that watched our lives would have to be not only omniscient and of genius intelligence, it also would have to be endowed with all the qualities of sensitivity that sometimes enable us to tell if our wives and colleagues are loyal or treacherous beneath their honeyed words and routine actions. Herman Kahn holds there is no limit to what computers can do,[19] but no one so far has suggested they can be programed to think illogically.

In any event, such a perfect machine could not be built and installed surreptitiously but would require a major national effort and the co-operation of its victims. Like the perfect police force devoid of popular support, it would be the culmination rather than the cause of a loss of political freedom.

In the meantime, nations spend billions of dollars encrypting and decrypting, eavesdropping and jamming, in a constant race both to seek and to hide information from

each other. Colonel Penkovsky reveals his secrets and his
speculations to the Americans while Mr. Philby, a Russian
double agent high in the British secret service, helps to organize the CIA. Governments control the television studios
and the printing presses, but leaflets attacking the Vietnamese war appear in American military installations repro-
duced on army Xerox machines using army paper. As in
the case of automation in industry, if we are moving toward a radical change in the over-all shape of society, we
have not passed any empirical bench marks as yet. Complete and accurate surveillance as a means of control is
probably a practical impossibility. What is much more
likely is a loss of privacy and constant inconvenience as the
wrong people gain access to information, as one wastes time
convincing the inquisitors that one is in fact innocent, or as
one struggles to untangle the errors of the errant machine.
The world of tomorrow will not be a 1984 world of almost
absolute control, but rather an intensification of the experience of those who have had difficulties over their income
tax or been incorrectly billed for a credit purchase or a
long-distance call. Not tyranny but chaos is its most likely
characteristic.[20]

What applies to surveillance as a means of control applies to the use of drugs and brainwashing—to intensive
psychological coercion. Such techniques, to be effective, require either that the subject co-operate or that he be physically isolated and under the control of the person wish-
ing to alter his ideas or behavior. Brainwashing, as opposed
to mere propagandizing, is a lengthy, expensive process,
which requires much skill and total control of the recipient's
environment.[21] A mild form of this technique was used by
the British in the Mau Mau crisis in Kenya; and in theory
this is the objective of all our "correctional" institutions;
the Communist Chinese have developed it into a fine art. But
brainwashing a majority would seem to be an impractical
and unlikely procedure.

Using drugs would be even more cumbersome. Hippie theorists have sometimes speculated about creating the millennium by putting enough LSD into a city water supply to turn on the whole population, but obviously the result would be pandemonium rather than control. Use of truth serums or will-destroying drugs in mass fashion still would require someone or something practically able to listen to and record the truth and to instruct the temporarily helpless in what they must do. On the other hand, control of key leaders might be gained by the use of such methods, if deception were added. Each congressman, instead of having his arm twisted by the President, could be administered drugs to control his will. Ideally, he would have to be simultaneously turned into an instant addict for some drug with pleasurable reactions so as to induce him to return after the first experience. But such methods of control, though theoretically possible, involve doing things the hard way. Greed, fear and pride are all available to the master manipulator. The use of drugs would seem to be an exceptional, though conceivable, means of control rather than a likely widespread practice.

Should the day come when all of the resources of technology, including medical-pharmacological technologies, are used to assault individual freedom, it will not come about exclusively by slow increment or through gradual erosion of liberties, but will require some overt political decision, at least in countries such as Great Britain and the United States. The common-law tradition is ambivalent and inconsistent in balancing freedom and social constraint, as on other matters, but recent judicial activity has been on the side of the individual.[22] Whatever the merits of the situation and the nature of actual enforcement practices, use of wire tapping by government agencies has had to wage an uphill fight for acceptance in the United States, and electronic eavesdropping, either publicly or privately sponsored, is under a judicial cloud. Rights of the

individual against self-incrimination have been increased
rather than narrowed, to the extent that a popular reaction
has set in. The courts generally are on the side of privacy
and freedom in these areas.

The great exception has been in the field of mental
health. Deviance that cannot be punished or curtailed on
criminal grounds is proscribed on allegedly medical ones.
The mental hospitals become centers of brainwashing
(however ineffective) for those whom society, or their relatives or associates with society's consent, deem to be deviant. Normal safeguards of law tend to be watered down
and the scientific prestige of the pseudo science of psy-
choanalysis and its cousins creates its own *imperium in
imperio*.[23] It is interesting to note that the Russians, too,
have caught on to this tactic, and, increasingly, dissident
intellectuals are sent not to prison but to sanatoria for
incarceration and rehabilitation.

Proponents of the possibility of a cowed and subser-
vient populace, a mass society created by technological
change, may feel that discussions such as the above are
cheap attempts to discredit their fears by a *reductio ad
absurdum*. Is not the real problem one caused by a monopoly of communications that creates a situation in which
everyone is so convinced of the basic rectitude of government policy that people need not always and everywhere
be spied upon or coerced by government personnel or machines, but will spy upon and coerce each other?

Such a situation is possible, of course; it has occurred
before in human history, and the Inquisition has its counterparts in the tyranny of small-town public opinion in
America even today. Advanced technology is not necessary
to produce conformity. Indeed, it could be argued that conformity (except for agreement about directly observable
facts) is harder to achieve in a technologized society. The
rationality underlying the world view of such a society is
always likely to spill over from purely instrumental means

of manipulating the environment to the questioning of social and political structures. The vast amounts of information about the environment, physical and social, that such a society must constantly process and digest is bound to contain data that will enable its inhabitants to come to their own conclusions, no matter how much a regime tries to structure their environment.

There is no question that as a result of modern technology the means of communication have become more centralized. Richard Fagan argues that in both the Soviet Union and the United States some .001 per cent of the population could perpetrate a hoax upon the other 99.999 per cent.[24] But such hoaxes are limited to particular questions of fact (the fake death of a President, false reports of an enemy attack) outside the citizens' direct experience and are necessarily of short duration. There always will be those in whose interest it is to question them. The difficulty of convincing all Americans of the validity of the Warren report has its counterparts in the disbelief with which citizens of Communist countries read their press, even though in general they may support the regime. Despite the weight of official skepticism, millions of American and Soviet citizens, including many sophisticated and technically trained persons, believe in the existence of UFO's. The more effectively governments control the channels of mass communication, the more likely is the existence of widespread rumors, unless populations are already convinced they have all the relevant facts. Interest, irrational desire and fear blunt perceptions so that even in open societies where information is readily available rumors spread. Millions of Americans (including a few congressmen) accepted the idea a few years ago that United Nations troops were going to be brought into certain southern states to enforce racial equality.

No society can be kept entirely closed. Electronic media can be completely controlled within the nation, and clandestine transmitters are relatively easy to detect, but nations can be penetrated from the outside.[25] Jamming is expensive and disruptive of one's own communications system. Only in a world state could the outside be kept out, since there would be no outside, save for extraterrestrial colonies that for any foreseeable future would be too dependent on earth support to be able to afford to be hostile. But control over other communications media within the nation has not been advanced by technology. Almost every day new means of communication become available as communication becomes the major activity of civilization. Before long, most homes will have their own duplicating equipment, and the day is probably not far off when all school children will be making their own movies with cheap hand-held cameras as a regular part of their education. Policing Xerox machines and home recorders is theoretically possible, but it presents the same problems as policing individual speech. The technological revolution has not restricted, but rather extended, the range of individual communication and the difficulties of controlling it.

Governments desirous of controlling public opinion would have to fall back upon positive controls, outweighing the opposition rather than destroying it. The resources available in modern society for these purposes are enormous. An increasing proportion of the population is in school at any given moment; at present in the United States almost as many persons are in school full time as are at work full time.[26] Yet the ability of teachers to influence students' attitudes, though great, is not unlimited, as any teacher knows. A natural war exists between students and teachers, especially where adolescents and the college generation are concerned. Students are influenced by their school experience, but as often by what their schoolmates do and think and what they see and read as by what they are formally taught. The role of youth in the Hungarian revolution and in dissent today throughout the world both East and

West is evidence that every modern society breeds its Berkeleys. The only way to prevent this is to emphasize docility and rote learning to the point where the ability of the educational system to produce the qualified technical personnel on which advanced societies rest is itself destroyed.

So also do mass communications have their built-in limitations. Experience indicates that Nazi Germany and the Soviet Union even in the Stalinist era were not able to control opinion entirely, partly because of the rumor effect already noted.[27] Studies in democratic societies indicate that a two-step flow of communications exists in which local- or group-opinion leaders influence how people interpret communications. Who these are may vary from a respected local banker when it comes to information about fiscal policy to a teen-ager when it comes to new fashions.[28] In addition, people are very stubborn in holding on to their ideas. Even the mass media can change them only slowly when it comes to fundamentals, if at all. The fact that the media have been overwhelmingly pro civil rights has apparently done little to keep millions, including many high on the socioeconomic ladder, from flocking to the banners of men such as George Wallace.

Perception follows interest; not only do people refuse to change certain ideas, but they refuse to become interested in certain topics. Saturation campaigns in the mass media fail to make citizens interested in such topics as the United Nations, which they assume, perhaps correctly, have little relevance to their daily lives.[29] The vast variety of special interests in any modern society leads to special "publics" with communications media and opinions of their own. There will always be a subtle difference in emphasis between a party journal such as *Pravda* and an army journal such as *Red Star*, and their readers will have somewhat different pictures of the universe. Only a society that set out to destroy itself by completely stifling all rationality, all initiative and all differences could exercise complete control over public opinion. There is certainly nothing in the nature of the new technological developments in communication as such that makes such a direction inevitable or even likely.

The Myth of the Scientific Elite

If there is no evidence to indicate that modern society, under the stimulus of technological change, is moving in the direction of total political control of the individual, what of the often associated contention that a scientific elite is developing that is gathering political power into its hands?[30] There is no question that scientists are more powerful than they were during the heyday of industrial civilization. The inventions on which industrialization was based were largely the products of tinkerers such as Watt, Ford and Edison. Only in its later stages was there a merger between science and technology, with science the dominant partner, and the professional, trained research scientist coming into his own. Scientists are more powerful today simply because there are more of them and they are highly paid and socially respected.

But this does not make them a political elite. Their numbers, though growing, do not make them a formidable voting bloc, even were they united, which they are not. They have fought bitterly among themselves (Oppenheimers versus Tellers) on the most significant aspects of both public and scientific policy. They have no independent power base, since they work mainly for the government or for private industries that they neither own nor control. Just as scientists are not becoming an economic elite—since the way to make money in the United States is not through salaries but through the use of capital—so, too, they are not becoming a political elite, for to gain political power one must be a politician or administrator.[31] Many scientists hold high positions in government, but these are not as scientists per se but as scientists turned bureaucrats. These men are hardly representative of the scientific community; they are often its least respected members, since they have deserted from, or are presumed to have failed at, the scientist's most sacred task, that of research and discovery.

The weakness of the power associated with the few scientific advisory posts in American government is notorious. The State Department is often faulted for making little use of its Assistant Secretary for Science and Technology, while the post of the President's Special Advisor for Science and Technology has been permitted to remain vacant for several years since its creation.[32] Many of the scientific projects on which the government has expended the most money have been ventures about which most scientists were highly skeptical.[33] At present, Congress is cutting deeply into support for projects and training programs that scientists favor. The brief period when a government and public, awed by the atom bomb, was willing to give science a blank check has come to an end. The scientific estate is now one among many in a pluralistic struggle for individual and group power, and far from the strongest.

It can, of course, be argued that while research scientists as such have limited influence, the world is run increasingly by technicians. Not only are management technicians taking over business and public administration and the communications industries, but political technicians, cool-eyed men such as Johnson, Nixon, Harold Wilson and Kosygin are taking over political life. But this is to stretch the definition of technique to the point of uselessness. Political life has always seen the rise of demagogues and charismatic leaders who attained followings without knowing quite how and who wielded power erratically, but the careers of such men usually have been short-lived. If to calculate rationally one's support and how to retain and extend it, to exercise quiet shrewdness about how to attain one's objectives with minimum difficulty, is the mark of the technician, then politics has been dominated by a technical elite at least since the time of the Roman republic. Certainly there is no evidence that persons of scientific background are gaining unusual influence in the councils of government in the world today. Economists and lawyers we have always with us in modern times. A few industrial managers have some power in the Soviet Union; many persons of scientific background are found among the French elite, especially since De Gaulle. But few scientists sit in the United States Congress or the British Parliament, even when physicians and engineers are so categorized, and few are found in the intimate councils of any chief executive. The professional politician is still on top, and the notion of a scientific elite a myth.[34]

Centralization and Decentralization

Has technological change led to a concentration of power in the hands of central governments or in those of a few top bureaucrats in government generally? Here the evidence is less clear-cut, but it certainly does not warrant an unqualified assertion that such is the case. As we have seen in the case of industry, electronics is a two-edged sword. It makes it possible for superiors to watch and communicate easily with subordinates, yet at the same time it enables decisions to be made almost anywhere, since almost anywhere can be a center of information and communication.

But the very speed with which messages can be transmitted has led to something of a communications overload at central headquarters; swamped by incoming stimuli, whether in the form of written reports or direct electronic messages, leaders are increasingly tempted to allow subordinates in the field to make more and more decisions, reserving only the most important ones for their personal attention. No statistics exist or could be practically collected that could demonstrate this fact, yet an increasing body of opinion and common experience seem to confirm it. Within American government, for instance, it is the state and local governments that have been growing most rapidly in expenditures and personnel since the end of World War II, if one discounts the federal government's military activities.[35] The governor may not be as sovereign a ruler as he once was, but who could contend that men such as Rockefeller, Reagan and Wallace have not affected the destinies of their states' citizens and enjoyed important influence in the national context?

What has happened is that the total activity of government has increased so greatly, just as the total activity of organized society has so increased in absolute terms, that more and more power is being utilized, while at the same time the lines of power and control are more and more intermeshed. State and local and federal governments are engaged in the kind of collaboration that has given rise to such descriptions as "marble cake federalism,"[36] while within the federal government interagency relationships also become more complex. The total social organism has a central nervous system, but so overwhelming are the desires and signals from its constituent parts, so involuntary most of the actions of its muscles and metabolic processes, that it is impossible to speak of it as being consistently directed by a single conscious will.

But technology by itself does not necessarily lead to bureaucratic dominance of government. The relationships between bureaucratic mechanisms and legislative bodies seem to reflect the institutional histories of their particular political cultures much more than any general social trend dictated by technological forces. The American Congress for generations has been the most powerful legislative body among those of the major powers, trying to control policy and administration in much greater detail than any other.

Despite the upper hand which the President retains in some aspects of foreign affairs (witnessed to by the frustrations of Senator Fulbright and his committee in their struggle with President Johnson), the American Congress continues to cut foreign aid, determine fiscal policy and budgetary details, deal with wars on poverty and civil rights much as it, or those whom it represents, see fit.

Elsewhere in the world nations give to their bureaucracies greater powers because they feel it locally necessary or desirable. But bureaucracy itself is subject to the same forces of decentralization as is government as a whole. The ideal type of modern bureaucracy as set forth by the great German sociologist Max Weber, despite its wide acceptance by social scientists, is hardly an adequate description of administrative reality.[37] In many underdeveloped nations where trained personnel are scarce, where bureaucrats enjoy unusually high social status, where interest groups are weak and communications poor, rigidity tends to be the rule with policies set at the top and followed at the bottom —at least on paper, though in practice this rigidity is modified by both ineptitude and corruption.[38] In most developed nations, notably the United States, the bureaucracy, like the legislature, is a matrix for pressures and opinions both from without and within, each adding an increment to a final decision which itself may be only part of a shifting process.

The sheer volume of activity leads to communications problems that make centralized direction difficult. Indeed, here as elsewhere in technological civilization, the paradox is that not uniformity but anarchy may present the greatest danger to man's ability to freely make and effectively implement rational decisions. As a British journalist wrote of the United States: the world of the future looks less and less like 1984 and more like a "technological Wild West."[39] This is not to say that rationality and efficiency dictate extreme centralization as the only alternative to anarchy, and

that a well-functioning technological society would con-
centrate power at the top. Experience to date indicates that
open societies are the most efficient, since the complexities
of life in an interrelated environment demand complete information freely disseminated and the flexibility to make
quick, on-the-spot, incremental responses. The Allied war
effort was better organized than that of the Nazis, despite
the latter's theoretically centralized dictatorship and alleged Teutonic efficiency;[40] Communist states seeking
greater economic productivity are moving in the direction
of more rather than less flexibility, while at the same time
evidence piles up of the dysfunctional aspects of rigidity
in their political systems.

Planning and Centralization

But does not a civilization based on technology depend on planning, and is not planning itself a centralized
process? Do we not plan more and therefore centralize
power more? No. Many persons think of planning as the
drawing of lines on a map or the putting of resources into
categories on paper, and then forcing reality to conform to
the planners' preconceived notions. It is possible to operate in this fashion, especially if one is dealing with nonliving objects; some architectural and engineering "plans"
may be thought of as executed in this way. But this is a
crude notion of planning indeed. Most plans make allowance for feedback from all the interests involved and from
all foreseeable contingencies, and recognize that plans will
need to be altered as the activity progresses. In many cases
what one speaks of as a plan is simply a system of accounts
that provides an inventory of what is actually being done
with all the resources available at a given time.

Planning is a bad word in some nonsocialist societies,
but every major nation in the world except the United
States and West Germany has an acknowledged economic

development plan and planning agency,[41] and business firms and individuals as well as governments plan for the future in various explicit ways. Most plans seek to take predicted behavior into account rather than to determine it, therefore individuals remain free to act as they would have did the plan not exist. Planning is not so much control in advance as a predetermination of reactions to possible contingent events.[42] In any case, the evidence does not indicate that the advances in statistical techniques and communications technologies of recent decades have had the effect of making the citizens of any major nation less free because they are subject to more centralized planning. Indeed, most nations have failed to plan adequately or to fulfill plans undertaken, and no one would think of Harold Wilson's Great Britain or Richard Nixon's America, beset as they are by economic, racial and political crises, as nations whose citizens' actions are rigidly predetermined by some monstrous machine. Quite the contrary.

Planning might be more effective were it not for the existence, already alluded to, of a variety of interest groups who have their own ideas about how the future should look. They are bolstered in their stand by the inability of governments to effectively coerce or convince them, because of the inherent limits of weaponry and communications and because of such hangovers from the industrial order as systems of law that give priority to individual rights, especially property rights, and the special freedom and power given the capitalist entrepreneur. Even where these particular latter elements are weakened or nonexistent, as in the socialist nations, planning is still intrinsically difficult, given the amount of information to be correlated and the problems of human unreliability and self-motivation.

Plans rigidly established in advance, to be really effective, would require absolute knowledge of all the consequences of any particular action and absolute control, and neither of these is possible. But the more attempts are made to plan, the more political conflict. Insofar as planning removes areas of activity from sheer chance or the impersonal influences of the market, the interests of individuals and groups are affected in a way that they can comprehend and seek to forestall. More planning therefore means more, rather than less, political conflict, as Bell and others have pointed out. This is true even in nondemocratic societies. The Red Army and Navy fight for their share of the defense budget just as bitterly behind the scenes as Americans struggle over rapid transit and freeways.

Planning and its associated phenomenon of rationality have not stifled political conflict but instead have changed its focus from conflict over means to conflict over ends. Many struggles of the past, even when they appeared to be deep-seated class and economic conflicts, were confused by the fact that it was not always easy to determine what the results of a particular policy would be. The development of the social sciences and information technology makes it increasingly possible to predict what the consequences of policies will be. Therefore, the disputes are about the justifications of policy, about the nature of justice, about values, about—if you will—ideology. At the same time, the increasing affluence created by technological advance tends to lower the temperature of the struggle over directly economic matters and gives people the margin of economic security that makes it possible for them to worry about other issues. People have always quarreled over noneconomic issues, even in the depths of poverty. Divorce laws were subjects of controversy long before abortion laws were challenged, and untold millions have died over such issues as Arianism, Nestorianism, Trinitarianism and similar theological questions. Increasingly, however, ideological issues are becoming the major or exclusive ones in modern societies, especially in the United States.[43] Technology has laid the basis for a radical alteration of the political order by underwriting the movement toward noneconomic issues. It has not, as some would hold, led to alienation and withdrawal from politics. Instead it has changed the content of politics.

Electronic Media and the New Politics

Electronics combines with relative affluence to make possible this increasing emphasis on noneconomic issues. This is what is behind all the talk about "image" politics and the triumph of style over content. If I hire an accountant or a plumber I may ignore his looks; if I am concerned about government being in the hands of the "right" kind of people, decent, intelligent and respectable as I define these qualities, then looks count. People have always preferred to be governed by those of acceptable race, religion, tastes and social background. All television has done is to allow vast numbers of people to judge the personal and cultural characteristics of an individual close up. Now that it is less respectable in the United States than it once was to pay overt attention to the most gross facts of social background, such as religion and national origin, the more subtle shadings must be judged by the voter, and television provides the means. But it has not created the voter's desire to judge a candidate's personality as well as his stands on issues. Image politics is as old as the republic, and the authors of *The Federalist* rest part of their confidence in republican government on the belief that the common people will elect to office persons they respect.

Electronics, however, has done more than make the image important. In a political sense it has also made the medium equal the message, to use McLuhan's famous catch phrase. Symbolic acts have always been important in politics; people have always spoken and demonstrated as a substitute for voting and fighting, as well as a prelude to them. What television has done is to blur the distinction between symbol and event. What the screen conveys is just as real as, perhaps more real than, the reality itself; the image overshadows the actual event. Therefore the viewer, confronted with images of riots in the cities and strife in Vietnam, seeks to balance them by images of his own creation—protest marches, draft-card burnings and so on—reacting in kind and often consciously aiming at the pseudo reality conferred by television coverage. Thus the electoral process loses some of its meaning. Why wait for the opportunity to change rulers in the hope that through this act one can affect events in the future? The unwanted event is here and now on the TV screen; it must be countered immediately by an event of one's own creation so that the bad image gives way to the good.[44]

The Breakdown of the Party Systems

Most modern Western parties are coalitions of interests—in the English-speaking nations, especially of economic interests; parties based on religion, ethnic origin or ideology were more at home in Europe. Today, when Continental parties appear to be becoming more pragmatic and economic in base, politics in America is tending to become more ideological. Traditionally, party leaders stayed away from volatile issues such as religion and morals if they could. In the British Parliament, with its tight party discipline, these were among the few things left to members' consciences, as in the case of divorce legislation. Yet how long can American parties, built on class and sectional alignments, hold together when the big issues are not merely taxes and wages but the meaning of work and the viability of the Puritan ethic; not merely foreign policy but, underlying that, pacifism and one's feelings about Che Guevara; not merely states' rights but race; not merely civil liberties but censorship, sex behavior and drugs? The struggle between liberal and conservative Republicans is hardly a simple matter of attitudes toward labor law and corporate taxation but rather a struggle between two ways of life, while Lyndon Johnson has typified all that many intellectuals and young people find repugnant in American society.

In the past, as new issues came to the fore, realignments did take place, but slowly and with a certain logic and coherence. Economic issues were both interrelated and capable of being compromised. Notwithstanding inconsistencies or irrelevancies, one could put work relief, high income taxes and the right to strike (or opposition to these) in the same package. But despite some psychologists' belief in the existence of entities such as the "authoritarian personality," it appears that attitudes toward East-West trade, race relations, conservation, abortion-law revision, toleration of homosexuals, policy toward Israel and church-state relations do not necessarily fit into a single neat syndrome. Insofar as they do, they run counter to economic alignments. Higher-income groups, generally more educated, are likely to be more liberal on cultural issues while less enthusiastic about social welfare and economic egalitarianism than the working classes.[45] George Wallace is well to the left of Richard Nixon on economic issues. The lines of alliance and hostility are so tangled as to hint that the two-party system itself may be on the verge of collapse, despite the factors in the electoral structure that bolster it, especially at the national level.[46] The two-party system has done much to keep America united (its great past failure led to the Civil War). Party discipline could be a major bolster to effective legislative support for planning to meet the problems presented by technology. Thus the extent to which technology promotes the breakdown of the party system, and with it a downgrading of the electoral process as the great lever by which public opinion influences government, could be another factor leading to chaos rather than hypercontrol in technological civilization.

The Breakdown of Nations

Along with the breakdown of parties may come the breakdown of nations. Cultural nationalism is not a modern phenomenon; it was present at the birth of the modern nation-state system and, as the struggles of the Poles, Czechs and Irish illustrate, was a major factor well into the twentieth century. But it seemed to be diminishing by mid-century in industrialized nations. Now it returns: Belgium and Canada are torn by strife and dissension. Scottish and Welsh nationalism increases rather than diminishes, and despite socialist solidarity and proletarian internationalism, Yugoslavia has problems of internal cohesion, while her Balkan neighbors scowl at each other.

One factor in this new nationalism may be the belief that on the international level technology has so concentrated power in the hands of a few states that for certain purposes it gives one just as much security or voice on the world scene to be a citizen of a tenth-rate power such as Wales as to be a citizen of a third-rate power such as Great Britain. But there are more direct technological influences. As we have seen, technology, by creating at least moderate affluence, has given people time to turn their attention to cultural issues. Nationalism may be supported by discontented workers, but it is led by the new-style well-to-do collegian or intellectual. What better cultural issue than preservation of one's heritage? Technology makes such preservation an even more immediately pressing problem. When written language was the medium of mass communication, and distant social interactions were limited, one could preserve one's culture in one's native village while maintaining limited contact with the outer world through a spoken language used on special occasions. Today, many children throughout the world spend hours each day glued to television sets.

The world is not yet a global village (how many Turkish television programs have you seen lately?), but the nation is. Modern electronics joins nations to each other, but its basic web, denser by several orders of magnitude than the global web, turns nations in upon themselves. To enter into the electronic village of another people is to lose one's soul just as surely as if one entered into their web of social and administrative interaction (witness Canada's strenuous and expensive attempts to promote a distinctively Canadian culture through subsidized TV). Subcultures therefore find political independence a necessary as well as a feasible alternative to being part of a larger nation if they are to survive.[47] They may retain economic bonds, but they need political autonomy to safeguard cultural autonomy, and they feel rich enough to sacrifice some economic goods for cultural ones. A technologized world, even with world government—or perhaps as a result of it—may see more and more national units emerging.

Failure of the Political System

To what extent can we say that the political system is being transformed by technology in a manner commensurate with the transformations that the new powers available to society are making in the basic situation of mankind? Hardly at all. Social inertia is at work in the political order just as in the economic. The political order is not changing in such a way as to provide the tools whereby the economic order may be reshaped to meet the challenges posed by the existential revolution. Business as usual has its counterpart in politics as usual. The bourgeois economic order was based on the premise of the unseen hand, the notion, as in Mandeville's *Fable of the Bees*, that private vice leads to public virtue. So, too, the political. It was expected that somehow justice and a viable political order would come out of the unrestricted interplay of group interests.

Both these abdications of conscious social control over the shape of society had their roots in the same belief, that freedom was the highest value and that it could best be achieved by leaving men alone to pursue their own interests. But it also assumed that there was enough room for error—enough economic surplus, enough areas of life inherently incapable of being dominated by politics—that men could walk away from their mistakes. It did not contemplate a situation in which my use of my economic freedoms makes the exercise of yours impossible, and in which every aspect of human life, including the provision of breathable air and drinkable water, requires a political decision. In short, it failed to recognize that freedom could only exist *within* the political and economic orders and not outside them, and therefore that the alternative to order might not be freedom but a chaos of inconsistent and destructive interactions.

The last decade at least has shown a breakdown, not an increase, in the ability of the political system to give meaningful direction to society. This is not to say that government actions do not, by commission and omission, influence the lives of individuals, but they do so in an increasingly formless way so that control of the reins of power seems more and more irrelevant, as the reins themselves become more slack. Thus while interest groups and citizens increasingly call upon government to do something, the government seems less and less capable of effective action. In the socialist states loss of faith in the efficacy of central planning is manifest; in the United States spokesmen of both left and right, extremists and moderates alike, speak with increasing favor of decentralization of governmental activity and with increasing skepticism of federal action, with the late Robert Kennedy and the Students for a Democratic Society sounding much like Ronald Reagan and the Young Americans for Freedom.

The American public-school system seems impotent to deal with the education of any but middle-class children, while Mayor Lindsay is considered something of an arch-radical for refusing to accept the general belief that New York City is ungovernable and perhaps even unviable.

Youth with deep social concerns and a sense of the magnitude of the problems facing the community do not, as their fathers did, join radical political movements aiming to seize control of the governmental structure, rather they attack the idea of structure itself or see the real revolution embodied in withdrawal from organized politics and society generally.

Everywhere the ability of the political system to channel popular wishes into some kind of meaningful decision-making grows weaker. The French political system is temporarily centered around a new emperor, Charles de Gaulle, ruling through a nobility of technicians, but this may be only a brief interim in traditional political disorder. In Great Britain the Labour party dispiritedly acts as the receiver of Conservative failure and increasingly lacks the gall to call the situation "socialism." In the United States there is an increasing feeling that the ground is shifting under the consensus that has underlain the political system for a generation, and men of varying opinions would endorse the sentiment that subtitles a book on the "Great Society" as *The Failure of American Liberalism*.[48] Many ask how healthy the American economy could be without the constant spur of military spending, which has been a major factor since the recession of 1938, at the same time they doubt both the wisdom of America's commitments abroad and her capacity to carry them out. Doubt about the nation's proper role in the world arena is coupled with bewilderment about racial problems at home; the essential success of the civil-rights movement has not brought racial harmony but has forced the nation to face up to the far more difficult problems of dealing with basic economic and social inequalities and with conflicts between black and white. General recognition exists that the New Deal and its ideas are as irrelevant as the *ancien régime,* and that the party system based on the Roosevelt era is coming apart, but nothing has yet taken its place and no adequate means exist for relating popular needs and desires to governmental action. The general lack of enthusiasm for either of the major candidates in the 1968 elections illustrates the increasing inability of the existing party system to provide adequate political leadership.

Thus the activity of government more and more seems not the incarnation of a popular will or of an ordered response to problems but a form of entertainment; politics more and more seems an arena in which interests and ideas clash with little intervention by the citizen spectators. In the United States, for instance, while vast sums of government money have been appropriated for man's conquest of outer space and the oceans, space and oceanographic policy have never become a subject of great popular interest or debate, despite their obvious significance. This is not because a small clique has withheld information or usurped decision-making power nor because the matter under discussion is inherently so complicated as to defy popular understanding; nor has apathy developed because the public is necessarily uninterested or not directly affected in the short as well as the long run; nor even because they are agreed on what should be done.

What has happened is that the political system simply has been unable to structure the issues and to relate them to the decision-making process in such a way as to enable the popular will to be expressed. As a result, scientists, private economic interests and military men have had a virtually free hand in forging policy out of their own conflicting but ultimately reconcilable interests. An existential revolution has been taking place through political default. Not only is it possible that things are being done that are not in the long-range interest of humanity (too much money spent on space and underwater exploration too fast or in the wrong way, new discoveries exploited in ways that have a negative effect on human development), but even from the standpoint of the proponents of progress for its own sake the situation is dangerous. A population that has supported space exploration because it appeared cheap may withdraw support irrationally when alternative needs come to the fore; those who have looked upon science as a weapon against foreign enemies may ignore it if international tensions ease. An almost unconscious commitment made out of ignorance and indifference is not likely to lead to the spiritual renaissance which so many of the prophets of progress see as the real justification of man's conquest of his environment.[49]

That the political system that was the product of industrial civilization has been unable to focus on major questions of policy in terms of the interest of the race is evidenced not only by its inability to control exploration of the terrestrial and extraterrestrial environment. This inadequacy is equally evident in the continuance of the accidental revolution in the domestic economy. Whatever may be its effects on the employment picture for the foreseeable future, the increased impact of automation and cybernation on the character of the economy and the quality and meaning of life cannot be denied. In the industrial era—especially in the United States and other nations committed to a *laissez-faire* economy—private short-run economic interest dictated which cities would grow and which countrysides would die, what would be produced for human consumption and what would not, what machines people would work with and how they would communicate and travel. Government made marginal adjustments, did things private enterprise found unprofitable, such as running comprehensive school systems, and tried to pick up the pieces.

Today the same forces are at work. Private economic interests will decide what industries will eliminate labor and what human functions will be replaced by the computer, which is to say they will decide what the future social and economic class system will look like, which humans may have the age-old function of productive labor taken away from them forever and be made wards of the species, and which of man's biological activities will quite literally become mechanized. As presently constituted the political order is simply incapable of making these fundamental decisions. This is not a case of failure to pass laws, appoint presidential advisory commissions, or anything else at that level. There is simply no basic acceptance of the legitimacy of such decisions being made by conscious action of the whole community rather than by the incremental decisions of individuals, and there is no institutional mechanism for eliciting, weighing and implementing popular decisions on such matters.

What is true of space and oceanographic exploration and the exploitation of automation and cybernation is, of course, also true to the same extent of any changes made in the economy by scientific advances and their social consequences. New power sources, new means of synthesizing food and raw materials through atomic manipulation, new building materials, new means of communication—everything that science can discover and technology create will be looked for or not, introduced or not, widely exploited or not, without reference to any standard other than private interest save when eccentric individuals or groups seek to impose their own personal convictions about the common good. But no means exist for the national community or the race as a whole to decide what shall be done.

Paradoxically, only in the field of biological and medical research do certain controls exist, legal and ideological relics of the preindustrial era. Thus what kind of surgery can be performed, what kinds of biological experimentation and manipulation will be made legal are still subject to social controls. The legal order has generally stood behind the right of the individual to retain control over his own body and the Hippocratic oath to preserve life has given cues to the medical profession as to what purposes their activity ought to serve. Thus today we see some medical men calling for restrictions on heart transplants on the grounds not that they are culturally undesirable but that they are physically dangerous, a fierce debate rages in legislative bodies as to whether abortion is simple therapy or potential murder and—spurred in part by the problems created by organ transplants—cries increasingly are heard for a more precise and sophisticated definition of the instant of death. Some social regulation of medical and biological technology will undoubtedly take place, but it may consist simply of providing a legal go-ahead for experimentation and change. It appears that the criteria will continue to be almost exclusively the physical well-being and the wishes of the individual patient, rather than the social welfare of the species. Suppose that tomorrow it was deemed possible to enable an individual to live forever, and he consented to the medical means necessary to this end. Despite the problems man-made immortality would pose for humanity, it is hard to believe that the individual or his physicians would be denied the opportunity to make him immortal. As in other areas, *laissez faire* remains the rule.

All indications are that *laissez faire* will continue to be the rule when embryonic therapy, sex determination, genetic control and similar techniques are introduced on a widespread basis. Paradoxically, artificial insemination is a private matter between doctor and patient, while many American states make fornication illegal and even proscribe certain forms of intercourse among the married. That the leading technological nation in the world chooses to regulate private biological relations in accordance with other persons' moral standards while not taking cognizance of biological activities that have an obvious social impact is an instance of cultural discontinuity that hardly augurs well for an integrated legal approach to the social problems posed by the revolution in biological sciences.

Nowhere are the problems posed by the inability of

the political order of pretechnological man to meet the crises caused by the existential revolution more obvious and immediate than in the area of ecology. Even the casual newspaper reader is aware of urban decay, crowded schools and recreational facilities, air and water pollution, traffic congestion and similar symptoms of a growing population with growing claims to limited resources. Public-opinion polls show that a substantial proportion of Americans at least consider some of these problems to be among their major concerns.[50] Yet despite the incorporation of some measures to sustain and rehabilitate the environment into certain "Great Society" programs, there are no adequate political instruments available for coping with such problems. As indicated above, the Great Society may well have represented a last attempt to begin dealing with some of these issues before their political ramifications were generally realized. But such beginnings were only possible (insofar as any of them survived the economies necessitated by the war in Vietnam) because the programs were voluntary in nature and the sums of money involved were so paltry that the burdens were politically negligible.

No attempt has been made to ask to what extent it is desirable or even economically feasible to repair damage that should never have been caused in the first place. Political answers do not exist to any of the basic ecological questions. Who should bear the cost of preventing air and water pollution: industry, the consumer, the general public? To what extent is private management capable of preserving scenic amenities? How shall we decide between industrial and recreational uses of the Hudson River or the Indiana dunes or the redwoods? Shall public policy aim at making life easier or more difficult for the man who desires to drive his own car to work? Shall it be designed to provide dwellings that consume open spaces or should it instead encourage the building of high-rise apartments? Shall limited educational resources be devoted to raising slightly the general level of competence or to assisting the most talented to fulfill their potentialities? When weather can be controlled, whose interests shall be served? To what extent shall providing goods and services for the American population as a whole, perhaps even for the world population, be emphasized as opposed to reducing pollution, congestion and the consumption of resources that have alternative public uses? Shall measures designed to cope with the effects of population growth be limited to these effects or should they include means for curtailing population growth itself? If the latter, what means of regulation—from subsidies and fiscal policy to outright coercion—shall be used? What effects would such policies have on the racial mixture of the population? Should public policy take cognizance of the trend in housing arrangements (already conditioned by various kinds of government intervention in the housing market) to segregate by age or stage in the life cycle as well as race? Is there an optimum rate of social change as well as a desired direction, and should the government consciously seek to influence the speed of change more directly?

All of these questions, all the subquestions that flow from them and all the related questions that have been left unstated involve major matters of human choice. Personal and group economic interests, status and power are affected by the answers. Moral and cultural and religious values are involved. Someone will be coerced or pressured, someone lose or gain in material and social status, someone be affected in the intimate details of his life, no matter how these questions are answered. What is basic, of course, is that this is true whether government does anything about any of our pressing ecological problems or not. Government intervention at any level will affect human life; so will governmental failure to intervene. Not only will change take place in any event, but it will also be change that is not completely voluntary on the part of most of the individuals affected. One is forced to breathe foul air if one lives in the cities even if no law requires it, and one's freedom is restricted almost as much if one is being forced to pay an economic premium for quiet, solitude or the avoidance of ugly or sordid neighborhoods whose degeneration government policy might have prevented.

Social choice is inescapable and freedom is conditioned at the individual level with or without government attempts to rationalize the environment, for certain choices cannot be made at the individual level. The ecological component of the existential revolution—the increasing density of the physical and human environment—makes it inevitable that some choices can be made only collectively. No one can breathe pure air out of doors unless society acts, or find adequate schooling within his means without social action. Only God can make a tree as yet, but ordinarily it takes a government to make a public park. The inability of the political system to deal adequately with ecological problems, especially when it comes to formulating comprehensive public policies through party programs and legislative action, means that certain choices are almost automatically ruled out, and that man's technological ability to cope with the situation is destroyed.

Herein lies the great paradox of the relationship of technological change and the political order, of existential revolution and social inertia. Let us assume that technological man, were he to exist, would apply to his own life the same standards of rationality that are associated with science and technology: the making of conscious choices based on knowledge of reality and its interrelations, the appreciation of the extent to which choice is conditioned by the inexorable facts of nature and of how freedom must be maximized within the limitations prescribed by those facts and an appreciation of the relationship between ends and means, parts and the whole. Then it is obvious that the present political order makes the emergence of technological man impossible.

It makes it impossible to do more than tinker with the

great problems facing the human species. All of these can be dealt with only by clear, conscious and sustained choices, implemented by informed and consistent social action. Space travel, use of the oceans, economic change, biological mutation—the political and administrative requirements such choices and action entail will necessarily overwhelm a political system geared to ignorance, arbitrariness and rule by special interests, and characterized by discontinuity and disjunction and general formlessness. Men have feared that technological man when he appeared would be a monster, a mere human gifted with Godlike powers to control himself, his environment, his fellows and the future evolution of the species itself. Existing political systems make such fears groundless. The political and governmental structures even in the most technologically advanced nations render man bewildered and impotent, a prisoner of his most primitive atavisms and the plaything of the fates.

The International Order and the Existential Revolution

This impotence is just as real on the international as on the domestic level, if not more so. A political order capable of dealing with the problems that the situation poses to the species as a whole does not exist, indeed is perhaps farther away than ever. At one time the great powers, through the concert of Europe and other mechanisms, were capable of imposing their will on lesser breeds in the many matters on which they were in agreement. The latter nineteenth century was the era of the Pax Britannica, and the world became part of one vast economic system centering on capitalist Western Europe and North America. When Sir Edward Grey said in 1914 that "the lights are going out, and we shall not see them lit again in our time," he was more right than he knew.

The League of Nations was impotent before serious crises, its successor the United Nations equally so. Prophets like Teilhard de Chardin who have saluted it as a portent, symbolizing the political incarnation of the Noosphere, are extremely premature. The overwhelming political fact of world politics in the late twentieth century is a divided world, with two great superpowers, the United States and the Soviet Union, and a third—mainland China—waiting in the wings. The fact of their power rests not on their resources or population alone but, above all, on technology. They alone have not only nuclear weapons but the ability to create whole weapons systems, to use them and to defend themselves in part against counterattack.

Yet the irony is that their great and almost exclusive military power is unable to establish world order. If the Soviet Union and the United States were united, even today, despite China's growing strength, they could rule the world. But their disunity makes them almost powerless. Small powers are encouraged to maneuver in the interstices created by great-power disorder. Albania and Rumania defy the Soviet Union, North Korea and Cuba defy the United States. The Viet Cong hold out against American might because nuclear weapons are too clumsy for effective political coercion of individuals and small groups and cannot be used to destroy those who have powerful protectors. Great powers are blackmailed by their allies as well as their enemies, as Saigon and Havana manipulate their protectors. Despite the admonitions of the Americans, Russians and British, other nations acquire nuclear weapons or seek to do so, creating a world in which any nation, however small, that is desperate enough can inflict horrible damage on any power seeking to control her. Indeed, within a few decades perhaps, international jewel thieves may be able to plant hidden bombs in New York or Moscow and threaten to destroy millions unless they are allowed to go their way. Peace, as never before, is not dependent solely on the logic of armament but on good will, good communications and political skill.

At the same time that military and political power

are dispersed, certain forms of economic power are becoming more and more concentrated. The full utilization of the dominant forms of technology demands large and affluent markets, as the architects of European unity have recognized. The brain drain, whereby the least developed nations lose their most technologically talented to the more developed and the latter to the most advanced (Indians go to Great Britain, the British come to the United States) calls attention to the fact that economically the world is becoming one system, and at a certain level the new technological civilization is even becoming planetary in scope, though its major points of concentration and its apexes of control will be in a few nations, most notably the United States. The increasing economic integration of the planet, coinciding with continued political disunity, simply adds to the increasing feeling that political life is unreal and the world, while coming closer together, is, in another sense, also coming apart.[51]

Nowhere is international economic interdependence illustrated more graphically than in the plight of the less developed nations. The existence of a world market renders them economically helpless before the technological development of the advanced countries. In time it may be possible that scientific advance can make the deserts bloom with desalinated water and the power from the released atomic energy of common minerals. But in the meantime living standards rise slowly if at all, especially where population growth continues unchecked, in part because technological civilization has passed by the undeveloped intellectually.

For the developing nations advance means learning to walk, and modern science and technology are designed to teach walkers how to fly. Thus people who need help in digging wells are induced or tempted to build hydroelectric dams, people who need better plows are shown how to use sophisticated and expensive fertilizer, nations needing industry but suffering from unemployment become the locus of automated factories, and hopelessness and resentment replace aspiration. Science, as Roger Revelle bluntly puts it, has done nothing for the poorer countries.[52] Even when they advance, they do so at a slower rate than those already ahead of them, so that the gap in living standards between the rich and poor peoples of the earth grows greater with every day, even when the latter are not on the road to emmiseration. At the same time a culture worldwide in its most superficial aspects contributes to a revolution of rising expectations. Left behind, drained of their most technologically advanced citizens, the underdeveloped nations are to the emerging world civilization what Appalachia and the Scottish Highlands are to the United States and Great Britain; the more populated countries such as India become the Notting Hills and Harlems of the new world.

Planning for humanity's needs on a world scale would mean solving all the problems of adequate national response to the existential revolution and more. Population control, allocation of scarce resources, choice between economic and noneconomic goals, all present the same problems, only on a vaster scale, with greater divergences of condition and interest and fewer factors of social and cultural cohesion to bridge them. If the political mechanism for coping with the dual ecological and existential revolution is weak at the national level, it is virtually nonexistent at the international level. Resentments and misunderstanding and local and ethnic pride, ignorance and special interests separate nations as much or more than they divide them. Nor is the earth brought together effectively by global communication; no American can see through the eyes of the Cuban or Russian TV viewer or the reader dependent on the Communist Chinese or Ethiopian press. No two persons' perceptions of reality are ever exactly alike; the fact that electronic and printed communications media are organized on a national basis reinforces differences along national lines. There is as yet no world culture. The world village created by electronics is a myth.

Thus it is clear that the political order at the international level is incapable of dealing with existential revolution. The space race is still that, despite the International Geophysical Year and repeated suggestions for American-Russian collaboration in space exploration.[53] Any direct benefits of space exploration will accrue to the powers who can afford it and carry it out, not to spectators. If space holds riches, the rich nations and those in economic control within them will reap the benefits, not the *campesinos* or the fellahin. This is more obviously and directly true in the case of the oceans. Voices have been raised in favor of UN control of ocean development, on the grounds that the high seas have always belonged to all mankind, and legislation has been introduced in the United States Congress looking to treaty agreements toward that end. But already the sea and the sea bed is being carved up by special treaties (as in the case of North Sea mineral rights) or by extensions of jurisdiction over the continental shelves. In time the sea will be fenced in the way the American West was, and the beneficiaries will not simply be the nations that have sea coasts, as opposed to those which do not, but the more technologically advanced among these maritime powers. Here, as in space, power breeds power, wealth breeds wealth.

The problems of utilizing science on an international scale are enormous. Not only exploiting space and the seas on a planetary rather than a national basis, not only deciding how to use science to make the resources of the earth able to support its total population, but even relatively simple everyday matters will be occasions for conflict. Once weather control is practicable, how shall we decide who gets rain and who sunshine, for instance? Hard enough to co-ordinate on a national basis (cloud seeding has already led to lawsuits in the United States), its potentialities as a source of international discord are obvious.

There is a tendency on the part of the advanced na-

tions to do as they will without consulting others affected—
the United States put millions of tiny needles into orbit a
few years ago, interfering with communications and astronomy, and, until scientists objected, the military contemplated giant mirrors in space to illuminate the battlefields
of Vietnam at night.[54] All of the nuclear powers have polluted the atmosphere with radioactive fallout without any
concern for humanity as a whole and with very little for
their own citizenry. Clearly, the international political order is in a state of advanced breakdown or, if one prefers,
hyperretarded primitiveness, which makes it incapable of
meeting what are obviously international problems.[55]

What of those issues that are increasingly relevant in
the advanced nations, yet do not concern most humans as
yet? What we do about controlling automation, organ transplants, genetic engineering and similar matters are of little
interest now to the peasants in the villages of the world. As
delegates to a recent international conference put it, why
talk to us of the effects of technology on the quality of life,
when we are on the verge of starvation, in part because of
technological backwardness?[56] But if man is to control his
own destiny, man—not only European or American man—
must do so. Asians and Africans are members of the common species, and a wrong evolutionary turning will affect
them as well as Americans and Europeans. Perhaps, though,
they will have the satisfaction of sitting back and watching
the peoples of the advanced nations lose their existential
identity, and of knowing that though poor, despised and exploited they themselves still carry the flag of humanity.

8

Technological Change and Cultural Lag

The existential revolution threatens virtually to destroy civilization as we have known it, to alter fundamentally the nature of man and his relation to the universe. Yet the economic institutions created by bourgeois man remain essentially unchanged despite rising uneasiness among prophets and public alike, as do the political institutions that would logically be the means through which the total community could meet the challenges posed by technological change. If technological man is coming into existence, he is not yet visible upon the economic or political landscape.

But perhaps we have been looking in the wrong place. Perhaps the very centrality and massiveness of modern economic and political institutions make them unamenable to adjustment to new pressures, and we should look elsewhere for the first signs of oncoming change. Perhaps it is in the cultural order that we shall first catch a glimpse of the new technological man. Perhaps education, family life, religion and art will give us some indication of the way in which man is changing in response to new pressures.

The relation of culture and technology, like the definition of culture itself, is a subject on which students of society have expended much energy in methodological quarrels. Economic life usually reflects technological change fairly rapidly and directly, though, of course, it conditions it as well. Political life, which always (implicitly at least) involves human volition, may or may not respond to technological change. Discussing the relation of technology to cultural life presents special problems. In one sense, culture refers to all the nonbiological aspects of human existence, including economics, politics and technology. In the popular usage it refers to man's personal life and values, his intellectual and his artistic expressions.

Proponents of the idea of technological or economic determinism use the concept of "cultural lag" to suggest that human beings are slow to respond intellectually to changes in the physical aspects of their existence. But such a concept assumes what it is the job of the social scientist to demonstrate—that there is a one-way relationship between two sets of social facts; it fails to allow for the possibility that culture not only reflects but conditions the physical side of human existence. Culture, too, is an independent variable or, to put it more felicitously, "Ideas have consequences."[1] The existence of technological change presupposes cultural acceptance. Indeed, technology is itself part of culture. As we have seen, the whole scientific and technological revolution that made industrialism possible and which in the view of many is now moving us into a postindustrial civilization was based on the acceptance of a particular view of life, of certain attitudes toward the nature of the universe and the meaning of human existence.

Thus the problem of the relation of contemporary culture and the existential revolution has two aspects: to what extent have the cultural norms created or retained by industrial civilization persisted despite technological change, that is, to what extent is "cultural lag" an empirical fact; and, secondly, what cultural changes would have to occur so that contemporary society could assimilate and cope with the existential revolution, that is, what would be an appropriate culture for technological man? The second question is most properly discussed later, when we attempt to evaluate the meaning of the existential revolution for contemporary man, and the response he must make if technological man is to become a reality, or, to put it another way, if humanity is to retain control of its destiny. But we cannot avoid touching upon this issue in passing; to describe the current cultural situation we need to know what might be—for contrast, even if not for actually passing judgment.

Cultural conditions are even more difficult to delineate than economic and political ones. We can establish relatively easily whether the production of automobiles has risen or the number of blue-collar workers has declined. We can look at voting statistics and determine to what extent party loyalty is weakening; in any event, we know whom the voters have chosen to rule. But culture is something else again. Does the presentation of Shakespeare on television mean that the cultural level is rising? Even assuming we know how many watched (and that Shakespeare is culturally "superior" to ordinary fare), we cannot know quite so easily what effect the performance has had upon the viewers.

Are big automobiles bought as status symbols or for their utility as forms of transportation? The pop sociologists and the advertising agencies may claim to know, but do the buyers themselves know? To assume unconscious motivation is dangerous; like many other concepts derived from the Freudian tradition in psychology, such an hypothesis is difficult if not impossible to test empirically. In dealing with economics and politics we have been on somewhat shaky ground, but it is possible to analyze trends in these areas with some degree of scientific validity. When dealing with cultural matters, although some hard data are available, evaluation is more subjective.

Nevertheless, it seems safe to say that in the area of culture, as in the others, technological man is more myth than reality. If we define culture for our present purposes as one's orientation toward the natural and social universe and one's role in it, the technological change that threatens to bring about an existential revolution has not led to the creation of new and appropriate cultural norms or social forms. Though stirrings exist among segments of youth and a few intellectuals,[2] the general response to technological change has been either the persistence of old patterns or their attenuation or breakdown with nothing being substituted for them. If any new pattern emerges, it is the absence of a pattern.

The Predicted Future of Culture

What cultural changes do the sociological prophets foresee as a result of current technological developments? Some who accept the concept of mass culture as a corollary of mass society postulate mass culture's continuation and intensification in a world-wide, homogeneous suburbia subject to all the spiritual myopia and desiccation that the intellectuals' notions of the "suburban way of life" imply. Some expect the culture of the future to reflect the rationality and order implicit in science and technology, which will present new means of orientation, while religion as an organized force will decline to the point of vanishing.[3] Herman Kahn and his associates assert that the new culture will be "sensate" (borrowing the term from the cultural philosopher Sorokin), based on hedonism (including the use of drugs) and a decline of the ethic of work.[4] Many assume that the family will decline in importance as its functions wither, that sexual life will be more permissive and open, while the concepts of male and female will change as the social roles of breadwinner and mother become less significant.[5]

Some see privacy on the decline[6] and alienation on the increase. Almost all agree with Erikson that "identity" will be the crucial problem of personal life,[7] and most hold that continued and accelerating social change will accentuate problems of personal and social adjustment, especially for youth deprived of meaningful models and aspirations.[8] Many look to an increase in cultural universalism, with the peoples of the world becoming more and more alike, while others see the new culture as more eclectic, varying within as well as among nations.

Not all of these projected futures are compatible and consistent, but most have in common the assumption that the world will become more "worldly," with rationality supreme in the work sphere, while personal life becomes increasingly a matter of individual will, even irrational will. The mechanized society becomes Apollonian, the personal sphere Dionysian. Virtually all the prophets, with the exception of the more dogmatic such as McLuhan, implicitly grant that their specific prophecies are less inherently reliable in these cultural matters than in others. Despite the fact that all assume technological change will play a role in molding future culture—or is already doing so—they make technology more a necessary, than a sufficient, condition for the changes they perceive, tending to base their cultural prophecies on straightforward extrapolations of current trends.[9]

Generally speaking, it can be said that the prophets of the new era are, despite the nature of the evidence, on more solid ground in their cultural than in their economic and political prophecies. Though, as we shall see, they grossly exaggerate the extent to which change has already taken place, their estimates of its general nature and direction are more sound. What is arguable, however, is what their predictions mean. For what emerges as the pattern of the future is not technological man so much as neoprimitive man trapped in a technological environment. The most certain thing that can be said about the future is that it will be culturally eclectic, but this could easily mean chaos rather than the emergence of a new human type. Rather than develop a new culture suitable for technological man, man may withdraw culturally before the existential revolution and end up living in cultural poverty and bondage, relieved by outbursts of frustration in much the same way as certain primitive groups (some American Indian tribes, for instance) who have been overcome by industrial civilization and deprived of a functioning culture.

Whatever the particular views of individual prophets, there is an increasing consensus that the hypothesis of mass culture, in the rigid form in which it was accepted a short time ago, cannot hold up, just as its parent theory of mass society has also had to be largely abandoned.[10] There is no question that the mass media form part of the cultural environment of everyone who lives in an advanced industrial society. Substantial portions of the population read such magazines as *Time* and *Reader's Digest* or watch the same network programs on television. Indeed, it can be argued that even if mass society is a myth, mass culture is not, since class distinctions have only marginal effects on patterns of cultural consumption. All classes tend to watch the same television programs, and one survey indicates that differences in reading habits between persons with postgraduate training and blue-collar workers is minor.[11]

Yet side by side with the mass media and their mass audience, cultural subgroups flourish and they influence their members to perceive the world—including the messages of the mass media—differently. Among the readers of *The Village Voice* and of *The National Observer* there is little overlap, though both groups are highly educated. *True* magazine reaches a different audience from *The New Yorker*. *Encounter* and *News of the World* represent different British subcultures. Many Americans leave TV to their children, and the various programing levels of the BBC represent sociological realities. In the United States the second most popular sport is stock-car racing[12] (whose very existence readers of the New York *Times* are only marginally aware of, if at all), while in increasing numbers Americans willingly desert their television sets to go hunting and fishing.[13]

Not only do separate publics exist, but also the creation of new publics is accelerating as factors such as class, education, religions, ethnicity and so on combine in new patterns. The survival of radio has been due in part to increasing specialization: some stations carry nothing but fundamentalist religious programs, others serve blacks or the Spanish-speaking, still others are devoted to the Top Forty favorites of the teen-agers or to telephone conversations with housewives and the elderly. Not everyone can have his own radio or TV station, but new specialized periodicals flourish, and the underground press is a success story which has attracted the attention of the *Wall Street Journal*, itself a deviation from the mass cultural norm.[14] Cheap electronic equipment makes home tape-recording possible and some envision the day when the underground film will be a universal phenomenon, with filmmaking a part of every high-school curriculum, displacing writing for many purposes as a means of communication and self-expression. Even Detroit's control of the automobile is not absolute; this important cultural artifact of the young is everywhere "customized" by hundreds of thousands of enthusiasts.[15]

Even where standardized products are commercially available on a mass basis, the range of individual choice among magazines and TV programs and clothes and sports and everything else is so vast that the possible combinations among them are virtually infinite. Each person can become his own subculture. Though many bits of communication are received by all, opinion polls constantly indicate that many do not share the common fund of information on even important public questions, and that attitudes on many matters differ widely. In culture, as in politics or economics, what we find is not conformity, standardization and centralized control, as the proponents of the mass-society hypothesis allege, but diversity to the point of incipient cultural breakdown.

The consequences of radically differing world views are not immediately serious since decisions about such traditional political and economic issues as balance of payments problems or foreign policy are usually made with only minor consideration of popular perceptions or wishes. But as the pressures of change force new "style" issues to the fore, public consensus on them may be so weak as to make public attempts to cope with these problems difficult.

Sex and the Family

But what of life at the personal level where cultural values are intimately expressed? Are deep-seated changes that reflect the changing existential situation evident here? One area in which observers claim to detect the beginnings of profound change is in sex and family life. Two forces, technological in origin, are supposedly converging to produce a new pattern of relationships.

The industrial system is generally presumed to have eliminated the family as a productive unit, destroying a role that it played in agricultural society and even, through the putting-out system, during the early days of industrialism. In industrial society the father was the worker, the mother or children only incidentally so, if at all. Each member of the family might work at a different occupation for a different employer. The family retained its function as a consuming unit, and as an agency for procreation and emotional support, but it lost some of its cement. Today new labor-saving machinery and above all, the beginnings of automation and the rise of the service industries have supposedly further eroded the basis of family life. A man's physical strength no longer gives him any economic advantage. A female bank teller is just as efficient as a male, a female physician is perhaps more acceptable to some patients. Women no longer need to be economically dependent on men.

Of potentially even greater significance than the changed economic function of the family (and the concomitant shift from the extended family common to most human societies to the nuclear family, limited to parents and their minor children, which is the norm for Western societies) has been the availability and increasing acceptance of a variety of contraceptive devices and techniques.[16] These have made possible a revolutionary change, the dissociation of sexual activity and procreation. Biologist Bentley Glass claims that the future will see "a total severance of human sexual life from the reproductive process."[17] Contraception makes the traditional family simply one among many possible ways of ordering sexual relations without disrupting society, and paves the way for real emancipation and equality for women. Contraception, combined with the lessened economic significance of the family as a productive unit and the increasing encroachment upon children's time of a variety of educational institutions and the growing moral influence of the peer group, has led many sociologists to predict that the family as it has existed will become extinct. And about time, too, some would add.[18]

The decline of the family appears to be partly if not wholly mythical, however. The family may not be a productive economic unit as such save in rare cases, but it is an important unit of consumption. Households rather than individuals are still the backbone of the consumer economy; it is they who purchase houses and most cars and major appliances, and who do most of the food shopping.[19] Though teen-agers who have their own money can usually spend it as they will, the wife's income is basic to the class position of many American families. A substantial number of families are in the middle or upper middle classes only because they have two regular incomes. If the family ceased to exist as a unit for pooling wages and expenditures the effect on economic and class status would be devastating.[20]

The fact that America and most of the Western world is still a bourgeois class-structured society redounds to strengthen the family. Adolescents may have some earnings of their own and pay more attention to their peers than to their fathers, but their class status—where they live, where they go to school and to a large extent who their peers are —is primarily determined by the class status of the family, especially that of the principal breadwinner. Despite universal public education, university scholarships, availability of jobs and so on, class membership remains largely a function of family membership. The difference between being a member of the Kennedy clan and a Negro high-school dropout is a function of economics and race, but it is through the family that the economic and racial structure of society is mediated and reinforced.

Nor has the family lost as much of its influence in conditioning behavior as is often imagined. Though the precise details are disputed by psychologists, the effect of early psychological conditioning upon a person's later life cannot be denied. By the time a child reaches the age where the peer group is important in setting standards most basic psychological traits are already established, and even after this point parental influence affects the extent to which peer-group standards are followed, and who the peer group is as well. Adolescent and postadolescent sexual behavior, for instance, though it may deviate from parental standards, is strongly influenced by them.[21] For preadolescents, parents remain important. Children may spend more and more time in group activity directly supervised by adults other than parents, but what this group activity is is largely determined by parents who decide on nursery and dancing schools, run car pools, and form the formal or informal groups that supervise the whole process of socialization, and this influence does not completely end even in adolescence.

Nor has the family entirely lost its function of serving as an extended kinship group, which provides material and emotional support to its members. Ties between parents and children ordinarily remain strong throughout the Western world even after the children are grown.[22] Visiting between parents and grown children tends to be frequent. Evidence indicates that even in America most grown children live within a short distance of their parents and see them regularly.[23] In addition, the existence of the automobile and the telephone have reduced effective distances and made continued social intercourse possible over long distances. The welfare state may mean less direct financial support of aged parents, but many young married couples would find it difficult to complete their college educations, make a down payment on a house, buy a new car or sometimes even send their children to private nursery school were it not for parental contributions to such projects. There is even good reason to question the proposition that family ties are looser and families more unstable than they were in the past. Divorce rates in the United States are not on the rise,[24] and historical studies indicate that the American family always has been loosely knit and footloose, perhaps even more so in the past than at present.[25]

The family is not about to disappear as a social unit as a result of the pressure of technological change. But can the family maintain itself in the face of the sexual revolution? The answer is that the sexual revolution, too, is largely a myth, at least so far as behavior is concerned. No evidence exists that the population as a whole engages in any more premarital- or extramarital intercourse than they did two or three generations ago, though behavior patterns of sub-groups may have altered somewhat.[26] What is evident, however, is a greater openness about sex, with overtly expressed standards becoming more congruent with actual behavior, as well as a greater willingness on the part of the less permissive to accept the existence of different standards of expression and behavior on the part of others.[27] But adultery and shotgun weddings are no invention of the twentieth century. Large population segments, especially outside major metropolitan areas in the United States, still remain rigid in their overt standards (and therefore in their legal ones) whatever their practices, and sexual analogues could be constructed for the old saw that Kansas would stay dry as long as the voters could stagger to the polls. Even among college students, long considered to be in the vanguard of the revolution, research shows little change in behavior patterns in recent years, especially among men.[28]

This latter observation, however, indicates one area in which something of a revolution is taking place, and that is in the acceptance of female sexuality, which in the past has been overtly denied in Anglo-American tradition and in certain class strata elsewhere. That sexual relations should be mutually satisfying is now openly accepted and is part of the more general trend of downgrading specialized functions of men and women. In middle-class America, and wherever its standards spread, men take a greater role in family chores traditionally reserved for women, especially child rearing. Older notions of masculinity and femininity are being altered. But if anything, this trend seems to strengthen rather than weaken family bonds.[29]

Middle-class America, where this tendency is most evident, has been referred to disparagingly as a child-centered society. Some would argue that the child is viewed simply as a status symbol, and not valued for its own sake; yet it is interesting to note that, in sharp contrast to Bohemian subcultures of the past, no Hippie gathering seems to be complete without small children underfoot, and even if some are brought up communally their presence indicates a continued acceptance of a nexus between sexuality and procreation. In his study of alienated youth Keniston found they wanted large families, partly as an attempt to create a private world as a buffer against the larger society and as a hedge against change.[30]

It would be useless to try to estimate the effect of technology upon the concept of romantic love, though the media have played a role in converting it into a mass dogma. Some evidence suggests that among those members of American society who are the raw material from which technological man might be expected to emerge—executives, professionals and the like—marriage exists largely as a utilitarian institution, closely tied to social status.[31] But this is certainly not a departure from the norms of aristocracies of the past.

One thing is certain: in whatever context it is expressed sexuality is not disappearing as a result of technological change. Nor has science completely eliminated the risks of sexual life, whatever its potential for doing so: the illegitimacy rate is rising steadily in the United States as is the incidence of venereal disease among the young.[32] But the concept of liberation has become a powerful myth.

Indeed, it can be argued that the mechanization of society has spurred the over-all eroticization of culture regardless of patterns of specifically sexual behavior. The body was opposed to the machine in the speculations about alienation of Feurerbach and the early Marx, and the supremacy of the organic served as a theme in the literary revolt against industrialism. When a cultural critic such as Gerald Sykes calls sex " 'the last green thing' in a world of steel and calculation,"[33] he may exaggerate, but sex forms a vital link in humanity's almost instinctual drive to construct an organic counterweight to the rational and mechanical aspects of technological civilization.

Sensate Culture and Drugs

What of the argument that the new society generally will become increasingly "sensate," in part as an implicit reaction against the encroachments of technological rationality in economic and social life? This whole argument is almost impossible to deal with in a meaningful fashion; the term "sensate" is so broad that statements employing it are virtually unfalsifiable. Certainly the kind of hatred of the flesh that has led ascetics of East and West to blind, castrate or otherwise mutilate themselves is increasingly viewed as psychological aberration. Belief in any realm of existence that is inaccessible to the senses is dismissed increasingly as meaningless if not actually erroneous. But what does "accessible to the senses" mean? The world view of modern physics is less and less accessible to the senses; even to the educated public the particles of the nuclear physicist increasingly resemble the Latin vocables that the medieval scholastics so delighted in manipulating. Is a building of Mies van der Rohe's or Oscar Niemeyer's more or less "sensate" than Chartres or the Roman Forum? Is the work of John Cage more or less "sensate" than that of Bach? When a scientist says that an experiment or theorem is "elegant" is this not an expression of sensual pleasure? To ask such questions is to realize how foolish they are. Mankind, especially the common man in affluent societies, may be reaching out for the pleasures of the senses that aristocracies have always enjoyed, but that does not mean that pleasures of the intellect are less valued.

The major solid evidence for the argument that sensateness is on the increase is the growing social acceptability of consciousness-altering drugs among the upper classes and the young, especially in the English-speaking world. Drug addiction is not a new phenomenon, many primitive cultures practice it, and in our own era much of the Orient still does. Narcotics addiction was widespread in late-nineteenth- and early-twentieth-century America. But narcotics and drugs such as nicotine and alcohol all essentially dull the senses rather than expand them, they are anodynes and retreats from experience rather than enlargements of it. What is new is the use of drugs for the discovery rather than the suppression of sensual experience.

But here again, as in the case of the sexual revolution, we must distinguish between appearance and reality. The actual extent of the use of marijuana and especially of the hallucinogenic drugs among the young appears to be exaggerated in popular accounts,[34] just as their spiritual or even their sensual benefits apparently are also. Much of the upsurge of publicity for drug use can be regarded as a brilliant advertising campaign on the part of the illicit drug industry, especially in view of its costlessness to the advertisers.[35] But while marijuana remains popular, the use of strong "psychedelic" drugs such as LSD is no longer as fashionable as it once was and seems to be tapering off. As in the case of extramarital sex, permissive attitudes have outstripped changes in behavior, so that even those who behave conventionally show increasing tolerance of deviant behavior. The willingness to explore or tolerate new patterns, however, as in the case of sex, can be regarded as an attempted assertion of the personal and individual against the system.

Just as sexual activity (assuming it has not been mechanized by how-to-do-it manuals) can represent a declaration of biological independence of the inorganic, so getting stoned and seeing visions is the ultimate rejection of the current television schedule. The probable result of current trends will be that drug behavior, like sexual behavior and family patterns, will vary considerably in future generations, with culture becoming more and more eclectic, a mosaic of subpatterns rather than a single set of integrated norms.

Alienation and Violence

Central to the argument that major cultural changes are afoot is the concept of alienation. Supposedly, industrialization creates alienation, and technological changes such as automation that presage the advent of post-industrial society simply extend and accentuate it. Measuring alienation is, of course, difficult. "Of happiness and of despair we have no measure," writes the psychoanalyst and sociologist Ernest van den Haag.[36] In a sense he is right, since even the individual is rarely sure that he is really happy or at peace with himself. But we do have *measures*. Some are purely attitudinal. For what it is worth, virtually all the public-opinion polls indicate that most Americans at least are basically happy with their lot in life and with their personal lives, whatever their feelings about such matters as taxes and foreign policy, and they rarely think about the latter except insofar as they expect to be directly affected. But a better index of alienation than answers to a pollster's questions is behavior. Are not rates of crime and mental illness, which can be logically viewed as evidences of alienation (before the Freudian revolution mental physicians were commonly referred to as "alienists"), on the increase in modern society, and can we not project these trends into the future and envision postindustrial society as racked by such manifestations of unease?

The answer would appear to be no. Statistics in these areas are notoriously bad, reflecting changes in definitions and methods of collecting data as much as any realities "outside" the collection process. But such data as exist do not indicate either that mental illness is increasing or that it is directly related to the pressures of life in an increasingly technologized society. Some of the increase in patient loads is the result of people living longer, in an era when the bodies of the aged can be kept going long after mental decay sets in. Some result from the institutionalization and medical recognition of what in the past were tolerated eccentricities. In any event, the total increase is neither substantial nor clear-cut.[37] Fairly clear evidence exists, however, that persons in "placid" rural societies suffer as much from mental problems as those living in the most technologized,[38] so that no increase due to technological advance is foreseeable, unless one assumes a critical threshold, as yet unreached, when the impact of technology will suddenly become unbearable.

The increase in crime, at least in the United States, is the result largely of statistical vagaries. Certain types of crime are increasing, others decreasing. What is striking is that crime, particularly those forms on the increase, is closely associated with youth. Areas with high birth rates must expect that crime rates will tend to rise along with the numbers of juveniles in the population. Insofar as evidence indicates any real rise in crime it can be considered largely a function of the age distribution of the population.[39]

Many have argued that there is a rising acceptance of violence in modern society, especially in the United States.[40] But the crime rate alone is not an ideal index of this. On the contrary, it can be plausibly argued that today—save in domestic quarrels and among racial minorities denied adequate police services—virtually every violent interpersonal act ends on the police blotter, which was certainly not true in nineteenth-century America. Crimes of unmotivated violence have increased and present a special pathological problem, but they are not statistically numerous. American intervention in the Vietnamese war and the brutality associated with the war have brought violence into the living room, but the effect of this on the public's consciousness and subsequent behavior cannot yet be assessed.

The major evidence for a climate of violence is in the media, but it is possible to argue that films such as *Bonnie*

and Clyde exist to provide vicarious satisfaction of desires
that are increasingly recognized as socially unacceptable,
instead of reflecting an acceptance of violence. However intrinsically plausible, this argument is not consistent with
the increase of overt sexual expression in the media, which
rather obviously correlates with an increasingly permissive
attitude. It is, of course, not impossible that daydreams of
violence are surrogates and daydreams of sex are not, but
psychological theory seems insufficiently refined to stipulate
how and why this could be so.

The belief that representation of violence, unlike that
of sex, reflects wishes that are recognized as unfulfillable is
given some plausibility by changing attitudes toward death.
To a society that increasingly believes that personal immortality, however desirable, is unlikely save through as yet
undeveloped scientific means, death becomes the ultimate
horror. This has led to what anthropologist Geoffrey Gorer
speaks of as the "pornography of death."[41] Death rather
than sex is the new unmentionable. Children are shielded
from it, euphemisms are used. Yet death is known to exist
and is universal as well as troubling. Therefore uneasiness
about it is relieved through a new form of "dirty joke" (*vide*
"black humor"), and anxieties over it find expression in its
sometimes covert, sometimes exaggerated, often unreal presentation in art and literature. Death by violence in books
or films is supposed to protect us from the reality of death
as we must personally deal with it, just as the happy end-
ing of the romantic love story of old protected us from the
realities of sex.

There is in any case no evidence that technological
man will be more violent than industrial man, to say nothing of preindustrial man, but there is always the danger that
the technologizing of violence will make it less real and
more palatable. Dropping a bomb on a city below can almost make one a voyeur of violence; it is both a less and
more violent act than slitting an enemy's throat. Many tech-

nicians who would find certain TV adventure series shock-
ing and would recoil in horror at the thought of striking
another have no compunction about preparing for nuclear
warfare.

The Revolution of the Young

Biological and anthropological evidence indicates that
aggression is widespread among, and possibly innate in,
man.[42] Certainly children in Western societies are prone to
express aggression through minor violence. A long tradition
in the West that emphasizes the connection between sexuality, especially male sexuality, and physical prowess
means that adolescent subcultures, possessing a high degree of sexual tension, are prone to express violence in certain situations, and there is no reason to attribute the
participation of youth in violent crimes to any toleration for
violence in the larger culture.

One way in which culture seems to be changing is in
the increasing role of the young as cultural pace-setters. As
Michael Harrington notes, Marx foresaw the proletariat
rising against the *bourgeoisie*; not that the real revolutionary class would be the teen-ager.[43] Yet just as technology created the industrial worker it has created the affluence that in turn has created the teen-ager. Affluence has
made it possible, indeed necessary, to postpone full-time
permanent productive labor at the same time that parents
can afford to provide spending money.[44] The result of leisure, parental indulgence and some income from self-em-
ployment, which is almost completely disposable at whim,
has created a vast teen-age market that has become the
economic basis of a constantly changing subculture. At the
same time, medical and nutritional advances have made
the adolescent healthier and sexually mature at an earlier
age than in previous history.[45]

Simultaneously, the schools have lost most of their

relevance through their own inadequacies, while the adult world generally has lost its role as social arbiter because change, largely technologically induced, is so rapid that experience is devalued and the bright adolescent probably understands the future in which he will have to live better than his parents. The result has been a vast amount of economic, sexual and sheer nervous energy searching for channels of release and threatening the adult world. Many of their elders view teen-agers as a barbarian horde ready to destroy civilization, while the latter and their spokesmen view youth as an oppressed majority.[46]

Some observers hold that widespread alienation exists among the young, resulting in a rejection of the society created by their elders and a refusal and inability to take a place in that society, and that this alienation has been caused in part by the new technology.[47] Keniston believes that the ego demands of a completely rationalized society can be borne only by a minority, and that American youth is turning away from technology and its values, turning toward the irrational, the organic, and the affective, refusing to grow up to be technological men. How far these data can be generalized is doubtful, however. The increase in overt expression of youthful hostility toward adult behavior and institutions in recent years has been closely related to particular issues such as civil rights, the war in Vietnam and the increasing bureaucratization of higher education, and cannot yet be demonstrated to stem from a general antipathy toward contemporary society.

Even insofar as alienation from the adult world has generalized rather than specific causes, its extent can be easily exaggerated. Most teen-agers, whatever cars they may drive or whatever concoctions they may eat, accept the standards of their elders in political, religious and moral matters. Some dissonance arises because often adult rationales are rejected at the verbal level, even though adult standards are followed in practice. Despite student agitation throughout the world, West and East, most students view education instrumentally, as a means to the economic good life as defined by the system created by their elders. In most nations, but especially in the United States and, despite appearances, the Soviet Union, most students are willing to go along with the *status quo* and even with the foreign policies of their homeland. Where alienation exists, it is among a minority. This minority may have considerable influence, but it is hardly a new social phenomenon attributable to changes in technology.[48]

In any case, although technology has made it possible for large numbers of youth to live the life formerly enjoyed only by the sons of the rich, the teen-age phenomenon is not directly tied to technological development. The influence of the teen-ager is largely a function of the birth rate and therefore will probably be transitory. If the world ever puts an end to the population explosion—or if it is already doing so as some assert—then the teen-ager is on the way out. If a stationary population plus medical advances means that the average age of death becomes eighty, then normally only 12 per cent of the population will be in the ten-to-twenty age bracket. Indeed, in such a world children might be relatively scarce and therefore cherished, and one scientist foresees a return to the extended family with aged relatives or friends moving in just to have children around.[49] In a world where they were so outnumbered youth would certainly lose much of the impulse and opportunity for effective rebellion against adult structures and standards.

The Myth of Suburbia

The myth of suburbia is the geographical equivalent of the myth of mass society and mass culture. It is true that most people want to live away from the central city; they like trees and single-family dwellings and prefer to travel by car.[50] But these preferences are of long standing in this country and are apparent within as well as outside most cities. But this is not really what the sociologists and pop sociologists have in mind when they talk of suburbia; for most of them suburbia is a particular state of mind, a setting in which a standardized "suburban" way of life imposes itself upon the inhabitants, forcing them to give up their individuality, their own "real" selves. But suburbia so conceived is more a projection of the fears and problems shared by many American intellectuals than a real place.

Following World War II, the rapid population increase made necessary a vast expansion of housing construction and this housing was built where the land was —outside the cities; also, as a deliberate policy, low downpayment, government-insured loans were virtually unobtainable for those who wished to buy any but new or almost new houses. So the newly formed families flocked to the suburbs and the suburbs came to be composed almost exclusively of young families with reasonably good credit ratings, which largely accounts for the much-bewailed suburban homogeneity. The explosive growth of population and of urbanization has meant that these relatively homogeneous suburbs often covered a larger area (and were farther from the center of the city) than the often equally homogeneous city "neighborhoods" in the past. Or perhaps it was because they were brand-new (good-size towns coming into existence where a few months before there had been only fields or woodland), with the houses looking much alike for blocks on end, that they were so visible to their intellectual critics who suddenly felt themselves in danger of being inundated by this (to them) faceless mass. Also, the growth of suburbia coincided with America's ceasing to be a country of first- or even second-generation immigrants, which meant the disappearance of many of the more overt cultural differences among people. People could now (with the obvious exception of the Negro) largely choose to be like one another if they wished—and the intellectual, who often had consciously cut himself off from his own roots, saw the whole population as rootless and adrift, looking only to their mirror-image neighbors for what to believe and how to act.

But there is no homogeneous suburban culture. This notion is the latter-day equivalent of the old American myth of the melting pot—and is just as spurious. There are upper-class suburbs and working-class ones, Jewish and Catholic and WASP and mixed ones; in time there may be Negro suburbs as well. The cultural life of suburbia reflects all the economic and social and ethnic and educational factors that make up any local population; it differs from the cultural life of the city only in that lower population densities make the provision of certain specialized cultural services less economically feasible. Probably no suburban shopping centers have bookstores specializing in French books and few provide first-rate tailors. But how many American cities do? If suburbs are well-to-do they attract good restaurants and specialty shops and even night clubs, just as certain sections of older cities do; if they are middle class or poor they attract Woolworths and Penneys. All that the suburbs completely lack are a few large-scale, specialized institutions such as museums, major art galleries, central libraries and, paradoxically, adequate parks. But so, too, do many large cities. The suburbs do not represent a homogeneous culture or a new one. Most leaders of post-industrial society live in the suburbs because they find them convenient or pleasant or a "good buy," but they bring their culture with them, and their lifeways are determined by their social class, income, occupation, education, ethnicity, religion and personal idiosyncracies just as they would be anywhere else.[51]

Tomorrow's Culture: Variety or Chaos?

What this survey of contemporary culture spells out is a society that has virtually no central integrating cultural institutions save those like the mass media that provide that minumum of sheer factual information individuals need to function in such economic or political capacities as they possess. Everyone knows who is running for President, what internal or external wars are under way or contemplated, what is happening to the cost of living and so on. Aside from this, individuals can dress as they please (off the job at least), dwell as they please (save where certain zoning controls exist), and eat, drink and amuse themselves as they see fit, barring crimes of violence against their fellow citizens. Some of these activities will cost money—as in the case of private schools; others will be possible only at the sacrifice of social and economic status, such as being a full-time dropout. But subcultures flourish and will continue to do so. Black Muslims, Amish, Hippies, rural Southern Baptists, ex-urbanites, homosexuals, Poles in Chicago, all will be allowed to go their own ways, save for certain pressures against overt racial discrimination in education and housing, which may yet prove ineffective and be tacitly abandoned. The only requirement will be to render unto the technological system that which is the system's, that is, not to throw sand into the machinery or otherwise interfere with the economically necessary activities of society. Here Ellul and his camp are correct: cultural activities in technological society may be completely free, since they do not seem to matter.[52]

Certain tensions between the individual and the whole will persist in this postindustrial society. Increasing emphasis on personalist ethics will lead to clashes between superegos that are highly autonomous and those that reflect general societal norms. The problem of the conscientious objector will appear in forms other than that of military service. Even Anglo-Saxon societies, despite their bias in favor of the individual, will in these cases seek to protect themselves against a chain reaction that might lead so many to drop out of an activity or to undertake active protest as to make it impossible to carry on what are regarded as functionally necessary activities. If a modern Carry Nation should smash cigarette vending machines because they spread cancer a real problem would arise.

Privacy also will present a problem. Fears that it will completely vanish are based on the twin postulates of overcrowding and absolute surveillance. But the population explosion may be contained before all private space vanishes, or social customs, as in crowded Great Britain or Japan, may redefine spheres of privacy. Absolute surveillance even with modern electronics would, as we have indicated, probably require expenditures of resources and personnel that would make it unfeasible. But there may be less privacy nevertheless.

The complete invisibility of the man who today lives in a large inner-city apartment house and has a private bank account may disappear in a more decentralized, yet more interconnected, world where electronics makes more and more things visible. Just as shrewd small-towners can tell you how much the leading lawyer paid for his house, how he prevented his son's shotgun wedding to the local grocer's daughter, why Mr. Smith had to be taken to the sanitorium and who Johnny Jones's real father is, so residents of the future may know much more about the private lives and fortunes of their fellows, though the rich may still have barred estates, and haylofts or their urban equivalents presumably still will exist. But such lack of privacy has been the case throughout most of human history. Perhaps, however, the people of postindustrial society will be less censorious in the use of their knowledge than men have usually been in the past.

Just as cultural variety persists within the most technologically advanced nations, so cultural variation is likely to be the rule among nations as well. Men may be able to understand their "similars" in other nations better than they do their geographic neighbors, just as middle-class Americans today may feel more at home in England or Sweden than in Watts or Harlem. But even in the world-wide mosaic, some differences of pattern will appear. As noted earlier, electronic communications are still organized on a national basis. Satellite transmitters of sufficient power might overcome this, but the incentive to provide them may not exist.

Two factors severely limit the extent to which the world will have a universal culture in any foreseeable future. First, postindustrial society may itself not be universal. A substantial portion of the world may fall back even in the movement toward industrial civilization. Already agricultural economists are urging that the United States stop shipping wheat to India, since millions of Indians will starve anyway, and save it instead for nations with more hope of development.[53] A single culture embracing both the famine-stricken world and the well-fed nations is an obvious impossibility. The Noosphere cannot exist half starved and half fed. Then, too, subtle differences may continue to distinguish the Soviet Union (to say nothing of Communist China) from the West. Life has a different *ambiance* in Castro's Cuba than in the United States, despite the fact that teen-agers dance to many of the same tunes. If much of the Third World rallies to the banner of an ideologically eclectic "communalist" revolution, substantial differences may continue to exist between their culture and that of postindustrial North America and western Europe, or even that of an increasingly bourgeois Soviet Union.

Communication and Education

The instruments of orientation and identity have changed little as a result of technological advance. As we have seen, the mass media increasingly have their rivals in a variety of specialized media from hand-held movie cameras to posters, but they remain large-scale enterprises with substantial domination of their markets, commercially oriented, and virtually uncontrolled by society as a whole.

In the case of the press, nearly absolute freedom presents little problem since monopoly is impossible and the newspaper is losing significance as a medium for communication of general information and ideas anyway. Electronic media, especially TV, are another matter. National monopolies, they have for practical purposes escaped government regulation in the United States at least. Despite technical requirements for licensing, and despite marginal attention to public-service programs, they present modern man with an image of himself as an infinite consumer, along with vicarious escape from contemporary society.

The mass media vary considerably in quality. The amount of variety and the degree of attention given to reality differ from location to location, especially in the United States, with its vast distances and commercially controlled media. To spend an evening in a motel in most cities and towns, alone with the local press and TV, is to realize that only a narrow segment of the outer world impinges on the routine of everyday local life. There is a tendency on the part of both the critics and the upholders of modern culture to base their judgments on the life that is led in the few metropolitan centers where they usually live, or indeed on life as it is lived in parts of those cities. But outside Paris, London, New York and Mexico City life may go on only little affected by mass culture, much less by any supposedly superior cultural influences.[54]

What is true of the media is equally true of the educational system. Despite teaching machines, TV lectures and so on, education has been only superficially changed by technological advance in this century. Most children in modern society are being trained by the same methods and in most cases inculcated with the same world view as they were a generation ago. A history textbook may mention the discovery of TV as well as the Korean war or the Suez intervention, but physics is still likely to be Newtonian and biology premolecular, and the eternal verities, including chauvinism and the Puritan ethic in some form, the substance of moral inculcation.[55] Modernity penetrates, if at all, only through the mass media.

Higher education remains the privilege of a relative few in Great Britain, France and West Germany. In the Soviet Union it is widespread but largely designed to produce conformist technicians. In areas such as India, the Philippines and other less developed nations it is bad almost beyond belief. In the United States the boom in higher education has done little to raise cultural levels among many attending classes, even when measured by the standards of previous centuries, much less the twenty-first in which those currently enrolled will spend part of their lives. The values and world view of today's collegian, especially in the United States, may be nearer to that of his parents than most prophets of technological man think. The Berkeleys and M.I.T.'s, the creative scientists and the Hippies, are the exception rather than the rule.

The Future of Religion

If one changes the focus from such instruments of orientation as the schools and the mass media to the content of orientation the picture remains essentially the same. The label "religion" covers a complex array of phenomena. Religious structures serve as means of orientation just as "religious" beliefs about cosmology or morals are part of the substance of orientation, and religious group adherence is a means of establishing personal and social identity. Religion—especially Christianity in the West, where modern science began—has served, as indicated earlier, as a basis for the idea underlying industrial civilization that the universe has meaning and must be conquered by man. Such convictions are not incompatible with postindustrial society and the emergence of technological man, yet it has been generally assumed by historians of culture that religion has declined as a result of acceptance of the scientific world view, and that this decline may be expected to continue into the future.[56]

Many reasons have been adduced for this decline, but essentially they are reducible to the belief that the inherent supernaturalism of religion is incompatible with both the practical materialism and the rejection of nonempirical cosmologies that are characteristic of modern man—what Max Weber has called "the disenchantment of the world."[57] For many people, it is argued, "the scientist has replaced the clergyman in the ministry of salvation;"[58] and, as Dietrich Bonhoeffer, a man of overwhelming influence on modern theology, wrote, "We are proceeding toward a time of no religion at all."[59]

In actual fact, the position of religion in the Western world has remained stable during the alleged transition from industrial to postindustrial society. Using statistics alone, it is possible to argue that the label "post-Christian" as applied to the modern era is inaccurate.[60] Actually, Christianity continues to spread in certain parts of the developing world, notably Africa, though this can be considered a true example of cultural lag, since both Christianity and Islam represent relative modernity in these areas. One consequence of the spread of industrialism and technology throughout the world has been that less and less are Christianity and "modernization" associated. One can now become "Westernized" without embracing Christianity, and as a consequence contemporary Christians can no longer assume that as "backwardness" recedes the world will become Christian. The result of the realization that Christianity will remain a minority religion in the world in any foreseeable future has been to force Christians to reassess their own concept of the role of the Church, and, partially as a consequence, the missionary impulse is faltering.

But what is most important to us is the position of reli-

gion in the advanced nations. Here a number of paradoxes
are evident. Though officially out of favor in socialist nations, religion retains a hold on parts of the population, even
some urbanized and educated elements, not least because
of widespread conviction of the inadequacy of the official
orthodoxy. In western Europe, the position of religion in
individual nations is not correlated with relative degrees of
technological advance, but seems to result from particular
historical factors. In Great Britain it is feeble; in Italy
equally so, save in the form of folk customs and superstition; but in France, Germany, Spain and other nations it
shows some strength. Its vitality as a social force seems
generally in inverse ratio to the extent of its recent identification with dominant political and social elements. But
strangely enough it is in the United States, forerunner of
the new technological society, that religion exhibits the
greatest strength.

The persistence of religion on the American scene is
not merely a matter of statistics of church membership
(which include almost two-thirds of the population, more
than in colonial times) or of avowed belief in God, which is
virtually unanimous.[61] For while students of religious behavior disagree in their estimates of the depth of the commitment of religious persons to a distinctive outlook on life,
sociological studies show that religious adherence is possibly the single most important social variable in determining behavior in a variety of situations.[62] Even if this partially reflects such intermediate variables as ethnicity or
other primary or secondary group affiliations, it is still
significant. The Catholic and the Jewish vote must still be
courted by politicians, whatever such terms actually mean.

The American situation in which religion and modernity coexist and even reinforce each other has varied historical and intellectual causes. One factor has been the lack
of an established church for a modernizing revolution to
struggle against. Another has been the dominant Protestant

emphasis on social action and personal ethical commitment as opposed to otherworldly concerns and dubious cosmologies, an emphasis that many Catholics have come to share. Especially significant is a virtual breakdown in the old quarrel between science and religion. The scientific approach to a total world philosophy has declined as science has become more mathematicized and more esoteric in its interests. The controversy over Darwinism could be called the last great struggle between science and religion,[63] because since then the nature of scientific teachings as well as religious teachings about the universe has become so obscure as to be intelligible mainly to professional specialists, and the common man can live with either, neither or with both at the same time. Both promise miracles and sometimes seem to deliver; how they do so is uninteresting to most people. What was required for compatibility was only that science stop attacking religion, which it has done now that it considers it irrelevant and no longer a constraining force, and that religion accept the world as important and progressive. Teilhard de Chardin is simply one among many recent religious thinkers who have ratified the secularization of the concept of Parousia, which this requires.

How stable is this modus vivendi? Leading scientists have always tended to be irreligious. Will an increase, however relative, in the power of the scientific community militate against religion? Probably not. Scientists are being drawn from a wider socioeconomic and ethnic spectrum and reflect their origins. An increasing number of Catholics are setting out on the scientific road to social and economic success, and it is interesting to note that most campus chapters of the Intervarsity Christian Fellowship, a fundamentalist Protestant group, are dominated by physical scientists.[64] Top scientists may be agnostics as before, but the lesser ranks especially see no incompatibility between laboratory or computer and church or synagogue. All this, however, may be subject to change. Now that the frontiers are in the life sciences rather than in geology, astronomy, paleontology and physics, conflicts between the scientific and the religious world view may be harder to compromise. That man is different in kind from a machine may be more fundamental to a religious world view than whether the earth circles the sun or vice versa.

The continued vitality of religious modes of thought is evidenced by the contribution that theologians and others sharing their perspectives have made to the discussion of the role of technology in human life and the significance of the existential revolution. Most have accepted technology, perhaps even somewhat too enthusiastically, but they have also realized that, as a Jesuit put it, "Our technological age . . . will require extensive recasting of our traditional Christian theology. It will make us discover a new concept of God . . . a new concept for Christology . . . and a new definition and function of the church herself."[65]

But the masses who make up the statistics of church membership may not be willing to follow their theologians into the syntheses that will enable religion to be meaningful to technological man in many areas. They already show signs of balking at the increasing social commitment of the clergy; salvation is still seen in exclusively personal terms in a manner parallel to and compatible with, though of course not derived historically from, the individualism of the decaying bourgeois civilization. It is possible that as the loss of the churches' intellectual and sociological functions becomes more apparent in the postindustrial era, religion may increasingly become the preserve of small groups based on self-selection rather than on birth or residential propinquity—a movement from "churches" to "sects" or perhaps to a multiplicity of sectlike groups within existing churches.

One leading sociologist of religion—himself an active Lutheran layman—holds that the twenty-first century will see the elimination of religion as a large-scale social force, with belief confined to small, closely knit, psychologically reinforcing groups who have shucked off the sociological and status concomitants of church membership for an implicitly purer intellectual and moral commitment.[66] The increasing growth of small sectlike communities of worship and service—the so-called "underground church"—among American Christians of even the most orthodox denominations is an indication this change may already be under way. As of today, however, there is no clear indication that technological change or the rising portents of the existential revolution have affected the religious orientations of the vast majority of Americans. Certainly the leaders of organized religion are doing virtually nothing to prepare their adherents for the shock waves of the future.[67]

Technology, the Arts and Education

What then of culture in the most common usage of the term: music, art, literature? How have the orientations toward the world that it provides been affected by recent technology? It might seem presumptuous even to ask whether or not such activities can provide orientation; but to the extent we assume they cannot we demonstrate our modernity. After all, it is not too long ago that Greek and Latin were regarded as the hallmarks of an educated Western man, because classical culture (in somewhat uneasy symbiosis with received Christianity) was considered to define the meaning of life. This era is gone forever.

That there is an inherent aural or visual beauty that the artist seeks to draw from nature, that form is anything other than our own subjective whim—these are ideas that are rejected almost automatically in the contemporary artistic world.[68] Even "socialist realism" is bowing to the times. Science and technology define reality, art does not. Classical music survives because its forms resemble those of mathematics that are the keys to nature in a neo-Pythagorean universe. But forms of electronic music in which the human composer is eliminated say, in effect, that the universe is self-defining and need only be presented. Representational painting has ceased to be serious art since the invention of the camera. The major job of the artist no longer is to seek reality but to tell of himself as perceiver.[69]

This is true of the novelist as well. The psychological case study or the anthropological or sociological monograph has tended to deprive the novel of one of its historic functions: telling us about man in society. Increasingly, the subject of the "serious" contemporary novel is the novelist's own sensibility—the novelist as perceiver. Social reality still survives to some extent in the work of playwrights, but even here form and substance are being submerged in the evanescent formlessness of the "happening."

Thus art at present provides pure sensual pleasure, entertainment, therapy and other valuable things, but it no longer serves, as it has in other civilizations, as a means for orientation or for integrating oneself with the social and physical environment. There are those who deplore this situation and have sought to find keys to a synthesis between science and the arts in many areas, especially in the mathematics of form. Gyorgy Kepes and his associates have been in the forefront of this attempt.[70] To the extent that they succeed art will have deep spiritual and intellectual significance for technological man; it will even help him come into existence by providing a basic element in his sensibility. To the extent that they fail art will be simply play, pleasurable in itself, but possibly another force for disorder in a chaotic world.

But if art and religion are either unchanging or simply falling apart, how can culture provide the new orientation to the universe that must be one of the marks of technological man? The only possible source for this new orientation would seem to be science itself. Yet little evidence exists that any scientific world view is taking over the integrating function in our culture, or even that such a world view is commonly shared by those who call themselves scientists. Science arose out of the marriage of natural philosophy and the activities of the technician. Yet today few scientists seem to feel the need for an explicit philosophy of the universe. The "big questions" seem scientifically uninteresting. Natural philosophy in the contemporary world has been reduced to cosmological speculations largely of interest to and capable of being discussed by astrophysicists, while philosophy of science has become increasingly synonymous with purely methodological questions. Some scientists accept the fact of order in the universe as primary, others reject it and regard science as the father of existential despair. For some scientists science has become the supreme value because it is supposed to be capable of leading mankind to a higher life. Others scoff at this claim as implying that history and hence the universe has some intrinsic meaning, yet in practice they act as if this were true by preferring scientific progress to all other values. Some place the highest value upon an untrammeled search for truth for its own sake; others would modify the search for the sake of other social values, though they might find it difficult to articulate in a systematic fashion what these values were or to defend their choices.[71]

The greatest hope for the role of science as a culturally integrating force in any future society lies with biology. The biological sciences, though not necessarily teleological, are at least holistic, and provide possible perspectives for man in searching for a relationship to his fellow creatures, his environment and his own life processes, as well as in controlling the development of his kind. To what extent biology is intrinsically capable of doing this job is a subject for later discussion, but the fact is that the biological sciences, like the sciences generally, have not become and are not becoming part of the cultural working equipment of modern man.

Man in contemporary society is increasingly aware of

the fruits of scientific discovery, but less and less of the means and of the world view of the sciences. The time when an educated man felt it necessary to be interested in and know something of the natural sciences passed with Jefferson and Franklin. To this extent, C. P. Snow is right: the educated nonscientist today knows even less about science than the scientist does about the humanities and the social sciences. But scientists themselves are in much the same position, not merely in terms of the specialties of their colleagues, but more importantly in lacking perspective on the whole scientific endeavor. One aspect of the increasing role of technology in our lives is that experts in all fields have become mere technicians: political scientists uninterested in politics, teachers of English literature who read nothing but professional monographs, as well as scientists who are only glorified lab assistants. Before science can provide new cultural orientations for an emerging technological man it must first not only be disseminated but thought about in humanly significant terms.

Cultural Disorder and the Existential Revolution

If religion, art and science are not changing in response to the oncoming existential revolution and preparing technological man to meet it, what orientation does society have toward the future? A sensate, materialistic, individualist attitude inherited from the industrial era. For all their faults, folk cultures had given some meaning to life. Even when they declined, working-class culture had a role in some countries, but, as Richard Hoggart has pointed out in the case of England, that too was destroyed by literacy.[72] There is little reason to believe that electronics can provide an adequate substitute. Immediacy of sensation provides a richness of shared experience that could be the basis for a magnum jump in personal growth and a newer, richer cultural life. But experience must be evaluated and ordered, however acquired, and this electronics alone cannot do. Over a century ago De Tocqueville predicted that "a kind of virtuous materialism may ultimately be established in the world, which will not corrupt, but enervate the soul, and noiselessly unbend the springs of action."[73] This description might well be applied to late-twentieth-century culture at all levels—that of the ruling elite and the populace as well.

Thus the cultural order, like the economic and political systems, provides no basis for dealing with the problems presented by the existential revolution, whether one regards them as promises or threats. Some hold that the concept of the future itself could, and in postindustrial society will, provide the basis for cultural integration of the society.[74] By having a common picture of what will be, we will have a means for coping with changes as they come. But "onward and upward" is hardly an adequate standard for evaluating choices and making decisions. And decisions must be made. We cannot assume the future, for there are many possible futures. We must, rather, in the words of the British scientist Dennis Gabor, "invent" the future.[75]

But we cannot invent it unless we have some idea of what we want to do. It seems certain that the exploration of space will continue, motivated by curiosity, desire for national advantage or private greed. So, too, the oceans will be made subject to man. But the conquest of space and the oceans can be simply the occasion for social disorder, cultural disorientation and perhaps international war, unless we first decide why we want to do these things. A mankind united by a utopian creed of making humanity conquerors of the universe might make mistakes and do terrible things in carrying out its desires, but this would be preferable to the mad scramble that the space and underseas races can become if carried on within the context of private capitalism, national aggrandizement and cultural disorder. It is true that there were poor in England prior to the colonization of America and that they are less poor today, but to spend billions on space while India starves will be a nightmare application of the assumption that every thing works out for the best in the end. Nor should one forget that conquest of the new world brought not only bullion to Spain but also a ruinous inflation that destroyed her social system and from which in a sense she has not recovered yet. Those who love the majesty of the open ocean may regret its becoming a farm or workshop for humanity; how much more should they fear its becoming a perpetual battlefield? Yet philosophy, science and religion are only haltingly beginning to address themselves to the question of why conquest should take place, and there is no reason to assume that either populations or governments are willing to listen.[76]

What is true of the conquest of the environment of space and ocean is also true of the conquest of the problems of scarcity. We have seen that the experts differ on whether cybernation and science can make the world a garden of ease or whether the planet is on the verge of famine and its social consequences. Actually, what appear to be diametrically opposed positions are not necessarily incompatible. Increasingly, there is general agreement on long-run prosperity and short-run disaster. But what is needed to bring inherent potentialities to fruition in a meaningful time framework is a sense of priorities, and this is lacking. Should science devote itself to the comfort of those now living and affluent or to those unborn or poor? Is it preferable for some men to live in a highly technologized world while others starve, or for all to attain a minimum level of development? It perhaps can be argued that grave differences in standards are necessary for progress, just as differences in levels of energy in a system are necessary if work is to take place, but the question is also one of whether humanity is primarily one species or many nations, and whether there is any optimum way of life.

Even within nations, what shall the effect of automation be? Shall all share its benefits or burdens, and, if so, how? These may appear to be exclusively political and economic questions, but they are unanswerable save in terms of some definition, however broad, of the good life, and this in turn depends on a concept of the nature of man. Literature and the arts, religion and science, which once purported to provide clues to man's nature, have either abdicated or answered that there are as many definitions as there are men, and that no common standards can be reached. To what extent man shall be placed in symbiotic relationship with the machine depends on one's prior conclusions about the extent to which man and machines differ, and this question economics and politics cannot answer. Gabor calls upon the humanists to tell us what futures we shall invent,[77] but they reply by cultivating their gardens or, increasingly, their private jungles.

The lack of a vision of human existence that can serve as a focus of integration is perhaps most clearly evident in the confusion as to what response shall be made to new developments in medicine and biology. Controlled breeding or controlled alteration or adulteration of the human form may or may not be desirable in themselves, but this is a decision that must somehow be made by the species as a whole. What would seem clearly undesirable is that new forms of humanity be considered private creations, brought into existence either in response to private economic needs or artistic whims. Yet, short of forbidding experimentation, humanity is powerless to direct it without some idea of where it wishes to go and how far. A society that carries eclecticism to the point where not only the total culture but the individual consciousness becomes a mere congeries of disassociated elements will find it impossible to make a collective decision as to what man shall make of man. One which allows individuals or the medical caste to make this decision for it will probably end by turning the community into a zoo without keepers.

From a long-range philosophical point of view the greatest failure of contemporary culture in meeting the challenge of the existential revolution lies in its inability to provide a framework for ordering and assimilating the new discoveries that enable man to affect his own biological nature. But from a short-range practical perspective its greatest inadequacy is its failure to come to grips with the ecological crisis. Throughout human history man and nature have stood in contrast to each other. Apollonian and Dionysian, classicist and modernist, the men of the Enlightenment and the Romantics, lovers of nature and dreamers of its conquest by science have quarreled or compromised or even collaborated. All of human art in every medium can be construed as expressing some facet of that quarrel, as can all the theories of philosophy and the creeds of religion.

Now the quarrel has come to an end. Man is standing over the prostrate but still writhing figure of nature, trying to decide whether to kill it, make it his slave or free it to become his partner. But regardless of the decision the relationship between man and nature can never be what it was. The difference between the subjective and the objective, between what is observed and what is made, between what is free and what is determined has almost been abolished. We stand on the verge of an era, of a plane of existence, in which there are no more givens and nothing is free save man's own consciousness and will.

What will man do with nature and himself? How will he order his relationships? Every conquest of nature now runs the risk of overkill, and the ultimate victim may be man himself. The central practical questions are, of course, political and economic. How many people shall there be? How shall they be distributed over the earth? Who shall decide this and who shall implement the decision? From answers to these questions there follow in part answers to others. How close shall men live, what proportions of their time shall be spent in work and leisure and how shall these be distributed among men? How much freedom and how much control shall exist within the political and social orders? At what level of society shall it be exercised? How much shall nature be coerced and how much seduced? How much shall man himself leave to chance and how much shall he determine?

In the age of autocreation, as one theologian styles it,[78] nothing is left to chance, for the creator is increasingly and necessarily omniscient. All the questions about human existence are seen to be part of a seamless web—cities and highways, education and work, art and science, breeding and dying. There are immense, perhaps insurmountable difficulties in creating a holistic picture of society that will provide the needed perspective for each individual decision, especially since the total equilibrium must be a dynamic one. But what is difficult can become impossible when there are no standards even of measurement, much less of ethical evaluation. Traditionally, man has found identity in his roles as a member of a family and a work group and a tribe, meaning through the reinforcing world view provided by his arts, his cosmologies and his religious rituals. In a world of complete cultural flux and discontinuity all man sees when he looks for guidance is a caricature of himself, like a child lost in an amusement-park fun house, with a thousand distorting mirrors and scrambled echoes of his own voice. In such circumstances, rebellion turns to self-destruction.

Technological man, then, does not exist. There is no new man emerging to replace the economic man of industrial society or the liberal democratic man of the bourgeois political order. The new technology has not produced a new human type, provided with a technological world view adequate to give cultural meaning to the existential revolution. Bourgeois man continues dominant just as his social order persists, while his political and cultural orders disintegrate. The existential revolution will not provide the challenge leading to the creation of a higher species, the "step to man" so many eagerly await. Rather it will be like a powerful ray striking an unprotected animal shambling through the forest, and this exposure will mean an assault on man's cultural and social "genes," which will produce a mutation all right, but a monster—and possibly an unviable one at that. Technological man does not yet exist. His job is to invent not the future but first of all **himself.**

9

Toward the Creation
of Technological Man

Technological man is more myth than reality. This is
the lesson that even as cursory a survey of modern society
as ours clearly points to. Bourgeois man is still in the saddle.
Or, to put it more accurately, things are in the saddle, since
bourgeois man is increasingly unable to cope with his problems. At the same time, an existential revolution is under
way that may destroy the identity of the human race, make
society unmanageable and render the planet literally uninhabitable. Bourgeois man is incapable of coping with this
revolution. The race's only salvation is in the creation of
technological man.

But what does this mean? What can it mean? Will
technological man be a new ruling class, performing a new
role based on new sources of power? For the most part,
no. Science confers power, but ruling classes perform
political roles, not scientific roles as such. Technological man
will not be a new ruling class in the usual sense of the
term. Will technological man then be a new personality
type—hyperrational, objective, manipulative? Not notice-
ably so. The link between certain types of society and

certain kinds of dominant personality types is easily oversimplified, and in any event we have had rationalistic, instrumental, hard-nosed human beings dominating Western
society since the beginnings of the modern era; the economic
man of the classical economists was such a type. Nor will
technological man be a new biological type, created either
by manipulation of man's genetic structure or by carrying
man-machine symbiosis to the point of altering human integrity. Such a development would mean that technological
man had failed to come into existence, and bourgeois civilization had fallen prey to the monsters of its own creation.

Technological man will be man in control of his own
development within the context of a meaningful philosophy
of the role of technology in human evolution. He will be
a new cultural type that will leaven all the leadership
echelons of society. Technological man will be man at home
with science and technology, for he will dominate them
rather than be dominated by them; indeed he will be so
at home that the question of who is in charge will never
even arise. To state that man should rule technology rather
than vice versa is almost a truism, of course. It serves no
intellectual function save implicitly to deny the contention
of those who argue that man cannot control technology and
of those who argue that he should not. But otherwise it is
an empty exhortation to virtue, fit more for the political
stump than as a basis for serious discussion of human
problems. Control technology yes, but in whose interest, in
accordance with what norms?

Any useful definition of technological man must therefore include within it some definition of what his outlook
on life will be. For to control technology, to control the
direction of human evolution, we must have some idea of
where we are going, and how far, else we will be mere
passengers rather than drivers of the chariot of evolution.
We are thus forced to try to do two difficult things, simultaneously to predict the future and to develop a new philoso-

phy of society based on the future's needs. But though technological man will create himself and cannot be programed in advance, the needs that call him forth go far toward defining both his task and the world view he must bring to it.

How can one possibly lay down a future philosophy for general acceptance? Even if such dominant world views as traditional Christianity, orthodox Marxism and classical liberalism have clearly failed to provide a rationale for dealing with the existential revolution, may they not simply be replaced not by a new philosophy but by a variety of conflicting value systems determined by individual histories, whims and tastes? Have we not defined lack of a common value system in the declining period of bourgeois civilization as part of our problem? Will not any new philosophy be intellectually arbitrary, capable of being spread, if at all, only through coercion or an irrational persuasion, which would be self-defeating since a unifying world philosophy for technological man must, above all, be based on shared perceptions and values?

Technological man, by definition, will be possessed of the world view of science and technology, which will themselves provide a standard of value for future civilization. At this point many readers may be tempted to throw up their hands. Those enamored of certain versions of Greek and medieval philosophy and of traditional religious systems will snort that values are either transcendent in nature or are derived from an analysis of the natural world which is essentially deductive and nonempirical in nature. Others will simply object that part of the whole mission of philosophy from Kant to Wittgenstein has been to show that values cannot be derived from natural philosophy: the belief that the "ought" cannot be derived from the "is" is now an elementary commonplace in every primer in ethics or the social sciences.[1]

But the matter is not so simply resolved. Many leading

modern philosophers, such as John Dewey, have argued from what man is to what he should do and be,[2] and many who formally deny that the data of existence provide ethical imperatives sneak their values in through the back door by appeals to common sense as a standard when all is said and done. Various subterfuges are used to get around the problem. Psychologists decide what is proper conduct through application of the concepts of "deviance" and "mental health," which are clearly based on the "is" of common experience. Skinner has been faulted by critics such as Joseph Wood Krutch for assuming in his utopia, *Walden Two*, that the problem of social values could be easily solved, since survival and health are universally acknowledged as values.[3] But what is the alternative to Skinner's position (in essence, that of Aristotle) save to locate values in a transcendent source communicating through mysterious forms of revelation that all men may not accept, in the irrational desires of the individual or in some innate knowledge implanted in the individual brain and available through individual introspection?

Fortunately, we do not have to answer all the fundamental questions about ethics that this discussion raises. The problem is not finding a sanction for values but simply defining them, which though a difficult problem is at least one capable of rational discussion. That is, we can assume we ought to do what is good for us if we can decide the latter. If our doctor tells us smoking will cause cancer this does not prove we should stop smoking. We have the option of preferring an earlier and possibly more painful death. If someone tells us the arms race is suicidal, he does not thereby prove that collectively we should eschew suicide.

In this sense, the "ought" can never be derived from empirically grounded predictions about the consequences of actions. Any preference for pleasure over pain, knowledge over ignorance, health over disease, and survival over destruction is incapable of justification unless we first agree that there is some inherent reason for respecting the order of nature that impels all creatures toward survival, activity and growth. Stated thus, the proposition that science cannot be the source of values is irrefutable.[4]

But what practical consequences does this have for most of mankind? Whether we choose to restrain the suicidal or masochistic is a problem in civil liberties, but few would deny that we should restrain the murderer or torturer. Problems arise from the fact that even if we admit that survival or happiness is desirable these may require different conditions for different people, since what makes me prosperous may make you poor. Not the nature of "goods," but their scarcity, allocation and occasional incompatibility present difficulties. So, too, at a general social level the problem arises of priorities among goods: granted that health and survival are both desirable, what happens if society must risk the health of all, or even just of some, in order to ensure its survival?

But these problems, however complex, may be more amenable to analysis and solution than we assume. Jeremy Bentham's hedonistic calculus may have to be rejected as simplistic, but Bentham did not have the resources of modern science (including the social sciences) to provide data as to what the effects of alternative policies might be, and he lacked computers to manipulate this data. Whether science can help us to reconcile conflicting values is a question that must be decided on the basis of experience and experiment, and the idea that it can help us cannot be dismissed out of hand through essentially irrelevant assumptions about the differences between the descriptive and normative orders. Dewey is certainly right in saying that a culture that permits science to destroy its values without permitting science to create new ones is a culture that destroys itself.[5]

The increasing knowledge of the order of nature provided by contemporary scientific discovery, the increasing power over that nature given to man by his technology and the fact that increases in population have raised the amount and intensity of human interaction to a new plane that bespeaks an evolutionary breakthrough, all combine to present technological man with the outlines of a new philosophy of human existence, a philosophy that can provide general guidelines that he can and must take advantage of if he is to retain control of his civilization.

Basic Elements of a New Philosophy

A basic element in this new philosophy is what might be called the *new naturalism,* which asserts that man is in fact part of nature rather than something apart from it, but that nature is not the rigid, mindless, deterministic machine that earlier eras conceived it to be. The totality of the universe is a dynamic process, a constant movement and becoming. Some scientists have gone so far as to contend that some form of mind exists in even nonliving matter,[6] but such an assumption is not necessary to the belief that the universe is, in a sense, a moving equilibrium of which man is a part.

However, man is not merely a part of nature, but the highest part, an element in a semidetermined system of nature with himself, for all practical purposes, private and undetermined, his mind the most complex thing in the universe. "If this property of complexity could somehow be transformed into visible brightness," writes a leading molecular biologist, "the biological world would become a walking field of light compared to the physical world . . . an earthworm would be a beacon . . . human beings would stand out like blazing suns of complexity, flashing bursts of meaning to each other through the dull night of the physical world between."[7] Man gains in dignity as he is seen as part of physical nature, while his most complex mechanical creations pale into insignificance.

Closely related to the new naturalism is the *new holism*, that is, the realization of how interconnected everything is. From the evolutionary philosophies of the nineteenth century has come the idea of becoming, which destroys the traditional distinctions between being and nonbeing, thus paving the way for the rejection of the Newtonian view of the world as matter in motion, a complex of forces exerted on objects, and of analogies based on leverage and weight and anything else associated with the primitive machinery of the early industrial era. The image of the mechanical universe must give way to the idea of process.

The basic concepts of process and system imply a recognition that no part is meaningful outside the whole, that no part can be defined or understood save in relation to the whole. There are few closed or isolated systems in nature and none in society, save for the desert islands of legend. Gestalt psychologists have always regarded the mind-body relationship as that of an integrated whole, but it is really mind-body-society-nature that is the totality.[8] All men are linked with each other and with their social and physical environments in a fantastically complex moving equilibrium, so that in thinking about social questions we must, in the words of M.I.T. president Julius Stratton, "advance from the anatomy of components to the physiology of the organic whole—which indeed is now the society itself."[9]

But this whole, the universal as well as the social, is a new kind of whole, determined not from outside but from within. For another element in the new world outlook is the *new immanentism*. Eastern philosophies have always stressed the immanent, leading to a pantheism not unlinked to the panpsychism of some modern biologists. But for the Western world, especially the Judaic-Christian tradition, God, the principle of order and change, was primarily outside. Though in theory He was everywhere, He

was envisioned as "up there" or "out there."[10] A civilization
whose world view was dominated by the physicist and the
mechanic could think of the Deity as a cosmic watchmaker,
of the universe as in some sense having been created and
set down. But the modern world view increasingly rejects
this viewpoint as the biological sciences come to the fore.
However physicists may look upon the development of the
physical universe as a whole, the world of living things is
somehow different. Nature here works another way, life is
antientropic. "The factory that makes the parts of a flower
is inside, and is not a factory but a development. . . . The
creative principle of the universe," John Rader Platt writes,
"is not an external but an internal one."[11] Nothing is isolated. Life exists within systems. And systems create themselves.

These three principles—the new naturalism, the new
holism and the new immanentism—provide the necessary
basis for the outlook that must come to dominate human
society if man is to survive the existential revolution already
under way. Technological man must so internalize these
ideas and make them so much a part of his instinctive
world view that they inform his personal, political and
cultural life. They in turn lead to certain further principles.
If man and nature are one, then society and the environment are one. Therefore, meaningful social policies must be
ecological in character, that is, they must be based on a
recognition that the interrelationship of men to each other
and to the total environment means that any decision, any
change, affects everything in the total system.

Thus, in a sense, nature has rights as well as man,
since its activity and that of man are inextricably inter-
mingled. The new holism, with its emphasis on process,
means that not only must every decision be seen in ecological perspective, but it must be recognized that there are
no individual decisions any more than there are actually
geometric points in the empirical world. Decision-making

is part of a seamless process. Man cannot become free by being outside or apart from the process. He is affected by what others do—that is, he is the subject of power—and he exercises power because his actions affect others. For in this holistic process every action of the whole passes through and is modified by the state of every cell or particle. Freedom consists in responding autonomously and authentically to the currents of life and action passing through one; the loss of freedom is not the loss of an impossible complete self-determination—which would necessitate standing outside the universe—but is a synonym for being bypassed and not being allowed to play one's part in shaping the whole.

For the whole shapes itself. This is the meaning of the new immanentism. Order is not imposed from outside in accordance with a predetermined plan of man or nature, it is a structure of interrelationships created by the constant activity of its own elements, which somehow always form a pattern as long as the whole survives. Men's actions, men's ideas and the technological forces that they set in motion are all part of this whole, and their activity leads to further development. Freedom is not outside but within nature, Dewey has said.[12] So, too, freedom does not exist apart from society. Planning is the selfconsciousness of the human element in developing patterns of interrelation—a self-consciousness that alone makes control and therefore freedom possible. Control over the elements in the total system —human and nonhuman—is effected by a constant process of adjustment, pressures and signals. As in nature, cells die or are destroyed; sometimes as in cancer they multiply out of control until checked; often signals are blocked or short-circuited rather than amplified. But there is no need for postulating an overseer who directs from outside; every part of the whole has power and influence, every living particle is a source of direction and life. This diffusion of power runs the risk of becoming a dissipation of responsibility as well[13] unless each participant constantly holds himself responsible not only for the immediate result of his particular acts but also for their ultimate impact upon the shaping of the whole.

Technological man, imbued through education and constant experience with the conviction that this is what the universe is like, will discover techniques and construct guidelines for dealing with the problems created for humanity by the existential revolution. From this basic world view he can derive ethical norms that, channeled through reformed institutional structures, can become the basis for policies that will make survival possible.

What norms can guide technological man in this task? They are not all derived directly from his basic outlook, but are nonetheless compatible with it and rest upon the same sets of data about the universe. The first of these norms is that man is part of nature and therefore cannot be its conquerer, that indeed he owes it some respect. As Albert Schweitzer said, a morality that deals only with the relation of man to man and not of man to nature is only half a morality.[14] Human self-knowledge is impossible in a world in which nature has been destroyed or so altered that it cannot speak to men. "Our goal," in the words of biologist Roger Revelle, chairman of the U.S. Committee for the International Biological Program, "should not be to conquer the natural world but to live in harmony with it.[15]

Secondly, ecological perspective dictates that man's economic and social life demands co-ordination if he is to survive, and his exploitation of natural resources must be determined by what is optimum for the total system. At the same time, the ability of the system to respond demands maximum freedom. Therefore, in purely cultural or individual matters where the linkage of behavior to the system is least direct, maximum freedom should be allowed. What this amounts to is combining economic and physical "planning" with cultural pluralism to the maximum extent possible.[16]

On an even more basic level, man must maintain the distinction between himself and the machines of his creation. Since man is superior in complexity to the physical universe, some presumption exists that this complexity has an evolutionary meaning that should be preserved. Linkages of man to machines and technologies that would make him irrevocably dependent on lower orders of reality would be antievolutionary. The great strength of man throughout his evolutionary history has been the flexibility that has resulted from his variety and his complexity. He has triumphed not merely because of his intelligence but also because of his allied versatility. Human flesh is weak, but man avoided the "error" of the crustaceans in protecting themselves in a way that made future development impossible. The human individual is weak, but man has avoided the dead end of the social insects, who have created a marvelous structure in which the nothingness of the individual and the inability to change are opposite sides of the same coin. Man's destiny lies in continuing to exploit this "openness," rather than entering into a symbiotic relationship with the inorganic machine that, while it might bring immediate increments of power, would inhibit his development by chaining him to a system of lesser potentialities. The possibilities of man as a "soft machine" are far greater and as yet little explored.[17] Man must stand above his physical technologies if he is to avoid their becoming his shell and the principles of their organization his anthill.

But not only must man stand above the machine, he must be in control of his own evolution. Those who think of man's destiny as a mindless leap forward forget that man is not only the sole creature capable of being conscious of evolution but the only one capable of controlling it, and this control must include the power to slow down and stop evolution if he so desires. Actually, some elements of physical technology may be already peaking, at least as far as their effect on society and man is concerned. If the population explosion is brought under control we may enter what might be called a "steady-state" form, wherein the unplumbed future would lie in biological science, and in man's mind. The final step to man would have been taken.[18]

In such a civilization man will have the task of finally finding himself, of fulfilling his role in the universe by becoming fully man. In the Old Testament, Yahweh reveals essentially nothing of Himself to the Hebrews save that "I am Who I am."[19] Man if he is in any sense akin to divinity has as his role becoming himself, doing his own thing. This means that the conquest of outer space should take second place to furthering man's forward movement to the conquest of "inner space."

How man can best explore himself remains a question. Some see mind-expanding drugs as the way[20] (a minor Hippie organ is called *Inner Space*). Arthur Koestler sees the primitive ape-brain as still existing as a "layer" of man's developed brain, and holds that only through drugs can the savage within us be sufficiently controlled so that we can avoid destroying ourselves,[21] just as the Hippies hold that only thus can the *bourgeoisie* be "turned on." A score of mystic and cultural traditions argue otherwise. But one thing is certain: in a world in which man controls his environment so as to provide for his physical needs and to conquer hunger and disease, the new frontier will be within.

Genetic engineering may have a role to play in perfecting the human body, but the untapped frontiers of knowledge and action lie in the mysterious and versatile computer that is the human brain. Much of what it can do in relation to the body and the external environment by the use of tools we already know through existent technology, but of what it can do directly we may have only an inkling. Newton was the last of the magicians, it has been said; in the world of technological man everyone would be a magician even by Newton's standards.²² But the basic point is that man's role is not to create a new creature, a new mutation of himself physically, but to exploit this still-unleashed marvel of flesh and bone and synapses that we hardly know.

The Reorientation of Culture

If this new vision of man as the intelligent self-conscious part of the universe, with full responsibility for himself and the universe, is valid, certain consequences for society must follow. Obviously, technological man cannot come into existence as the dominant human type without the reorientation of human culture. The new naturalism, the new holism and the new immanentism must become as much the dominant and energizing themes of this new civilization as the world views of medieval Christianity or bourgeois mechanistic materialism were in earlier eras. Education, art, relations between the sexes and the generations, literature, philosophy and religion—all elements of culture—must reflect the new world view not only explicitly but in terms of their own internal processes and styles.

How can this be achieved? Save for education (and here only to a limited extent), none of these components of culture is subject to centralized control. One can decide that all children deserve an education that frees their minds from mechanical forms and constraints and sensitizes them to their parts in mankind's constant interaction with the total universe, but one cannot prevent parents and painters and preachers from reflecting a sterile past if they choose. Yet it does not matter that it is not possible to centralize control over cultural activities, for the new immanentism itself should tell us that change and restructuring must come from within, and that the points of leverage are everywhere. Unless the new outlook spontaneously permeates civilization, mankind will fail in any event.

But how can this new world view become dominant while the cultural pluralism that appears to be both the emerging pattern of tomorrow and, to some degree, an innately desirable one, also exists? The answer is that the level of integration is the totality. Uniformity is not necessary to unity any more than every piece of a mosaic must be the same color and texture or every cell in a body must have the same function. What is required is that all participants in technological civilization recognize that there is a whole that they do not totally represent, and that the one intolerable action is the claim of any individual or group within it to dominance and universality, for this would quite literally short-circuit the total cultural process.

Individuals or groups contribute by being themselves while recognizing that although their "selfhood" is relative yet the very tenuousness of its identity must necessarily be maintained. Political groups in democratic societies are coming to realize slowly that they can and must tolerate and encourage differing viewpoints, that the interest of the whole demands that each group holds to its own views and interests. In the ecumenical age of the West, religious groups are slowly coming to the same conclusion. Tolerance of ambiguity and diversity in culture is a cultural recognition of the fact that it is the absence of entropy that makes activity possible; homogeneity cannot lead to a higher harmony, but only to that cessation of activity we call death.

But to say that only by arising spontaneously can the new vision of the world arise at all is not to deny that everyone who possesses it must seek to share it. In many areas of life, such as international relations and control of environmental pollution, the fact that bourgeois civilization still persists is a pressing and immediate danger. The men who will be national rulers or citizens, intellectual leaders or consumers in the year 2000 are in school right now, so the time for reform is now.[23] It may be that only outside formal educational processes can the job be done: perhaps we should hope that McLuhan is right in his insistence that electronic media have already superseded the schools and are reorienting human consciousness to the total environment.

A new culture will have to be reflected in radical changes in our economic and political systems. Traditional societies distribute goods and make economic decisions with reference to traditional norms rather than rational bargaining for the most part. If these norms are based on experiences with the physical and social environment that still hold valid, they survive; if not, they die. The market system of bourgeois capitalism is much more self-conscious, rational and flexible. Supply and demand are adjusted to each other and production therefore tends to come into equilibrium with needs, at least of those individuals with any economic power. But the decision-making process of the market suffers from a fatal flaw: it is individualistic and antiholistic. Only the immediate economic interests of the buyer and seller are used as standards. Consequences for other parties—employees or suppliers, persons in other industries or nations, taxpayers and the unemployed—are all neglected. It is assumed that an "invisible hand" will direct everything to the common good.

But this assumption becomes less tenable as the growing complexity of a society based on technological advance and increased population density creates an ever-thicker pattern of interaction and interdependency, one which requires means for consciously taking the interests of others into account. Someone must clean up the tin cans when deposit bottles are no longer used, someone must clear the polluted air, find jobs for the technologically unemployed or alternative uses for products no longer in demand. The faster the rate of change, the larger the increments of change—the less breathing space between decisions, so to speak—the more difficult life becomes. Until now we have

managed to live with the results of market decisions; someone has come along to clean up the wreckage. But, even
so, problems of equity remained. Why should all clean up
the debris left by a few? Or, since quite often the few
pay for adjustments without realizing it, would they rationally and freely choose to have their party in the first place
if they knew the real cost of the fiddler?

In any event, the pace of technological change is increasing and population continues to grow so that it is less
and less possible to rely on serendipity. Man must take
over control of his society. But the problem of making decisions so that they reflect the total needs of the system
rationally considered and distribute gains and losses with
some equity cannot be solved by the simple substitution
of purportedly socialist regimes for capitalist ones. Though
in principle socialist governments represent the interests of
the whole, in practice decisions are made in terms of immediate expediency, the interests of particular leaders or
departments and the same uncritical acceptance of any
technological change that promises growth in productivity
that applies in capitalist societies. The struggle against
polluting Lake Baikal is in principle the same struggle as
that against polluting Lake Tahoe, and the socialist USSR
has, on the whole, perhaps done less well with its ecological
problems than has the capitalist United States. Military
needs are preferred to human needs in socialist as well as
in capitalist nations, and interest groups go their own ways
to virtually the same extent.[24]

What all societies need is a system of social accounting
that will make clear the total costs to the system of each
possible outcome of the decision-making process (including, of course, failure to change) and the incidence of
gains and benefits to all concerned.[25] Such accounting is no
longer impossible, thanks to refinements in data collecting
and computerization of results, but there are still those who
would argue that it would be meaningless or undesirable.

It can be held, for instance, that there is no way of structuring the outcome of decision-making to give optimum benefit to all, no possibility of acceptable compromise. A sophisticated, logical argument demonstrates that no standard of measurement can represent the desires of all conflicting elements adequately.[26] Combining individual orders of preference into common standards of social priorities is extremely difficult. So, too, it may be argued that value choices—including such matters as the desire for fresh air or the avoidance of ugliness—cannot be reduced to common terms with such economic matters as taxes, wages and profits. Finally, it can be held that individuals and groups will be unwilling to accept less than total satisfaction of their specific demands upon the society.

These objections to the possibility of an acceptable level of agreement on common social priorities and activities are weighty but hardly conclusive. Legislative bodies and private groups using formal decision-making processes have for generations arrived at decisions that, while perhaps blurring the logic of choice, have been psychologically acceptable to participating individuals and interests, in part because preferences themselves change in the process of discussion and decision. Nor is it impossible to devise means for taking into account and weighing the importance which individuals and groups attach to "noneconomic" goods. By actually or hypothetically forcing a choice between them and intrinsically quantifiable values, the desirability of such goods can be measured. Real-estate agents have rough ways of determining clients' preferences among architectural styles and the value attached to a "good address" or a good school district; economists are able to weight the monetary value of leisure by testing under what circumstances workers will work overtime; and voters often express their preferences for lower taxes over additional amenities.

What stands in the way of making society more rational in its choices is less the intrinsic difficulty of the task than the lack of the will and the techniques necessary to make over-all social decisions. Some possible techniques for decision-making already have been advanced; an example is the "mixed scanning" that the sociologist Amitai Etzioni holds will be necessary in the "active society," the society that consciously controls itself.[27] But above all there must be a willingness to exercise self-control. To say that rational planning by sharpening our perception of clashes of interest will make compromise difficult calls attention to an important characteristic of the politics of the future, but to conclude that compromise will become impossible is to foreclose discussion; if human nature is unchangeable then social systems are likewise unreformable. But if technological man comes into existence he will necessarily have to recognize that individuals and groups cannot always get all that they want from the totality, and he will necessarily be rational enough and sufficiently cognizant of the absolute importance of keeping the total system in equilibrium to render even the most difficult problems of social choice solvable. If this sounds utopian, one can only agree with the biologist John Rader Platt, who has observed that utopia may be the only viable social system in the world to come.[28]

What applies to domestic politics applies to international politics as well. But here the clash of interests is not only more overt and intense than it is domestically, but the common psychological identifications that help to make solutions possible on the domestic level are less available. Yet room for hope exists. Man may yet come to accept a holistic view of the world community. Lack of international communication is no longer primarily a function of technology but of how society chooses to use it; world-wide communication is inherently feasible, and technology presses toward universalism. Various political devices have been suggested for making world government possible—from international political parties that would engage in struggles for delegates to world bodies across national lines, thus restructuring emotional identifications,[29] to various improvements in the power of currently existing bodies such as the United Nations. The gradual breaking up of many larger nations may, paradoxically, make world government easier to achieve: an independent Flanders, Scotland or Quebec might be more inclined to world citizenship than larger or more nearly self-sufficient nations.

But however it may be implemented institutionally, basically the change will be one in attitude. An ecological outlook on the world will see all problems as interdependent; and immanentist view will recognize that significant change in the nature of the world can result from intensification of incremental changes that go on all the time—what some students of world politics refer to as a "functional" approach to international unity. A hopeful straw in the wind is the increasingly international style of youth and the identification with other persons across national lines that they increasingly manifest.[30] The joint exploration of the oceans offers possibilities for co-operation as well as conflict; so does the conquest of space that, symbolically especially, holds forth the image of humankind as a unity engaged in expanding its forntiers. As man increases his controls over biological processes, more thought will have to be given to mankind as a species, which should redound to feelings of political solidarity. Science itself—despite nationalism and careerism—possesses elements of a functioning international community whose attitudes could and would have to become part of the character of technological man if he is to come into being.[31]

If it is clear that a new philosophy involves new norms for decision-making, and that new social and political institutions are needed to convert these into policies and practices so that education, the economy and the domestic and international political orders can become the social tools through which technological man can develop his self-awareness and exercise his powers, it is less clear what precise policies are best suited to deal with the crisis pre-

sented by the existential revolution. This in part is as it
should be, since the future will remain open as long as
man is man.

But certain lines of policy suggest themselves as flow-
ing from all we have been saying so far. Man's greatest
need is not to transcend his species as such but to develop
it fully. We want to envision great-great-grandchildren
who will resemble us, not because we aim at a symbolic
immortality as individuals, or because we feel that the human race is perfect, but because we do not yet know what
this race can do, and can only talk meaningfully of its
fullest development if it retains its basic identity. Man is
not a superape; he is no longer an ape at all. Before we
abandon man for a machine-man or a genetic mutant, we
should learn what he can do in his present form once liberated from hunger, fear and ignorance. Nor should we
forget Pascal's warning that in seeking to become angels
we may become less than men.[32]

The Need for Controls

Continuity of the species means some continuity of
social and cultural institutions and processes. Too rapid
change leads to disorientation. If the future is absolutely
unpredictable, any meaningful activity becomes impossible, and perhaps we should seek to slow down the rate
of social and cultural change, as men such as Arnold
Toynbee have advocated.[33] On the other hand, certain things
are changing inevitably anyway: short of sterilizing half of
those now living we cannot prevent a substantially larger
population in the near future. Since civilization is an interrelated whole, if we wish to retain other elements of human culture we must make some adjustments to the
changes we cannot prevent. This need to adjust in order
to preserve is something a wise conservatism has always
known, and is what has distinguished it from sheer inertia
and obscurantism.

Certain controls may be necessary if we are to preserve any freedom at all. Of paramount importance is the control of technological and economic innovation. Control does not mean that new techniques will not be introduced, but rather that they will be channeled in such a way as to serve the general rather than simply a private good. A society where talent produces new goods for sale and new means of destruction while cities decay and children baffle the educational system is no more innovative than one in which technological resources are devoted to the development of the depressed segments of the population and to enhancing the environment. Means must be found to channel technological advance into areas where it has the greatest potential for social usefulness.

This may not be as difficult as might be imagined. Government already directly or indirectly controls most research and technical innovation even in capitalist nations; the problem is to put technological men in power rather than men of a previous breed who do not have any sense of how these scientific resources might best be used. Paradoxically, the control of technological change might be the supreme opportunity that technology affords for human progress. If technology compels men "to be more men" and "reveals the nature of nature more clearly," as one philosopher of science puts it, it does so by calling forth our highest powers, forcing us to use reason to decide what nature is and what it is for. But this is a challenge that the race cannot shirk. "To despair of reason is to despair of man."[34] Controlling technology in all its ramifications may be the supreme test of our species' adulthood.

Several conflicting priorities exist in the use of space and the oceans. Some access to nature in an untouched state is a scientific as well as a spiritual need. Both space and the oceans—especially the latter—must be used in such a way that they are not turned into mere dump heaps.[35] Economic exploitation of both must serve the common good of the race. The oceans must be used in a way that bene-

fits not alone the richer nations, best equipped technologically to exploit them, but the poor as well. Treaties for
international control must aim not merely at orderly exploitation but at the principle that the oceans are a common
world resource, to be used to equalize living standards
rather than to perpetuate or accentuate conditions of
economic inequality.[36]

The economic problem of space exploration does not
stem primarily from the need to distribute its potential
economic benefits, which have been grossly exaggerated at
least as far as any immediate future is concerned, but
rather lies in the alternative use of resources now devoted
to space exploration. A less feverish and costly endeavor
would make possible diversion of resources—including
scarce scientific talent—elsewhere. A planet that spends
billions to put one or two men on another planet while
children starve, not only in India but within the borders
of the major powers, has carried the antientropic drive too
far and perhaps should consolidate before moving onward.

Population control, conservation not of natural resources but of nature itself, and biogenetic policy are closely
interrelated issues. The problems presented by the population explosion are so dramatic as to have already excited
widespread popular concern throughout the world. It is
quite possible that total world population could increase
several times over and high living standards in terms of
food and material artifacts be maintained within the developed areas of the world. Severe famines and widespread
poverty can exist in the poorer nations without necessarily
disturbing living standards elsewhere. The notion that the
"Third World," the "nonwhite" races or the "underdeveloped" will rise up in wrath against the rich is largely a
propaganda cliché. In a world of nuclear weapons, population size loses most of its meaning as a factor in national
power and the rich would undoubtedly defend themselves
against despoliation to the death.

But even if most or part of the world can keep on

multiplying without famine becoming universal, sooner or later growth must stop. Even if the world becomes a mere anthill, using the most advanced technology imaginable to recycle every bit of air for breathing, creating food out of rocks and energy out of sea water, the sheer mass of flesh will ultimately make further growth impossible. We will have reached "standing room only," and interplanetary or even interstellar migration offer little hope of a solution. Growth will have to stop and a steady state be achieved wherein death and birth rates are equal, as they have probably been throughout most of human history. But long before this point is reached, man will have destroyed every vestige of his natural environment, completely lost touch with his animal heritage and changed from an individual into a social insect in all but appearance.

Since putting an end to growth is inevitable, the only question is when.[37] Given the laws of compound interest, it will not be too many generations before stoppage becomes mandatory. The problem therefore is one of whether we can halt population growth prior to the total destruction of man's relationship with nature and before his historic culture becomes meaningless. There is a "wisdom in wildness," writes Charles Lindbergh (himself a distinguished contributor to science and technology), and technological man would agree.[38] If wilderness is necessary to the human spirit, we face a problem of crisis proportions. But even if the problem is reduced to one of simply carrying off wastes that pollute water and air and endanger life, health or economic efficiency, it is still a serious one, all psychological and aesthetic questions aside.

Yet it is easy to understand why resistance to controls exists. The more fundamental habits of behavior are the more resistant they are to change. Procreation, especially, involves intimate individual concerns. Any social policies in this area will mean, for modern Western man, a sharp break wth tradition. Advocates of population control have suggested a variety of ways in which this might be accomplished. Some would use punitive sanctions such as a negative income tax or, in the case of those too poor to pay taxes, sterilization after they produce children beyond their quota. Others look to positive means, such as a bonus for not having children, on the theory that it is less onerous to choose between two goods—a child or financial gain—than between a child and financial loss—a good and an evil. The solution advanced by the economist Kenneth Boulding, as we noted earlier, is that each human being at birth should be given the right to have one child, and that these rights could be used, bought or sold.[39] This proposal would maximize choice, but Boulding ignores the problem of those who produce outside the system and the punitive sanctions necessary to underpin it.

It has also been suggested that technological means could be used, such as putting contraceptive substances into the water supply, thereby making the having of a child require special permission by placing control of the antidote under public auspices.[40] These suggestions are not all as outlandish as they seem. Most human societies, including our own, arranged marriages until recently. In the West the combination of the tradition that no one married until he could support a wife—which meant owning land in some areas—with severe penalties for illegitimacy, were an effective social mechanism of population control. In Victorian England mass infanticide was practiced by consciously tolerating and even encouraging high infant mortality rates, especially in foundling homes.[41] In recent years large numbers of couples in Western society who have adopted children have accepted the intrusion of social inspection and decision with regard to their fitness to be parents with minimal aftereffects.

Yet there is no question that a general and rigorous and open policy of population control would be regarded by most people as revolutionary, especially since many of them do not yet find the consequences of unlimited growth impossible to bear and have little regard for or knowledge about the future. Present evidence indicates that most prosperous Westerners now want families of about three or four children, which would constantly refuel the population explosion.[42] Therefore family planning, to be an effective check on growth, will require some degree of social control.[43]

If population growth is not checked, then every other aspect of life will necessarily have to undergo revolutionary change simply to insure human survival over the next several generations. Societies that refuse to change their breeding habits will have to change how they eat, dwell, work and use their leisure, and freedom of procreation will be paid for by a loss of other freedoms. Here is an area where even an enlightened conservative might feel that one alteration in existing patterns was a cheap price to pay to prevent the total restructuring of human life.

If population growth in the developed nations posed an obvious threat to economic growth and material living standards, it might be relatively easy to elicit popular for measures to curb the birth rate. But what if the result of uncontrolled growth is instead the overcrowding of cities, highways and recreational facilities, and the destruction of humanity's age-old contract with the natural environment that gave our species birth? Then the political problem becomes more difficult. An aesthetic attachment to privacy, solitude and the wilderness is a minority position in bourgeois civilization. In any democratic system, these values will have to be maintained by complicated political maneuvering—through convincing the majority that minority tastes have economic benefits for the whole, by trading off concessions in some areas of policy for preservation of what cannot be replaced and similar stratagems.[44] But these are stopgap measures. Unless technological man assumes a steady state as an optimum for population growth and manifests a reverence for wilderness and history as necessary elements in total culture, postindustrial society will become an anthill society. Fortunately, the scientific community has been generally ardent in its support of pollution controls and conservation, and an increase in scientific comprehension by the public may cause this attitude to spread.[45]

Feelings about genetic controls, however, are more divided. The scientific community, even more perhaps than other professional groups, is suspicious of lay controls; this despite the many scientific activities that are supported by public funds. The medical profession, especially, enjoys an elite status that in capitalist nations has led them to try to maintain control not only of the content but of the financing and distribution of medical care. Most scientists have rejected suggestions—inspired by recent publicity over the synthesis of DNA and the rash of heart transplants—that in the United States a commission be set up on the ethical and social aspects of biological research.[46] This is in partial contrast to the widespread support that scientists have given to American participation in the International Biological Commission,[47] which is concerned with maintaining the quality of the world environment.

This apparent inconsistency in scientists' attitudes stems from the fact that scientific discovery and its consequences are separated in the thinking of most scientists. Research must remain under the control of scientists rather than laymen. But for obvious economic and legal reasons the consequences of research may be subject to social controls; some scientists have even taken the position that what the military do with their discoveries is none of the scientists' concern. But the distinction between discovery and its application may be an unreal one in practice, even if we deny the conclusion of men such as Ellul that all knowledge will eventually be used.

If human beings are involved in biological research—having their organs transplanted, being administered new drugs—the very act of experimentation has social consequences;[48] the first test-tube baby will be a human being with a claim on citizenship. Biological research can enable mankind to determine its own genetic future. Obviously, a society that does not control these developments has lost control of itself. Just as war is too important, in Clemenceau's oft-quoted phrase, to be left to the generals so the future form of the race is too important to be left to the professionals in the life sciences.[49]

Technological man has yet to emerge. Bourgeois man still dominates the world—just as much in nominally socialist as in capitalist nations. Industrial society is not so much being transformed into a postindustrial, technological society as it is breaking down—economically, politically and culturally. Rigidities in social institutions and attitudes create a society comparable to a geological formation with fault lines where slippage is inhibited and great earthquakes therefore necessarily build up. The existential revolution is building up pressures that can lead to cataclysm, or it can be converted into what Platt calls a "cultural shock-front," after the passage of which man will enter upon a new and stable plateau of existence where he can finally become Man.[50] If technological man comes into existence not only among scientists and technologists but in all walks of life in all advanced nations—and there are signs that he is emerging, like the seed beneath the snow—the existential revolution can become an instrument for liberation rather than destruction.

A world society could be based upon a realization that man is part of nature, yet something special in it—a mere reed, in Pascal's words—but a thinking reed, and that his problem is not to overcome nature but to live in a more subtle and conscious harmony with it, not to transcend his animal nature but to recognize that spirit and flesh are one and that the total human being must be activated and developed to new intensities and planes of activity. Such a world could become the launching pad for the next and final step in man's evolutionary process, where he becomes not a new creature but finally fully himself. For his destiny is not to become enslaved by his own creations or to lose himself in some cosmic nirvana, but to exploit fully all the intricacies of his individual self. It is to complexity, to individuation and to a new and more inclusive unity that the universe moves—to the transfiguration rather than the loss of identity of the individual human and the species.[51] If technological man can create a world society wherein man and his environment are in balance, man can abandon the age-old fight against nature for survival and accept nature as a companion, just as an adolescent can abandon the struggle against his parents to assert his adulthood and in time can become their friend. Then man can turn to his real purposes, which are play and cultivation of the deeps of the inner space of the individual and society.

Technological man will be his own master. Prior to his emergence, the outlines of technological civilization must remain dim save for the knowledge that it will have to rest upon a unified view of the universe, on ecological balance and on fidelity to the essential identity of the human species. Technological man will create his own future, and it may contain some surprises even for him. The Dominican mystic Meister Eckhart wrote at the beginning of the long journey that brought Western man from the cocoon of medievalism through industrial civilization to our own day and its choice between chaos and transfiguration, but his words have timeless meaning: "There is no stopping place in this life—no, nor was there ever one for any man, no matter how far along his way he'd gone. This above all, then, be ready at all times for the gifts of God, and always for new ones."[52]

The new gifts are all about us today, and the newer ones in store are unpredictable in their nature and their timing. Upon man's ability to recognize them for what they are and to convert them into what his development requires rests not only his future but, for all we know, that of all of creation.

Notes[*]

1 What Is and What Is To Be

1. Hannah Arendt, *Eichmann in Jerusalem.*
2. Cf. Richard L. Rubenstein, "Judaism and the Death of God."
3. Isaac Asimov (ed.), *More Soviet Science Fiction*, pp. 9–11; Don K. Price, *The Scientific Estate*, pp. 4–6; H. Bruce Franklin, quoted in "Helpful Role Given to Science Fiction," in the New York *Times*, November 20, 1967.
4. For example, the futurist movement in Italy from 1909 to World War I, a group of artists and writers who embraced the machine in a violently antihumanist fashion, helping pave the way for fascism. Lewis Corey, "Marquis de Sade—the Cult of Despotism," pp. 26–30; also Joshua C. Taylor, *Futurism.*
5. "Systems Analysis and Social Policy," address by Fred S. Hoffman at annual meeting of American Association for the Advancement of Science, New York City, December 27, 1967, as telecast over NET eastern network.
6. See Daniel Bell (ed.), "Toward the Year 2000: Work in Progress," special number of *Daedalus*, 96 (Summer, 1967).
7. Herman Kahn and Anthony J. Weiner, *The Year 2000.*
8. Foreign Policy Association, *Toward the Year 2018.*
9. In the latter nation, Werkgroep 2000 publish the journal *Katernen 2000* in Amsterdam.
10. On methods see Kahn and Weiner, *The Year 2000*; Bertrand de Jouvenel, *The Art of Conjecture;* and T. J. Gordon and Olaf Helmer, *Report on a Long-Range Forecasting Study*, especially pp. 5–6. On the

[*] Publication data for books and articles will be found in full in the Bibliography.

futurists generally, see Bell, "The Study of the Future"; William H. Honan, "They Live in the Year 2000"; and Max Ways, "The Road to 1977." For a skeptical view of the futurists see Robert A. Nisbet, "The Years 2000 and All That."

11. Bell, "Notes on the Post-Industrial Society" and his essay in Eli Ginsberg (ed.), Technology and Social Change, pp. 44–59.

12. Zbigniew Brzezinski, "America in the Technetronic Age" and "Toward a Technetronic Society."

13. Harvey Cox, The Secular City.

14. J. K. Galbraith, The New Industrial State.

15. Kenneth Keniston, The Uncommitted, pp. 365 ff.

16. Most notably in Marshall McLuhan, Understanding Media.

17. Jacques Ellul, The Technological Society.

18. Romano Guardini, The End of the Modern World, pp. 73–74.

19. The phrase is that of Raymond Aron, in The Epoch of Universal Technology.

20. George Gaylord Simpson, The Meaning of Evolution, p. 286.

21. Robert Heilbroner in Foreword to Ben B. Seligman, Most Notorious Victory, p. ix.

22. Quoted in Walter Sullivan, "Our Future Is Incomputable," New York Times, March 26, 1967.

23. Unidentified medical research worker, quoted in "The New Medicine and Its Weapons," Newsweek, April 24, 1967, p. 68.

2 Technology and Industrial Man

1. On animal behavior see Konrad Lorenz, On Aggression, and Leslie Reid, The Sociology of Nature.

2. "Herr Eugen Duhring's Revolution in Science" reprinted in Lewis S. Feuer (ed.), Marx and Engels: Basic Writings on Politics and Philosophy, p. 280.

3. Lewis Mumford, The Myth of the Machine.

4. Marshall D. Sahlins, "The Origins of Society."

5. Sherwood L. Washburn, "Tools and Human Evolution," p. 63. Robert L. Braidwood argues that not man but pre-sapiens "man" invented tools, since tools made man man ("The Agricultural Revolution"). See also Charles F. Hockett and Robert Ascher, "The Human Revolution," and Hockett, "The Origins of Speech." On primitive technology see Alvin Gouldner and Richard A. Peterson, Notes on Technology and the Moral Order, and Melville Herskovits, Economic Anthropology.

6. A notable exception has been Carroll Quigley, The Development of Civilizations.

7. Ogburn's most important work includes Social Change, the Social Effects of Aviation, Technology and International Relations (ed.), and, with M. F. Nimkoff, Technology and the Changing Family. Also of interest is his "Technology as Environment."

8. Leslie White, The Science of Culture, p. 365.

9. Daniel Bell, "The Year 2000," p. 643.

10. James Mellaart, "The Beginnings of Village and Urban Life," in Stuart Piggott (ed.), The Dawn of Civilization, p. 63. For the early

historical period I have drawn most extensively on the following: V.
Gordon Childe, *Man Makes Himself, Social Evolution* and *What
Happened in History;* Jacquetta Hawkes and Sir Leonard Woolley,
Prehistory and the Beginnings of Civilization; Grahame Clark, *World
Prehistory.*

11. Karl Wittfogel, *Oriental Despotism.* The phrase itself is Marx's.
12. Robert M. Adams, "Early Civilizations, Subsistence, and Environment," in Carl H. Kraeling and Robert M. Adams (eds.), *City Invincible,* pp. 269–295.
13. Charles Singer, "East and West in Retrospect," in Singer et al., *A
History of Technology,* Vol. II, pp. 754–755.
14. Leo Strauss, *Natural Right and History,* pp. 81–119.
15. Authorities are unable to agree on when Hero lived, the range in
dates is from 200 B.C. to A.D. 300. In any event, he was a product
of Greek culture in a slave-based society.
16. For the Greek, Roman and early medieval periods I have leaned
most heavily on Quigley, *The Development of Civilizations,* and
William McNeill, *The Rise of the West.* No really serviceable history
of technology exists. The five-volume Oxford *History of Technology*
by Singer, Holmyard, Hall and Williams has been described by Lynn
White, Jr., as "as much a codification of error as of sound information," and he has referred to the literature on technology generally
as "mostly rubbish." See his remarks in Carl F. Stover (ed.), *The
Technological Order,* p. 102. T. K. Derry and Trevor I. Williams,
A Short History of Technology is, in effect, a shorter version of the
Oxford opus. Melvin E. Kranzberg and Charles W. Pursell, *Technology
in Western Civilization* is a collection of readings. More popular or
specialized books include Roger Burlinghame, *Backgrounds of Power;*
Fred Cottrell, *Energy and Society;* A. R. Ubbelohde, *Man and
Energy;* Russell Lord, *The Human Use of the Earth* (about agricul-
ture); John W. Oliver, *History of American Technology;* and Joseph
Needham's magistral *Science and Civilization in China.*
17. For the medieval period I have drawn on the work of McNeill and
Quigley, on Lynn White's *Medieval Technology and Social Change,*
and on Lewis Mumford's *The Culture of Cities* and *Technics and
Civilization.* On the growth of industrialism I have in addition relied
on Karl Polanyi, *The Great Transformation,* and on the work of
John U. Nef, *Cultural Foundations of Industrial Civilization, The
Conquest of the Material World* and *War and Human Progress.*
18. Nef, *War and Human Progress,* p. 233.
19. On the intellectual bases of the scientific-industrial revolution see
Nef, *Cultural Foundations of Industrial Civilization;* Jacob Bronow-
ski and Bruce Mazlish, *The Western Intellectual Tradition;* Lewis
Feuer, *The Scientific Intellectual;* Herbert Butterfield, *The Origins of
Modern Science,* 1300–1800 and "The Scientific Revolution"; Hannah
Arendt, *The Human Condition;* and Leonard Marsak (ed.), *The Rise
of Science in Relation to Society.* On the later spread of science and
industrialism see also Richard H. Shryock, "American Indifference to
Basic Science during the Nineteenth Century"; Irving Zeitlin, "Aspects of the Scientific-Industrial Revolution in America"; and George
Basilla, "The Spread of Western Science."
20. On the relationships between religion and the scientific-industrial

revolution see especially Max Weber, *The Protestant Ethic and the Spirit of Capitalism;* R. H. Tawney, *Religion and the Rise of Capitalism;* Lewis P. Feuer, *The Scientific Intellectual;* Robert K. Merton, *Social Theory and Social Structure,* pp. 329–346; Norman O. Brown, *Life Against Death;* and Ernest Benz, *Evolution and Christian Hope.* Also Lynn White, Jr., "The Historical Roots of Our Ecological Crisis."

21. Noted by Mumford, *Technics and Civilization,* pp. 13–14.
22. Alfred North Whitehead, *Science and the Modern World,* pp. 13–20.
23. Quoted in Peter Michelmore, *Einstein,* p. 128.
24. Nef, *War and Human Progress,* p. 12.
25. Nef, *The Conquest of the Material World,* p. 136.
26. *Ibid.,* p. 219.
27. Richard McLanahan, *Images of the Universe,* p. 91 ca.
28. Whitehead, *Science and the Modern World,* p. 98.
29. On science and the revolution see Henri Guerlac's essay in Phillip G. Frank (ed.), *The Validation of Scientific Theories,* pp. 171–191.
30. Cf. Robert Gilpen, Jr., *France in the Age of the Scientific State.*
31. W. H. G. Armytage, *The Rise of the Technocrats,* p. 166.
32. *Ibid.,* p. 100. Lynn White Jr., suggests that St. Francis of Assisi should be regarded as the patron saint of ecologists. "St. Francis and the Ecologic Backlash."
33. Sir Robert Wilson-Watt, in Stover, *The Technological Order,* p. 1.
34. Kenneth E. Boulding in H. G. Halcrow (ed.), *Contemporary Readings in Agricultural Economics,* p. 197.
35. Herbert Croly, *The Promise of American Life.*
36. On the problem see Charles Hyneman, *Bureaucracy in a Democracy.*
37. The relationship between society, culture and personality is a complex and controverted subject. See Hans Gerth and C. Wright Mills, *Character and Social Structure;* Anthony F. C. Wallace, *Culture and Personality;* Alfred E. Lindesmith and Anselm L. Strauss, "A Critique of Culture-Personality Writings"; Melford E. Spiro, "Culture and Personality."

3 The Machine and Its Critics

1. Michael Harrington, *The Accidental Century.*
2. See Herbert Marcuse, *One-Dimensional Man;* also Robert Wolff, Barrington Moore, Jr., and Herbert Marcuse, *A Critique of Pure Tolerance.*
3. Alvin M. Weinberg, "Can Technology Replace Social Engineering?" and "Can Technology Stabilize World Order?"
4. Edmund Burke, *Reflections on the Revolution in France,* p. 110.
5. See G. K. Chesterton, *William Cobbett;* G. D. H. Cole, *The Life of William Cobbett.*
6. Asa Briggs (ed.), *William Morris: Selected Writings and Designs,* p. 306.
7. Quoted in Raymond Williams, *Culture and Society 1780–1950,* p. 25.
8. *Ibid.,* p. 78.
9. Matthew Arnold, *Culture and Anarchy,* p. 13.
10. Morris Goran, "The Literati Revolt against Science," p. 379.
11. Quoted in Williams, *Culture and Society,* p. 154.
12. Quoted *ibid.,* p. 166.

13. On these movements see Hilaire Belloc, *The Servile State*, and Francis W. Coker, *Recent Political Thought*.

14. See T. S. Eliot, *The Idea of a Christian Society* and *Notes Toward the Definition of Culture*. For a political analysis of his thought see Francis W. Coker, "Some Recent Criticisms of Democracy."

15. Lawrence's most explicitly political statement is *The Plumed Serpent*, although the anti-industrial theme is apparent throughout his works.

16. For an overview of British attitudes see Mark R. Hillegas, *The Future as Nightmare*; Gerald Leach, "Technophobia on the Left: Are British Intellectuals Anti-Science?"; C. P. Snow, *The Two Cultures*; Herbert L. Sussman, *Victorians and the Machine*.

17. Leo Marx, *The Machine in the Garden*, p. 3.

18. Quoted in W. H. G. Armytage, *The Rise of the Technocrats*, p. 147.

19. William Kornhauser, *The Politics of Mass Society*, p. 37. On mass-society theory and its origins see Kornhauser, *ibid*. Also, Arthur Mitzman, "Anti-Progress: A Study in the Romantic Roots of German Sociology"; Edward Shils, "Daydreams and Nightmares: Reflections on the Criticism of Mass Culture" and "The Theory of Mass Society"; Leon Bramson, *The Political Context of Sociology*.

20. See especially Weber's *The Theory of Social and Economic Organization*.

21. Bramson, *The Political Context of Sociology*, p. 79.

22. Robert Redfield, *The Primitive World and Its Transformations*, "The Folk Society," and other works.

23. On this subject see Harold Rosenberg, "America's Post-Radical Critics," in George B. Huszar (ed.), *The Intellectuals*.

24. Lewis Feuer, "What is Alienation? The Career of a Concept," pp. 119 ff.

25. Erik Erikson, *Childhood and Society*, p. 242.

26. For instance, Gerald Sykes, *Alienation*; Maurice R. Stein, Arthur J. Vidich and David Manning White (eds.), *Identity and Anxiety*; Eric and Mary Josephson (eds.), *Man Alone*; Kenneth Keniston, *The Uncommitted*; Dwight G. Dean, "Alienation: Meaning and Measure"; Melvin Seeman, "The Meaning of Alienation."

27. William H. Whyte, *The Organization Man*; Vance Packard, *The Status Seekers*.

28. Harvey Wheeler, "Danger Signals in the Political System," p. 299.

29. Rudolph Allers, in Robert Paul Mohan (ed.), *Technology and Christian Culture*, pp. 38, 43.

30. Herbert Marcuse, *One-Dimensional Man*, p. 9.

31. Ben B. Seligman, *Most Notorious Victory*, pp. 362–363, 375.

32. Dwight Macdonald, in Bernard Rosenberg and David Manning White (eds.), *Mass Culture*, p. 62.

33. Edward Sapir, quoted in Winston White, *Beyond Conformity*, p. 19.

34. Rosenberg, *Mass Culture*, p. 12.

4 The Prophets of The New

1. Jacques Ellul, *The Technological Society*.

2. Marshall McLuhan, *Understanding Media*, p. vii.

3. Bertram Gross, *Space-Time and Post-Industrial Society*.

4. Amitai Etzioni, *The Active Society*, p. viii.
5. Daniel Bell, "The Post-Industrial Society," p. 28.
6. Victor Fuchs, "The First Service Economy."
7. Cf. Fritz Machup, *The Production and Distribution of Knowledge in The United States*.
8. Charles A. Reich, "The New Property."
9. Robert E. Lane in "The Politics of Consensus in an Age of Affluence" and "The Decline of Politics and Ideology in a Knowledgeable Society" sees us moving in this direction.
10. On utopianism see especially Ernest Benz, *Evolution and Christian Hope*; Norman Cohn, *The Pursuit of the Millennium*; Fred L. Polak, *The Image of the Future*; Nell Eurich, *Science in Utopia*; Howard Bruce Franklin, *Future Perfect*; Thomas Molnar, *Utopia: The Perennial Heresy*; George Kateb, *Utopia and Its Enemies*.
11. Olaf Stapledon, *Last and First Men*.
12. Leon Trotsky, *Literature and Revolution*, p. 251.
13. *Ibid.*, p. 253.
14. *Ibid.*, p. 254.
15. *Ibid.*, p. 255.
16. *Ibid.*, p. 256.
17. For Marx's views on the machine see Karl Marx, *The First English Translation of Marx's Notes on Machines*.
18. Igor M. Zabelin, quoted in the New York *Times*, January 9, 1967, "Population Rise Linked to Space Age."
19. See Erich Fromm (ed.), *Socialist Humanism*; also Mulford Q. Sibley, "Socialism and Technology."
20. C. P. Snow, *The Two Cultures: And a Second Look*; also his review of Herbert Butterfield, "The Rise of Modern Science, 1300–1800," in *Scientific American*, 203 (September, 1960), p. 252.
21. See McLuhan, *The Mechanical Bride*; also Neil Compton, "The Paradox of Marshall McLuhan."
22. McLuhan, *Understanding Media, The Medium is the Massage* and "Address at Vision '65."
23. Gerald Sykes, *The Cool Millennium*, p. 67.
24. Skinner sums up his own ideas in "Freedom and the Control of Man." See also Carl R. Rogers and B. F. Skinner, "Some Issues Concerning the Control of Human Behavior". Some critical commentaries are: Harold V. Rhodes, *Utopia in American Political Thought*, pp. 59–70; George Kateb, *Utopia and its Enemies*, pp. 156–179; Floyd Matson, *The Broken Image*, pp. 69–81; Joseph Wood Krutch, *The Measure of Man*, pp. 57–71.
25. William Gilman, *Science: U.S.A.*, p. 54.
26. Richard Landers, *Man's Place in the Dybosphere*, p. 74.
27. *Ibid.*, p. 83.
28. *Ibid.*, p. 230.
29. *Ibid.*, p. 24.
30. *Ibid.*, p. 209.
31. *Ibid.*, p. 240.
32. *Ibid.*, p. 252.
33. Harvey Cox, *The Secular City*. For a discussion of Cox's ideas see Daniel Callahan (ed.), *The Secular City Debate*.
34. Thomas Altizer, *The Gospel of Atheistic Humanism*.

35. The secondary literature on Teilhard is already immense and is still growing. As an introduction see Michael F. Murray, *The Thought of Teilhard de Chardin;* the *Teilhard Conference Proceedings;* Ernest Benz, *Evolution and Christian Hope;* Robert T. Francoeur's essay in Christopher Derrick (ed.), *Cosmic Piety* and Christopher F. Mooney's essay in John Courtney Murray, S.J., (ed.), *Freedom and Man,* and Stephen Toulmin, "On Teilhard de Chardin."
36. Teilhard de Chardin, *The Phenomenon of Man,* p. 220.
37. Teilhard de Chardin, *The Future of Man,* p. 31.
38. *Ibid.,* p. 39.
39. *Ibid.,* p. 40.
40. *Ibid.,* p. 169.
41. *Ibid.,* p. 115.
42. *Ibid.,* p. 173.
43. *Ibid.,* p. 146.
44. *Ibid.,* p. 147.
45. Teilhard de Chardin, *The Phenomenon of Man,* p. 244.
46. Teilhard de Chardin, *The Future of Man,* p. 137.
47. Harvey Cox, sometimes viewed as sharing Teilhard's uncritical future orientation, has shifted his position somewhat, saying that "a stern, puritanical march toward the future leaves us no room for enjoying the here and now."—Quoted in the New York *Times,* March 24, 1968, " 'God is Dead' Doctrine Is Losing Ground to the Theology of Hope!"
48. Teilhard de Chardin, *The Future of Man,* p. 137.
49. *Ibid.,* p. 139.
50. *Ibid.*
51. *Ibid.,* p. 228.
52. *Ibid.,* p. 119.
53. *Ibid.,* p. 42.
54. *Ibid.,* p. 17.
55. *Ibid.,* p. 51.
56. *Ibid.,* p. 113.
57. *Ibid.,* p. 46.
58. *Ibid.,* p. 145.
59. *Ibid.,* p. 121.
60. *Ibid.,* pp. 110, 122; *The Phenomenon of Man,* p. 286.
61. *Ibid.,* p. 229.
62. Teilhard de Chardin, *The Future of Man,* p. 44.
63. Ernest Benz, *Evolution and Christian Hope,* pp. 77–82.
64. On Clarke see G. Smith, "Astounding Story: About a Science Fiction Writer."

5 The Existential Revolution

1. In assessing the future I have leaned most heavily on Herman Kahn and Anthony J. Weiner, *The Year 2000;* T. J. Gordon and Olaf Helmer, *Report on a Long-Range Forecasting Study;* Daniel Bell and his associates who prepared the special issue of *Daedalus,* "Toward the Year 2000: Work in Progress" (Summer, 1967); Walter Gilman, *Science: U.S.A.;* Nigel Calder (ed.), *The World in 1984;*

Arthur C. Clarke, *Profiles of the Future; Wall Street Journal, Here Comes Tomorrow;* Sir George Thompson, *The Foreseeable Future;* Foreign Policy Association, *Toward the Year 2018;* and Sergei Gouschev and Michael Vassilev, *Russian Science in the 21st Century.* Not all of these prophets are in agreement, of course. See also Stuart Chase, *The Most Probable World,* and Harrison Brown, James Bonner and John Weir, *The Next Hundred Years.*

2. Gordon and Helmer, *Report of a Long-Range Forecasting Study,* p. 25. Clarke's estimate is between 2050 and 2060 (*Profiles of the Future,* p. 235).

3. Gordon and Helmer, *Report,* p. 25.

4. For early and somewhat timid looks at the impact of space travel on humanity see Lincoln P. Bloomfield (ed.), *Outer Space: Prospects for Man and Society;* Lillian Levy (ed.), *Space: Its Impact upon Man and Society;* Harold Leland Goodwin, *Space: Frontier Unlimited;* and Howard J. Taubenfeld (ed.), *Space and Society.* But see also Arthur C. Clarke, *The Promise of Space.*

5. On the oceans see Harris B. Stewart, Jr., *The Global Sea;* Marine Technology Society, *Exploiting the Ocean;* John Bardach, *Harvest of the Sea;* Elisabeth Mann Borghese, "The Republic of the Deep Seas"; and Athelstan Spilhaus, "Oceanography: A Wet and Wondrous Journey."

6. "Dolphins Operate Sea Lost and Found," New York *Times,* March 23, 1967.

7. "Breathing Water Seen in 5 Years," Washington *Post,* November 12, 1967.

8. See D. S. Halacy, Jr., *The Weather Changers;* Thomas F. Malone, "Weather Modification"; and W. R. Derrick Sewall, "Humanity and the Weather."

9. Gordon and Helmer, *Report,* p. 21.

10. Alan Westin, "The Snooping Machine."

11. On man's future biological self-control see John D. Roslansky (ed.), *Genetics and the Future of Man;* Jean Rostand, *Peut-on Modifier l'Homme?;* Max Gunther, "Second Genesis"; Kurt Hirschorn, "On Re-Doing Man"; Dwight J. Ingle, "The Biological Future of Man"; Hermann J. Muller, "The Prospects of Genetic Change"; and Albert Rosenfeld, "Will Man Direct His Own Evolution?"

12. "Brain Renewal Object of Science," Washington *Post,* May 3, 1968.

13. "Genes Are Held Able to Cure Disease," New York *Times,* October 22, 1967.

14. "There Is Peril, Too, In Growing Technology," New York *Times,* March 24, 1968.

15. Kahn and Weiner, *The Year* 2000, p. 56.

16. John Heller, quoted in Max Gunther, "Second Genesis," p. 117.

17. *Population Bulletin,* 15 (March, 1959), p. 21, quoted in Alvin M. Weinberg, *Reflections on Big Science,* p. 4.

18. Edward S. Deevey, Jr., "The Human Population."

19. For instance, Harrison Brown as quoted in the New York *Times,* April 23, 1967. Estimates differ radically, in part because base figures are uncertain in many areas. The official United Nations estimate is about seven billion by 2005. See also Philip M. Hauser, "Population," in Foreign Policy Association, *Toward the Year 2018.*

20. By 1967 the American birth rate had dropped to 17.9 per thousand; our lowest on record, but far above the replacement rate. "U.S. Birth Rate Drops to New Low," Washington *Post,* February 26, 1968. The white American rate, however, is close to the replacement level, as are those of Sweden, Norway, Japan, Great Britain and France. "Birth Rate Decline," New York *Times,* April 29, 1968.
21. William B. Shore, et al., *The Region's Growth,* p. 16.

6 Technological Change and Economic Inertia

1. Arthur Koestler argues that it is possible to find evidence of three stages in human mental development which overlay each other in the physical structure of the brain. (*The Ghost in the Machine*).
2. As one cultural critic puts it, reflecting the influence of Teilhard, "America is a special avant-garde point in the 'hominization' of our planet, and her problems are those of the whole human race, only in concentrated form," (Walter Ong, S.J., *Frontiers in American Catholicism,* p. 102.)
3. "The Census—What's Wrong With It, What Can Be Done" *Trans-Action,* 5 (May, 1968), pp. 49–56.
4. Increasingly, of course, top stars are paid in percentages of a film's profits or are classified as part-owners of the films in which they appear. Both tax laws and the changing structure of the industry are confusing the distinction between employee and owner, illustrating how arbitrary such classifications are.
5. Ben J. Wattenberg and Richard J. Scammon, *This U.S.A.,* p. 29.
6. Daniel Bell, "Notes on the Post-Industrial Society: I," p. 28.
7. Victor Fuchs, "The First Service Economy," p. 7.
8. Wattenberg and Scammon, *This U.S.A.,* p. 199.
9. Christopher Jencks and David Riesman, "On Class in America."
10. Bell, "Post-Industrial Society: I," p. 30.
11. *Ibid.,* p. 34 *ca.*
12. Bell, "Notes on the Post-Industrial Society: II," p. 104 *ca.*
13. Bell, "Post-Industrial Society: I," pp. 32–33.
14. Quoted *ibid.* Over half the research scientists in the United States are employed by the Department of Defense (Raymond J. Mack, *Transforming America,* p. 107). See also Murray L. Weidenbaum, "Measurements of the Economic Impact of the Defense and Space Programs."
15. Seymour Melman, *Our Depleted Society.*
16. See Donald A. Strickland, "Physicists' Views of Space Politics."
17. For a critical account of the military intellectuals see Irving Louis Horowitz, *The War Game.*
18. See Homer E. Newell and Leonard Jaffe, "Impact of Space Research on Science and Technology"; D. S. Greenberg, "Civilian Technology: NASA Study Finds Little 'Spin-off'."
19. Address of Fred S. Hoffman, "Systems Analysis and Public Policy," annual meeting of American Association for the Advancement of Science, New York City, December 27, 1967, and commentaries. Also "Systems Analysts Are Baffled by Problems of Social Changes," New York *Times,* March 24, 1968.

20. "McNamara Departure Means Failure in Managerial Faith," Washington *Post*, February 28, 1968.
21. Wattenberg and Scammon, *This U.S.A.*, p. 257.
22. Cf. William Kornhauser, *Scientists in Industry*.
23. Paul Goodman, *Growing up Absurd*, Chapter One.
24. Roger Starr and James Carlson, "Pollution and Poverty: The Strategy of Cross-commitment," p. 124.
25. Yale Brozen, quoted in "No Automation Tomorrow," *The Public Interest*, 10 (Winter, 1968), p. 134. See also Dean Champion and Edward Z. Dager, "Automation Man in the Counting House," and W. D. Brinkloe, "Automation and Self-Hypnosis."
26. Sebastian de Grazia, *Of Time, Work, and Leisure*. See also Harold L. Wilensky, "The Uneven Distribution of Leisure."
27. Harold J. Barnett, "The Myth of Our Vanishing Resources."
28. For some pessimistic views of population and resources see Kenneth Boulding, "Is Scarcity Dead?" and Luther J. Carter, "World Food Supply: PSAC Panel Warns of the Impending Famine."
29. John Kenneth Galbraith, *The New Industrial State*, pp. 198–210.
30. See Donald A. Schon, *Technology and Change*, and Peter F. Drucker, *Landmarks of Tomorrow*.
31. Ben Seligman, *Most Notorious Victory*, pp. 312–317.
32. Jean Gottmann, *Megalopolis*.
33. On income distribution and class structure see especially T. H. Bottomore, *Classes in Modern Society;* Reinhard Bendix and Seymour Martin Lipset (eds.), *Class, Status and Power;* Gabriel Kolko, *Wealth and Power in America;* Jencks and Riesman, "On Class in America"; Ralf Dahrendorf, "Recent Changes in the Class Structure of European Societies"; and "The Embourgoisement of American Labor," *The Public Interest*, 10 (Winter, 1968), pp. 133–134.
34. Oscar Gass, "A Washington Commentary." These figures seem to be generally accepted by analysts. Conservative economist Henry Wallich calculates that in 1957 the top 5 percent received 20 percent of all American income (*The Cost of Freedom*, p. 107).
35. Gass, "Washington Commentary."
36. Bottomore, *Classes in Modern Society*, p. 30–31.
37. Harvey Swados in Stein, Vidich and White, *Identity and Anxiety*, p. 199.
38. "The Myth of the Happy Worker", in *A Radical's America;* also Frank Marquart, "The Auto Worker."
39. Seligman, *Most Notorious Victory*, pp. 217–220.
40. On working conditions in modern industry generally see Robert Blauner, *Alienation and Freedom;* Georges Friedmann, *Industrial Society;* and Herbert A. Simon, *The New Shape of Automation*.
41. Bottomore, *Classes in Modern Society*, p. 84–85.
42. William H. Whyte, Jr., defines the organization man as one who "belongs" to the organization, that is, internalizes its norms, and who accepts the social ethic, "that contemporary body of thought which makes morally legitimate the pressures of society against the individual" (*The Organization Man*, p. 7).
43. Roy Lewis and Rosemary Stewart, *The Managers*.
44. Walter Guzzardi, Jr., *The Young Executives;* Edward E. Lawler, III, "How Much Money Do Executives Want?"

45. Milovan Djilas, *The New Class.*
46. Donald J. Bogue, "The End of the Population Explosion." Fellow demographer Philip Hauser considers his estimates absurd; see Foreign Policy Association, *Toward the Year 2018,* p. 146, fn.
47. Daniel J. Eleazer, "Are We a Nation of Cities?" For a "procity" view see Jane Jacobs, *The Life and Death of Great American Cities.*
48. On the economics of suburbanization see Editors of Fortune, *The Exploding Metropolis;* H. Wentworth Eldredge (ed.), *Taming Megalopolis;* and Gottmann, *Megalopolis.*
49. Nicholas Von Hoffmann, points out the skillful advertising campaign mounted by purveyors of illegal drugs through the use of the musical and art world and the mass media to spread their message that "turning on" is the thing to do. "The Acid Affair," Washington *Post,* October 17, 1967.
50. See Andrew Hacker, "Power to Do What?" in Irving Louis Horowitz (ed.), *The New Sociology* and his "A Country Called Corporate America."
51. Medical care is a prime example of class differentials in living standards, but the picture is not a simple one. See Charles Kadushin, "Social Classes and the Experience of Ill Health"; Ruth Lamb Coser, "The Cost of Medical Care"; and "The Moneyed and Affluent Are Found to Live Longer," Washington *Post,* July 10, 1966.
52. Kenneth Boulding, "Where Are We Going If Anywhere?" p. 166. What sanctions could or would be used against those who exceeded their quota Boulding does not say.
53. "Threats to the Treasures of the World's Oldest Lake," New York *Times,* July 2, 1967, and Justice William O. Douglas, "An Inquest on Our Lakes and Rivers," p. 177.
54. "Soviet Urban Sprawl Defies Official Efforts to Curb the Growth of Cities," New York *Times,* November 13, 1966.

7 Technology and the Rediscovery of Politics

1. Ben B. Seligman, *Most Notorious Victory,* p. 375.
2. Jacques Ellul, *The Technological Society,* p. 318. See also his *The Political Illusion.*
3. Franz L. Neumann, "Approaches to the Study of Political Power," p. 170.
4. Marshall McLuhan, "Address at Vision '65," p. 204.
5. Daniel Bell, "Post-Industrial Society: II," p. 106; "Post-Industrial Society: I," p. 34. See also Peter Drucker, "Notes on the New Politics."
6. Cf. Daniel P. Moynihan, "The Relationship of Federal to Local Authorities."
7. Hanah Arendt, *The Human Condition.*
8. Discussion, Bell, "Toward the Year 2000," *Daedalus* (Summer, 1967), p. 674 *ca.* See also Martin Shubik, "Information, Rationality and Free Choice in a Democratic Society."
9. Robert E. Lane, "The Decline of Politics and Ideology in a Knowledgeable Society" and "The Politics of Consensus in an Age of Affluence."

10. Bell, "Post-Industrial Society: II," p. 103.
11. Peter Drucker, "Notes on the New Politics," pp. 28–30.
12. Don K. Price, *The Scientific Estate.*
13. On the persistence of groups in modern industrial society and their influence on government see for example, Henry Ehrmann (ed.), *Interest Groups on Four Continents;* Corinne Lathrop Gilb, *Hidden Hierarchies;* David Truman, *The Governmental Process;* Samuel Beer, "Group Representation in Britain and the United States"; and Charles Perrow, "The Sociological Perspective and Political Pluralism."
14. Carl J. Friedrich and Zbigniew K. Brzezinski, *Totalitarian Dictatorship and Autocracy,* p. 10.
15. For a contrary view see Ellul, *Propaganda.*
16. David Riesman, "Some Observations on the Limits of Totalitarian Control."
17. See Alan Westin, "The Snooping Machine."
18. Norbert Wiener, *God and Golem, Inc.,* pp. 72–73.
19. In Mary Kersey Harvey (ed.), "Life in the Year 2000," pp. 143–144. On computers and their limitations see Norbert Wiener, *The Human Use of Human Beings;* J. Bronowski, "The Logic of the Mind"; Max Gunther, "Computers: Their Built-In Limitations"; Robert McClintock, "Machines and Vitalists"; and Marvin L. Minsky, "Artificial Intelligence."
20. On privacy and its future see Alan Westin, *Privacy and Freedom* and "Science, Privacy and Freedom"; and Harry Kalvin, Jr., "The Problems of Privacy in the Year 2000."
21. On psychological coercion and the related use of drugs see Aldous Huxley, *Brave New World Revisited;* Robert J. Lifton, *Brainwashing and the Psychology of Totalism;* and Gardner C. Quarton, "Deliberate Attempts to Control Human Behavior and Modify Personality."
22. See Samuel H. Hofstadter and George Horowitz, *The Right of Privacy.*
23. See Thomas Szasz, *Law, Liberty and Psychiatry* and *Psychiatric Justice.*
24. Richard R. Fagan, *Politics and Communication,* p. 44.
25. Especially with satellite transmitters. See "Propaganda Called a Peril of Communication Satellites," New York *Times,* May 5, 1966.
26. Wattenberg and Scammon, *This U.S.A.,* p. 238.
27. Raymond Bauer and D. Gleicher, "A Word-of-Mouth Communication in the Soviet Union"; Paul Kecskemeti, "Totalitarian Communications as a Mean of Control"; and Peter Rossi and Raymond Bauer, "Some Patterns of Soviet Communications Behavior." Note also the chapter on Hungary in the revised edition of Hannah Arendt's *The Origins of Totalitarianism.*
28. See Elihu Katz and Paul F. Lazersfeld, *Personal Influence;* David Riesman, *The Lonely Crowd;* and Elihu Katz, "The Two-Step Flow of Communication." On modern communications generally see Lewis Anthony Dexter and David Manning White (eds.), *People, Society and Mass Communication;* and Marshall McLuhan, *Understanding Media.*
29. Shirley A. Star and Helen MacGill Hughes, "Report on an Educational Campaign."
30. This belief is widely expressed today; cf. Ralph Lapp, *The New*

Priesthood. For earlier expressions of the idea that modern society is destined to be dominated by a technical elite see Thorstein Veblen, *The Engineers and the Price System,* and James Burnham, *The Managerial Revolution.*

31. The increasing use of scientists in nonscientific work has, of course, led to an increase in the number of those attracted to science for extrascientific reasons. See Norman Storer, "The Coming Changes in American Science."

32. On the scientific weakness of the State Department see Eugene B. Skolnikoff, *Science, Technology and American Foreign Policy.*

33. See Donald A. Strickland, "Physicist' Views of Space Politics," and Michael Maccoby, "Government, Scientists and the Priorities of Science."

34. A huge literature is growing up on the relations of science and politics. As an introduction see Bernard Barber, *Science and the Social Order;* Norman Kaplan (ed.), *Science and Society;* Robert Boguslaw, *The New Utopians;* J. Stefan Dupre and Sanford A. Lakoff, *Science and the Nation;* Donald S. Greenberg, *The Politics of Pure Science* and "The Myth of the Scientific Elite"; Morton Grodzins and Eugene Rabinowitch (eds.), *The Atomic Age;* Sanford A. Lakoff (ed.), *Knowledge and Power;* Ralph Lapp, *The New Priesthood;* H. L. Nieberg, *In the Name of Science;* Don K. Price, *The Scientific Estate;* Avery Leiserson, "Scientists and the Policy Process"; and Wallace S. Sayre, "Science, Scientists and American Science Policy."

35. It is estimated that over a quarter of a million people hold local elective public office in the United States. Allen M. Potter, *American Government and Politics,* p. 79.

36. The phrase is that of the late Morton Grodzins.

37. On bureaucracy and freedom see Mary P. Follett, *Dynamic Administration;* Harvey Wheeler, *The Restoration of Politics;* Reinhard Bendix, "Bureaucracy and the Problem of Power"; Alvin P. Gouldner, "Metaphysical Pathos and the Theory of Bureaucracy"; and Dwight Waldo, "Development of Theory of Democratic Administration."

38. On public administration throughout the world see Ferrel Heady, *Public Administration in Comparative Perspective,* and Nimrod Raphaeli (ed.), *Readings in Comparative Public Administration.*

39. Paul Johnson, "London Letter," *New Statesman,* 75 (1968), p. 476.

40. Arnold Toynbee makes this point in his introduction to his *Survey of International Affairs, 1939–1946: Hitler's Europe;* pp. 7–8. See also *ibid.,* pp. 11–164, *passim.*

41. Albert Waterston, *Development Planning,* pp. 39–40.

42. On planning and freedom see Raymond A. Bauer (ed.), *Social Indicators;* Robert Boguslaw, *The New Utopians;* Robert A. Dahl and Charles E. Lindblom, *Politics, Economics and Welfare;* Bertram Gross (ed.), *Action Under Planning* and "National Planning"; F. A. Hayek, *The Constitution of Liberty;* Joseph Rosenfarb, *Freedom in the Administrative State;* William Withers, *Freedom Through Power;* Barbara Wooten, *Freedom Under Planning;* and Charles E. Lindblom, "Economics and the Administration of National Planning."

43. This is viewed somewhat negatively by John F. Bunzel, *Anti-Politics in America,* and more positively by Paul Jacobs and Saul Landau (eds.), *The New Radicals,* and Jack Newfield, *A Prophetic Minority.*

For background see Walter Dean Burnham, "The Changing Shape of the American Political Universe"; Joseph R. Gusfield, "Mass Society and Extremist Politics"; and Harvey Wheeler, "Danger Signals in the Political System."

44. McLuhan touches on this problem in *War and Peace in the Global Village.*

45. Seymour Martin Lipset, *Political Man*, pp. 97–176.

46. See Jack Dennis, "Support for the Party System by the Mass Public."

47. On the relationship of nationalism and communication in the broadest sense see Karl W. Deutsch, *Nationalism and Social Communication.*

48. Marvin E. Gettleman and David Marmelstein (eds.), *The Great Society Reader: The Failure of American Liberalism.*

49. See J. V. Reistrup, "Religious Revival at Cape Kennedy," Washington *Post*, March 16, 1967.

50. "Poll Finds Crime Top Fear at Home," New York *Times*, February 29, 1968. Respondents perceived the following problems also locally pressing: education (including crowded schools) second, transportation third, and sanitation eleventh.

51. On the general impact of technology on international politics see Carlyl P. Haskins, *The Scientific Revolution and World Politics* and "Technology, Science and American Foreign Policy." On the future see Ithiel de Sola Pool, "The International System in the Next Half-Century." Many close observers believe that no area of politics is less susceptible to being managed by rational means. See Thomas C. Schelling, "PPBS and Foreign Affairs"; and Albert Wohlstetter, "Scientists, Seers and Strategy" and "Technology, Prediction, and Disorder."

52. "Scientific Revolution seen Bypassing Poorer Nations," Washington *Post*, December 28, 1967, and "Another Opinion: The Failure of Western Science," New York *Times*, December 31, 1967. But see also *Scientific American, Technology and Economic Development.*

53. See Don E. Kash, *The Politics of Space Cooperation*, and Allob Frye, "Politics: The First Dimension of Space."

54. "Scientists Oppose Orbiting Mirrors," New York *Times*, May 26, 1967.

55. For a discussion of suggested bases of world community see W. Warren Wagar, *The City of Man.*

56. "A Rich-Poor Division Is Evident at Church Parley," New York *Times*, July 14, 1966.

8 Technological Change and Cultural Lag

1. The title of a book by Richard Weaver.

2. Recent developments are brilliantly analyzed in Theodore Roszak, "The Counter Culture."

3. So much is the decline of religion taken for granted that it is rarely mentioned. Kahn and Weiner in *The Year* 2000 take note of the prediction of Sorokin and others that a religious revival in the postsensate period is possible, p. 43.

4. Kahn and Weiner, *The Year* 2000 generally. See also Sorokin, *The Crisis of Our Age.*

5. On the decline of sexual differences see Marshall McLuhan and

George B. Leonard, "The Future of Sex," and Charles E. Winick, *The New People.*

6. Cf. Harry Kalvin, Jr., "The Problems of Privacy in the Year 2000."

7. Erik Erikson, *Childhood and Society,* p. 282; also his *Identity.*

8. For instance, Kenneth Keniston, *The Uncommited.*

9. For example, Virginia Held, "The High Cost of Culture," and Nigel Calder, *The World in 1984,* Vol. II, pp. 85–101.

10. On mass culture see, *inter alia,* Bernard Rosenberg and David Manning White (eds.), *Mass Culture;* Jules Henry, *Culture Against Man;* Norman Jacobs (ed.), *Culture for the Millions;* Winston White, *Beyond Conformity.* Also Lewis Corey, "Nightmares, Daydreams and Professor Shils"; Edward Shils, "Daydreams and Nightmares"; Irving Kristol, "High, Low, and Modern"; Henry Rabassiere, Some Aspects of Mass Culture"; and Harold Rosenberg, "Pop Culture and Kitch Criticism."

11. Harold W. Wilensky in "Mass Society and Mass Culture" argues that mass culture is a possibility even if mass society is largely a myth.

12. Tom Wolfe, *The Kandy-Kolored Tangerine-Flake Streamline Baby,* p. 135.

13. On American use of leisure, see De Grazia, *Of Time, Work and Leisure;* Eric Larabee and Rolf Meyerson (eds.), *Mass Leisure;* and Ruell Denny and David Riesman, "Leisure in Urbanized America," in Paul K. Hatt and Albert J. Reiss, *Reader in Urban Sociology.*

14. "The Underground Press Succeeds by Intriguing Rebels and Squares," *Wall Street Journal,* March 4, 1968.

15. Wolfe, *Kandy-Kolored.*

16. Summarized in "Freedom from Fear."

17. Quoted in "There Is Peril, Too, in Growing Technology," New York *Times,* March 24, 1968.

18. For example, Barrington Moore, Jr., *Political Power and Social Theory,* pp. 160–178.

19. Wattenberg and Scammon, *This U.S.A.,* p. 39 *ca.*

20. *Ibid.,* p. 171.

21. Ira L. Reiss, "How and Why America's Sex Standards Are Changing."

22. Michael Young and Peter Willmott, *Family and Class in East London.*

23. Alvin L. Schorr, "Selfish Children and Lonely Parents."

24. Wattenberg and Scammon, *This U.S.A.,* pp. 42–43. Historian William L. O'Neill sees no relationship between the rising divorce rate in the nineteenth century and industrialization. "1946 Called Peak for Divorce Rates in U.S. in Century," New York *Times,* February 15, 1968. Since divorce rates are highest among the least affluent, there is no reason to expect them to increase with rising living standards.

25. Frank F. Furstenberg, Jr., "Industrialization and the American Family." For another view see W. F. Ogburn and M. F. Nimkoff, *Technology and the Changing Family.*

26. Reiss, "How and Why America's Sex Standards are Changing." Dr. Alfred Kinsey himself denies technology has had a major impact upon sexual behavior to date. "Collegians Attitudes on Sex Unchanged," Washington *Post,* December 29, 1967.

27. See "Anything Goes" and "Sex and the College Girl," New York *Times,* January 7, 1968. For expressions of newer attitudes see Robert H. Rimmer, *The Harrad Experiment* and the symposium "Religion and the New Morality."

28. Reiss, "How and Why America's Sex Standards Are Changing," and the report "Virginity in College," *Trans-Action*, 2 (March-April, 1965), p. 24. Some evidence that standards are changing is found in Vance Packard, *The Sexual Wilderness*, however.

29. On the allegedly changing role of women see Winick, *The New People;* Bruno Bettelheim, "Women: Emancipation is Still to Come." On the future of women see Buckminster Fuller, "Goddesses of the Twenty-First Century," and Mary Kersey Harvey (ed.), "Life in the Year 2000."

30. Keniston, *The Uncommitted*, p. 227.

31. John F. Cuber and Peggy B. Harroff, *Sex and the Significant Americans.*

32. On illegitimacy see "Study Reports Illegitimate Births Have Tripled," New York *Times*, March 14, 1968. Between 1960–1965 white rates went up 26 percent. Venereal-disease rates are more difficult to health measure since many cases go unreported, but the consensus of public officials seems to be that there is a rapid rise, especially among younger age groups.

33. Gerald Sykes, *The Cool Millennium*, p. 15.

34. Gallup Poll, *Reader's Digest*, November, 1967. See also, however, Richard Goldstein, *1 in 7: Drugs on Campus*, and Norman E. Zinberg, "Facts and Fancies about Drug Addiction."

35. Nicholas Von Hoffman, "The Acid Affair," Washington *Post*, October 17, 1967. See also his *We Are the People Our Parents Warned Us Against.*

36. The title of one of his chapters in Ralph Ross and Ernest van den Haag, *The Fabric of Society*. On measuring alienation see Ephraim Harold Mizruchi, "Alienation and Anomie" in Irving Louis Horowitz (ed.), *The New Sociology;* Dwight Dean, "Meaning and Measurement of Alienation"; Gwynn Nettler, "A Measure of Alienation"; and Melvin Seeman, "On the Meaning of Alienation."

37. Bernard Berelson and Gary A. Steiner, *Human Behavior*, pp. 635–640; John A. Clauson, "The Sociology of Mental Illness" in Robert K. Merton *et al.* (eds.), *Sociology Today;* and "Suicide and the Welfare State," *The Public Interest*, 2 (Winter, 1966), pp. 114–115.

38. See, for instance, Joseph W. Eaton and Robert J. Weill, "The Mental Health of the Hutterites" in Eric and Mary Josephson, *Man Alone.* Also see A. R. Mangus, "Personality Adjustment in Rural and Urban Children" in Hatt and Reiss, *Reader in Urban Sociology.*

39. On crime see Daniel Bell, *The End of Ideology*, pp. 137–158; T. R. Fyvel, *The Troublemakers;* and James Q. Wilson, "Crime in the Streets" and "Why We are Having a Wave of Violence."

40. See Max Lerner, "Climate of Violence"; also the special section of *Esquire*, "Why Are We Suddenly Obsessed with Violence?"

41. See his essay in Maurice R. Stein *et al.*, *Identity and Anxiety.*

42. Konrad Lorenz, *On Aggression*. Also J. D. McCarthy and F. J. Ebling (eds.), *The Natural History of Aggression*, which illustrates the tendency of biological scientists to think of man as naturally aggressive, while social scientists do not.

43. Michael Harrington, *The Accidental Century*, pp. 19–20, 22.

44. The situation of the teen-aged poor, especially Negro youth, is, of course, different, though the "generation gap" exists in various forms among the poor as well as the affluent.

45. Cf. Joshua Lederberg, "Kids Today Grow Up Faster, Should Rights Come Sooner?" Washington *Post*, February 10, 1968.

46. Edgar Z. Friedenberg, "The Image of the Adolescent Minority," and Nat Hentoff, "Youth—The Oppressed Majority."

47. See Kenneth Keniston, "Youth, Change and Violence," especially pp. 233–234; also his *Young Radicals* and *The Uncommitted*.

48. On contemporary youth see Erik Erikson (ed.), *Youth: Change and Challenge*; Edgar Z. Friedenberg, *Coming of Age in America*; Paul Goodman, *Growing Up Absurd*; and, for Britain, F. Musgrove, *Youth and the Social Order*.

49. John Rader Platt, *The Step to Man*, p. 198.

50. Bennett M. Berger, "Suburbia and the American Dream."

51. For various views of "suburbia" see Bennett M. Berger, *Working Class Suburb*; William Dobriner, *Class in Suburbia* and his edited *The Suburban Community*; Herbert Gans, *The Levittowners*; William J. Newman, *The Futilitarian Society*; John R. Seeley *et al.*, *Crestwood Heights*; Robert C. Wood, *Suburbia*; and Scott Greer, "The Social Structure and Political Processes of Suburbia." Maurice R. Stein, *The Eclipse of Community*, provides valuable perspective for the whole argument about suburbia.

52. See his remarks in Carl F. Stover (ed.), *The Technological Order*, p. 13 *ca*. The most recent example of large-scale cultural deviance within industrial society is the Hippie movement, which has inspired and been fed by a vast literature. See among the bibliographical items especially those written by Berger, Davis, Hinkle and Roszak; also the discussion of their predecessors, the "Beats" in Goodman, *Growing Up Absurd*, pp. 170–190.

53. Paul Ehrlich, "The Fight Against Famine Is Already Lost."

54. See generally W. H. Ferry, "Masscomm as Educator."

55. On science education see B. F. Skinner, "Teaching Science in High School—What Is Wrong?"

56. Cf. William Barrett, *Irrational Man*, pp. 20–31.

57. From Max Weber, p. 148 *inter alia*. The phrase is borrowed from Schiller.

58. Robert E. Fitch, "The Scientist as Priest and Savior," p. 368.

59. Dietrich Bonhoeffer, *Prisoner for God*, p. 123.

60. Cf. Walter Ong., S.J., *In the American Grain*, pp. 147–164.

61. Some 97 percent of Americans still claim belief in God, though some studies indicate only 45 percent attend church regularly, and 67 percent believe religion is losing its influence on American life. See Washington *Post*, April 15, 1967, December 23, 1967, December 26, 1967, and May 25, 1968, and New York *Times*, March 20, 1968. For varying aspects and interpretations of religion today see Donald R. Cutler (ed.), *The Religious Situation*.

62. Cf. Gerhard Lenski, *The Religious Factor*.

63. Robert M. MacIver in John G. Burke (ed.), *The New Technology and Human Values*, p. 58.

64. Price, *The Scientific Estate*, pp. 115–116.

65. Herbert Rogers, S.J., quoted in "Computer Age Splits Church Writers," Washington *Post*, October 15, 1966.

66. Peter Berger, quoted in "A Bleak Outlook Seen for Religion," New York *Times*, February 25, 1968.

67. For a variety of views on the future of religion see Robert Adolfs,

O.S.A., *The Grave of God;* Myron M. Bloy, Jr., "Technology and Theology" in Robert Theobald (ed.), *Dialogue on Technology;* Donald Brophy (ed.), *Science and Faith in the 21st Century;* Arend Theodor Van Leeuwen, *Christianity in World History* and *Prophecy in a Technocratic Era.* Also Thomas F. O'Dea, "The Crisis of the Contemporary Religious Consciousness"; Michael Novak, "Christianity: Renewed or Slowly Abandoned?"; and Rodney Stark and Charles Y. Glock, "Will Ethics Be the Death of Christianity?"

68. See Erich Kahler, *The Disintegration of Form in the Arts.*

69. On current trends see Richard Kostelanetz, *The New American Arts.*

70. See his six-volume "Values and Vision" series and his "The Visual Arts and the Sciences." Also especially worth attention are the articles of William R. Cozart and Jacob Landau in Robert Theobald, *Dialogue on Technology,* and Lancelot Law Whyte, *The Next Development in Man.*

71. However, a growing literature in this area is becoming available. See especially Jacob Bronowski, *Science and Human Values,* and C. P. Snow, "The Moral Un-Neutrality of Science."

72. Richard Hoggart, *The Uses of Literacy.* Also see Raymond Williams, *The Long Revolution,* and Brian Wicker, *Culture and Liturgy.*

73. Quoted in Hoggart, *The Uses of Literacy,* p. 141.

74. Cf. Margaret Mead, "The Future as the Basis for Establishing a Shared Culture."

75. See Gabor's *Inventing the Future* and his article of the same title.

76. For two views of the merits of space exploration see Max Born, "Blessings and Evils of Space Travel," and Martin E. Marty, "A Humanist's View of Space Research."

77. Gabor, *Inventing the Future.*

78. Karl Rahner, S.J., in Brophy, *Science and Faith in the 21st Century,* p. 15.

9 Toward the Creation of Technological Man

1. For example, Eugene J. Meehan, *The Theory and Method of Political Analysis,* p. 47. For some recent critiques of the effects of this attitude see Kenneth Boulding, "Philosophy, Behavioral Science, and the Nature of Man," and Christian Bay, "Politics and Pseudopolitics." See also T. H. Weldon, *The Vocabulary of Politics.*

2. Cf. especially Dewey, *The Quest for Certainty.* His views are criticized in Morton White, *Social Thought in America,* pp. 203–219.

3. *The Measure of Man,* pp. 90–91. Marx, of course, had to struggle with a similar problem. See Howard L. Parsons, "Value and Mental Health in the Thought of Marx."

4. A more subtle problem arises in defining health, happiness or even survival, which we cannot go into here save to note that it is a problem for all men, not for technical philosophers alone.

5. Paraphrased by Henry H. Villard in Morse and Warner, *Technological Innovation and Society,* p. 197.

6. Cf. the discussion in Theodosius Dobzhansky, *The Biology of Ultimate Concern,* pp. 12–34.

7. Platt, *The Step to Man,* p. 151.

8. See Roszak, "The Counter Culture," Part IV. For some approaches to the total problem of man in nature see Marston Bates, *The Forest and the Sea;* Nigel Calder, *Eden Was No Garden;* Lynton C. Caldwell, *Planned Control of the Biophysical Environment;* William R. Ewald, Jr. (ed.), *Environment for Man;* Aldous Huxley, *The Politics of Ecology;* S. Dillon Ripley and Helmut T. Buechner, "Ecosystem Science as a Point of Synthesis"; Paul B. Sears, "Utopia and the Living Landscape"; Paul Shepard, *Man in the Landscape;* and Philip L. Wagner, *The Human Use of the Earth.* On man himself see Jacob Bronowski, *The Identity of Man;* Alexis Carrell, *Man, the Unknown;* and P. B. Medewar, *The Future of Man.*

9. M.I.T. commencement address, 1964, in Burke, *The New Technology and Human Values,* p. 94.

10. This traditional attitude is under severe attack by contemporary theologians even in orthodox churches. See Leslie Dewart, *The Future of Belief.*

11. Platt, *The Step to Man,* p. 183.

12. Paraphrased by Herbert J. Muller in Burke, *The New Technology and Human Values,* p. 44.

13. Cf. Warner R. Schilling, "The H-Bomb Decision."

14. Quoted in Bates, *The Forest and the Sea,* p. 254.

15. Quoted in "How Man Changes His World," New York *Times,* September 24, 1967.

16. As Joseph Rosenfarb points out, "An economy being planned does not necessarily involve a planned culture," *Freedom and the Administrative State,* p. 87.

17. The term comes from a different context, William Burroughs' novel, *The Soft Machine,* but is relevant here.

18. Platt, *The Step to Man,* p. 187.

19. Exodus, 3:14, *The New Jerusalem Bible.*

20. William Braden, *The Private Sea;* Timothy Leary, *The Politics of Ecstacy;* also Rev. George B. Murray, S.J. and Jean Huston, "L.S.D.: The Inward Voyage."

21. This is the general thesis of Koestler in *The Ghost in the Machine.*

22. For an interesting if controversial approach to this point see L. Pauwels and J. Bergier, *The Morning of the Magicians.*

23. On suggested reforms see Lynton C. Caldwell, "Managing the Scientific Super-Culture"; Robert S. Morison, "Education for Environmental Concerns"; and E. V. David, Jr. and J. G. Truxal, "The Man-Made World."

24. On specific problems of controlling the effects of science and technology on society see Barry Commoner, *Science and Survival;* H. Wentworth Eldredge, *Taming Megalopolis;* Nigel Calder, "Tomorrow's Politics"; LaMont C. Cole, "Can the World Be Saved?"; Rene J. Dubos, "Scientists Alone Can't Do the Job"; Amitai Etzioni, "On the National Guidance of Science"; Wilbur H. Ferry, "Must We Rewrite the Constitution to Control Technology?"; Julian Huxley, *The Human Crisis;* Henry Jarrett (ed.), *Environmental Quality in a Growing Economy;* John Lear, "Policing the Consequences of Science"; Roger Revelle, "Outdoor Recreation in a Hyper-Productive Society." For basic perspectives see Joseph Wood Krutch, *And Even If You Do;* Yves R. Simon, *Philosophy of Democratic Government,* pp. 260–322;

Oswald Spengler, *Man and Technics;* Andreas G. Van Melsen, *Science and Technology;* also Denis de Rougemont, "Man v. Technics"; Lynton C. Caldwell, "Biopolitics"; and Richard L. Means, "Why Worry About Nature?"

25. On problems and techniques of decision-making see Raymond A. Bauer, *Social Indicators;* David Braybrooke and Charles E. Lindblom, *A Strategy of Decision;* Robert A. Dahl and Charles E. Lindblom, *Politics, Economics and Welfare;* Bertram Gross (ed.), *Action Under Planning;* also Todd A. La Porte, "Politics and 'Inventing the Future' "; and Roger Starr and James Carlson, "Pollution and Poverty."

26. Kenneth Arrow, *Social Choice and Individual Values.* For a critique see James Coleman, "The Possibility of a Social Welfare Function."

27. Amitai Etzioni, *The Active Society,* pp. 282–309 and "Mixed-Scanning."

28. Platt, *The Step To Man,* p. 200.

29. *Ibid.,* p. 51. Something similar has been suggested by Arthur I. Waskow. See "Peaceful Strife Expected by '99," New York *Times,* February 12, 1968.

30. Keniston, "Youth, Change and Violence," p. 233. This is perhaps less true in the developing nations than the developed. Most developing nations are currently going through a kind of xenophobia not unlike that exhibited by the developed nations in the nineteenth century.

31. Michael Polanyi, "The Republic of Science."

32. See also the warnings of Carlyl P. Haskins, "Organ Transplants Bring Warning on Life's Values," Washington *Post,* January 29, 1968.

33. "Toynbee Urges Man to Slow Rapid Pace of Change," New York *Times,* March 14, 1967.

34. Van Melsen, *Science and Technology,* Vol. II, pp. 306–308.

35. On the problem presented by space travel see Carl Sagan *et al.,* "Contamination of Mars."

36. A U.N. committee on the subject was convened by U Thant on March 18, 1968. See also Luther J. Carter, "Deep Seabed" and J. V. Reistrup, "Davy Jones' Locker Tempts the World."

37. As the distinguished conservative economist Wilhelm Ropke puts it, "If it has to stop eventually, why not now? Why must the earth be first transformed into an anthill?" *A Humane Economy,* p. 44.

38. Charles A. Lindbergh, "The Wisdom of Wildness."

39. Kenneth Boulding, "Where Are We Going If Anywhere?" pp. 166–167.

40. For various suggestions see Platt, *The Step to Man,* p. 105; "Annual Bonus Is Urged For Not Having Babies," New York *Times,* March 2, 1968; "Zoologist Urges Taxes On Diapers," New York *Times,* May 29, 1968. Institution of a form of easily dissoluble childless marriage, in addition to more permanent procreative unions, has also been urged. "Overcrowding Crisis Due in 1970's, According to Experts on Population," Washington *Post,* July 15, 1967.

41. William L. Langer, "Europe's Initial Population Explosion."

42. "The Irrepressible Family," *The Public Interest,* 3 (Spring, 1966), pp. 127–128.

43. Kingsley Davis, "Population Policy"; also Margaret Snyder, "Behavioral Science and Family Planning."

44. See Aaron Wildavsky, "Aesthetic Power or the Triumph of the Sensitive Minority Over the Vulgar Mass."

45. The pages of *Science* and the *Bulletin of the Atomic Scientists* reflect this. The American Association for the Advancement of Science recently set up a committee on human-environmental relations. See Dale Wolfle, "The Only Earth We Have."

46. Joshua Lederberg does so in "Legislation on Transplants Should Begin With Specifics," Washington *Post*, January 28, 1968. See also "Transplant Controls Urged," Washington *Post*, February 28, 1968; " 'Genetic Engineering' Fears Discounted," Washington *Star*, March 8, 1968; "Scientist Doubts Genetic Abuse: Calls Research the Best Defense," New York *Times*, March 9, 1968; "Naive Howls on Medical Research," Washington *Star*, March 14, 1968; "Dr. Bernard Rejects Curbs on Doctors," Washington *Post*, March 9, 1968.

47. Despite this support American participation has been less than adequate, even though spurred on by the House Subcommittee on Science, Research and Development, chaired by Representative Daddario. See "House Panel Asks U.S. Aid for World Study of Man's Effect on Earth," New York *Times*, March 20, 1968; and Philip M. Boffey, "International Biological Program."

48. On experimentation on humans see M. H. Pappworth, *Human Guinea Pigs;* Bernard Barber, "Experimenting with Humans"; Walter Goodman, "Doctors Must Experiment with Humans"; P. D. Medewar, "Science and the Sanctity of Life"; and Edward Shils, "The Sanctity of Life."

49. Some scientists such as Lederberg realize this, as in his "Society, Not Science, to Decide When to Cure Some Diseases," Washington *Post*, December 30, 1967, though he is less than enthusiastic that this is the case.

50. Platt, *The Step to Man*, p. 195.

51. Cf. George Gaylord Simpson, *The Meaning of Evolution*, pp. 307–308.

52. Quoted in Huston Smith, "The New Age," p. 18. Eckhart lived circa 1260–1328.

Bibliography

The bibliography is designed both to reflect works consulted in the preparation of this book and to introduce readers to additional material on the topics discussed. Especially cogent or stimulating books and articles are denoted by an asterisk (*). For reasons of space, short newspaper articles cited in the footnotes are omitted, thus slighting the fine job of science reporting being done by several American newspapers, notably the New York *Times* and Washington *Post*. Coauthored material is listed only under the name of the senior author. Articles in magazines that do not run material in continuous sequence are cited by the initial page only. Editions cited are not necessarily the original publication of a work.

1. Books

Adolfs, Robert, O.S.A. *The Grave of God.* Translated by N. D. Smith. New York: Harper and Row, 1967.

Amis, Kingsley. *New Maps in Hell.* New York: Harcourt, Brace, 1960.

Apter, David E. *The Politics of Modernization.* Chicago: University of Chicago Press, 1965.

Altizer, Thomas. *The Gospel of Atheistic Humanism.* Philadelphia: Westminster Press, 1966.

Ardrey, Robert. *African Genesis.* New York: Atheneum, 1961.

Arendt, Hannah. *Eichmann in Jerusalem.* New York: The Viking Press, 1963.
———. **The Human Condition.* Chicago: University of Chicago Press, 1958.
———. *The Origins of Totalitarianism.* Revised Edition. New York: Meridian Books, 1958.
Armytage, W. H. G. **The Rise of the Technocrats.* London: Routledge and Kegan Paul, 1965.
Arnold, Matthew. *Culture and Anarchy.* London: Smith, Elder, 1875.
Aron, Raymond. **The Epoch of Universal Technology.* London: Encounter pamphlets, 1964.
———. *The Industrial Society.* New York: Praeger, 1967.
——— (ed.). *World Technology and Human Destiny.* Ann Arbor: University of Michigan Press, 1963.
Arrow, Kenneth. *Social Choice and Individual Values.* New York: Wiley, 1963.
Asimov, Isaac (ed.). *More Soviet Science Fiction.* New York: Collier Books, 1962.
Auzias, Jean Marie. *Clefs Pour La Technique.* Paris: Seghers, 1966.
Baltzell, E. Digby. *The Protestant Establishment.* New York: Random House, 1964.
Barber, Bernard. **Science and the Social Order.* New York: Collier Books, 1962.
——— and Hirsch, Walter (eds.). *The Sociology of Science.* Glencoe: The Free Press, 1963.
Bardach, John. *Harvest of the Sea.* New York: Harper and Row, 1967.
Barrett, William. **Irrational Man.* London: Mercury Books, 1964.
Barringer, Herbert R., Blanksten, George I., and Mack, Raymond W. (eds.). *Social Change in Developing Areas.* Cambridge: Schenkman, 1965.
Bates, Marston. **The Forest and the Sea.* New York: Random House, 1960.
Bauer, Raymond A. *Social Indicators.* Cambridge: The M.I.T. Press, 1966.
Bazalon, David T. *Power in America.* New York: New American Library, 1967.
Bell, Daniel. *The End of Ideology.* Glencoe: The Free Press, 1959.
Belloc, Hilaire. *The Servile State.* New York: Henry Holt, 1946.
Bendix, Reinhard, and Lipset, Seymour Martin. (eds.). *Class, Status and Power.* Glencoe: The Free Press, 1953.
Benjamin, A. Cornelius. *Science, Technology and Human Values.* Columbia: University of Missouri Press, 1965.
Benz, Ernest. **Evolution and Christian Hope.* Translated by Heinz G. Frank. Garden City: Anchor Books, 1968.
Berelson, Bernard, and Steiner, Gary A. **Human Behavior.* New York: Harcourt, Brace, 1964.
Berger, Bennett M. *Working-class Suburb.* Berkeley: University of California Press, 1960.
Berkner, Lloyd. *The Scientific Age.* New Haven: Yale University Press, 1964.
Bernal, John Desmond. *The Social Function of Science.* Cambridge: The M.I.T. Press, 1967.
Blau, Peter, and Scott, W. Richard. *Formal Organization.* San Francisco: Chandler, 1962.
Blauner, Robert. *Alienation and Freedom.* Chicago: University of Chicago Press, 1964.

Bloomfield, Lincoln P. (ed.). *Outer Space: Prospects for Man and Society.* Englewood Cliffs: Prentice-Hall, 1962.
Bloy, Myron B., Jr. *The Crisis of Human Values.* New York: Seabury Press, 1962.
Bock, Edwin A. *The Last Colonialism?* Bloomington: Comparative Administration Group, American Society for Public Administration, 1967.
Bogart, Leo. *The Age of Television.* New York: Ungar, 1958.
Boguslaw, Robert. *The New Utopians.* Englewood Cliffs: Prentice-Hall, 1965.
Bonhoeffer, Dietrich. *Prisoner for God.* New York: Macmillan, 1955.
Borsodi, Ralph. *Flight from the City.* New York: Harper, 1933.
———. *This Ugly Civilization.* New York: Harper, 1933.
Bottomore, T. H. *Classes in Modern Society.* New York: Pantheon, 1966.
———. *Elites and Society.* New York: Basic Books, 1964.
Boyko, Hugh (ed.). *Science and the Future of Mankind.* Bloomington: Indiana University Press, 1961.
Braden, William. *The Private Sea.* Chicago: Quadrangle, 1967.
Bramson, Leon. *The Political Context of Sociology.* Princeton: Princeton University Press, 1961.
Braybrooke, David, and Lindblom, Charles E. *A Strategy of Decision.* New York: Macmillan, 1963.
Briggs, Asa (ed.). *William Morris: Selected Writings and Designs.* Baltimore: Penguin Books, 1962.
Brinton, Crane. *The Anatomy of Revolution.* New York: Vintage, 1957.
Bronowski, Jacob. *The Identity of Man.* New York: Messner, 1956.
———. *Science and Human Values.* New York: Messner, 1956.
———, and Mazlish, Bruce. *The Western Intellectual Tradition.* New York: Harper and Row, 1960.
Brooks, Norman. *The Next Ninety Years.* Pasadena: California Institute of Technology Press, 1967.
Brophy, Donald (ed.). *Science and Faith in the 21st Century.* New York: Paulist Press, 1967.
Brown, Harrison. *The Challenge of Man's Future.* New York: The Viking Press, 1954.
———, Bonner, James, and Weir, John. *The Next Hundred Years.* New York: The Viking Press, 1957.
Brown, Norman O. *Life Against Death.* Middletown: Wesleyan University Press, 1959.
Bryson, Lyman. *Science and Freedom.* New York: Columbia University Press, 1947.
Bunzel, John. *Anti-Politics in America.* New York: Knopf, 1967.
Burke, Edmund. *Reflections on the Revolution in France.* New York: Dolphin Books, 1961.
Burke, John G. (ed.). *The New Technology and Human Values.* Belmont: Wadsworth, 1967.
Burke, W. T. *Ocean Sciences, Technology and the Future International Law of the Sea.* Columbus: Ohio State University Press, 1966.
Burlinghame, Roger. *Backgrounds of Power.* New York: Scribner's, 1949.
Burnham, James. *The Managerial Revolution.* New York: John Day, 1941.
Burroughs, William. *The Soft Machine* (a novel). New York: Grove Press, 1966.
Butterfield, Herbert. *The Origins of Modern Science: 1300–1800.* New York: Macmillan, 1956.

Calder, Nigel. *Eden Was No Garden*. New York: Holt, Rinehart and Winston, 1967.
——— (ed.). *The World in 1984*. Vols. I and II. Hammondsworth: Penguin Books, 1965.
Caldwell, Lynton C. *Planned Control of the Biophysical Environment*. Bloomington: Comparative Administration Group, American Society for Public Administration, 1964.
———, assisted by Vandivort, Martha B. *Science, Technology and Public Policy. A Selective and Annotated Bibliography*. Bloomington: Institute of Public Administration, Indiana University, 1965.
Callahan, Daniel (ed.). *The Secular City Debate*. New York: Macmillan, 1966.
Campbell, Francis Stuart (E. V. Kuhneldt-Leddihn, Pseud.). *The Menace of the Herd*. Milwaukee: Bruce, 1943.
Carrell, Alexis. *Man the Unknown*. New York: Harper, 1939.
Carrington, Richard A. *A Million Years of Man*. Cleveland: Meridian Books, 1963.
Chase, Stuart. *The Most Probable World*. New York: Harper and Row, 1959.
Chesterton, G. K. *William Cobbett*. New York: Dodd, Mead, 1926.
Childe, V. Gordon. *Man Makes Himself*. New York: Mentor Books, 1951.
———. *Social Evolution*. London: C. A. Watts, 1951.
———. *What Happened in History*. Baltimore: Penguin Books, 1964.
Clark, Grahame. *World Prehistory*. Cambridge: Cambridge University Press, 1961.
Clarke, Arthur C. *Childhood's End* (a novel). New York: Ballatine Books, 1963.
———. *Profiles of the Future*. New York: Bantam Books, 1964.
———. *The Promise of Space* (a novel). New York: Harper and Row, 1968.
———. *2001: A Space Odyssey*. New York: Signet Books, 1968.
Coffin, Tris. *The Armed Society*. Baltimore: Penguin Books, 1964.
Cohn, Norman. *The Pursuit of the Millennium*. New York: Essential Books, 1957.
Coker, Francis W. *Recent Political Thought*. New York: Appleton-Century-Crofts, 1934.
Cole, G. D. H. *The Life of William Cobbett*. London: Home and Van Thal, 1947.
Commoner, Barry. *Science and Survival*. New York: The Viking Press, 1967.
Cook, Fred J. *The Corrupted Land*. New York: Macmillan, 1966.
———. *The Warfare State*. New York: Macmillan, 1962.
Cottrell, Fred. *Energy and Society*. New York: McGraw-Hill, 1955.
Cox, Donald W. *America's New Policy Makers*. Philadelphia: Chilton Books, 1964.
Cox, Harvey. *The Secular City*. New York: Macmillan, 1965.
Croly, Herbert. *The Promise of American Life*. New York: Macmillan, 1909.
Cuber, John F., and Harroff, Peggy B. *Sex and the Significant Americans*. Baltimore: Penguin Books, 1966.
Cutler, Donald R. (ed.). *The Religious Situation*. Boston: Beacon Press, 1968.
Dahl, Robert A., and Lindblom, Charles E. *Politics, Economics and Welfare*. New York: Harper, 1953.

Dahrendorf, Ralf. *Class and Class Conflict in Industrial Society.* Stanford: Stanford University Press, 1959.

Dasmann, Raymond F. *The Destruction of California.* New York: Macmillan, 1965.

Davis, William O., and Schuman, Jack N. (eds.). *ESSA: Science and Engineering, July 13, 1965 to June 30, 1967.* Washington: Government Printing Office, 1968.

Day, Lincoln H., and Day, Alice Taylor. **Too Many Americans.* Boston: Houghton Mifflin, 1964.

De Grazia, Sebastian. *Of Time, Work, and Leisure.* New York: Twentieth Century Fund, 1962.

De Huszar, George B. (ed.). *The Intellectuals.* Glencoe: The Free Press, 1960.

Dekker, Albert. *The Discovery of Nature.* New York: Simon and Schuster, 1965.

Derrick, Christopher (ed.). *Cosmic Piety.* New York: Kenedy, 1965.

Derry, T. K., and Williams, Trevor I. **A Short History of Technology.* New York: Oxford University Press, 1961.

Deutsch, Karl. *Nationalism and Social Communication.* Cambridge: The M.I.T. Press, 1966.

———. *The Nerves of Government.* New York: The Free Press, 1963.

Dewart, Leslie. *The Future of Belief.* New York: Herder and Herder, 1965.

Dewey, John. *The Quest for Certainty.* New York: Milton, Balch, 1929.

Dexter, Lewis Anthony, and White, David Manning (eds.). *People, Society and Mass Communications.* New York: The Free Press, 1964.

Djilas, Milovan. *The New Class.* New York: Praeger, 1957.

Dobriner, William. *Class in Suburbia.* Englewood Cliffs: Prentice-Hall, 1963.

——— (ed.). *The Suburban Community.* New York: Putnam, 1958.

Dobzhansky, Theodosius. **The Biology of Ultimate Concern.* New York: New American Library, 1967.

Domhoff, G. William. **Who Rules America?* Englewood Cliffs: Prentice-Hall, 1967.

Drucker, Peter F. *Landmarks of Tomorrow.* New York: Harper, 1959.

Dupre, J. Stefan, and Lakoff, Sanford A. *Science and the Nation.* Englewood Cliffs: Prentice-Hall, 1962.

Ehrmann, Henry J. (ed.). *Interest Groups on Four Continents.* Pittsburgh: University of Pittsburgh Press, 1958.

Eisenstadt, S. N. *Modernization.* Englewood Cliffs: Prentice-Hall, 1966.

Eldredge, H. Wentworth (ed.). **Taming Megalopolis.* Vols. I and II. Garden City: Anchor Books, 1967.

Eliot, T. S. *The Idea of a Christian Society.* New York: Harcourt, Brace, 1949.

———. *Notes Toward the Definition of Culture.* New York: Harcourt, Brace, 1940.

Ellul, Jacques. *Propaganda.* Translated by Konrad Kellen and Jean Lerner. New York: Knopf, 1967.

———. *The Political Illusion.* Translated by Konrad Kellen. New York: Knopf, 1968.

———. **The Technological Society.* Translated by John Wilkinson. Introduction by Robert K. Merton. New York: Knopf, 1964.

Erikson, Erik H. *Childhood and Society.* New York: Norton, 1962.

—— (ed.). *Youth: Change and Challenge.* New York: Basic Books, 1963.

——. *Identity: Youth and Crisis.* New York: Norton, 1968.

Ettinger, Robert W. *The Prospect of Immortality.* New York: Doubleday, 1964.

Etzioni, Amitai. **The Active Society.* New York: Rinehart and Winston, 1961.

——. *Complex Organizations.* New York: The Free Press, 1968.

——. *The Moon-Doggle.* New York: Doubleday, 1964.

Eurich, Nell. *Science in Utopia.* Cambridge: Harvard University Press, 1967.

Ewald, William R., Jr. (ed.). **Environment for Man.* Bloomington: Indiana University Press, 1967.

Fabun, Don. *The Dynamics of Change.* Englewood Cliffs: Prentice-Hall, 1967.

Fagan, Richard R. *Politics and Communication.* Boston: Little, Brown, 1966.

Feuer, Lewis S. *The Scientific Intellectual.* New York: Basic Books, 1963.

Follett, Mary P. *Dynamic Administration.* Edited by H. C. Metcalf and L. Urwick, Bath: Management Publications Trust, 1941.

——. *The New State.* New York: Longmans, 1918.

Foreign Policy Association. **Toward the Year 2018.* Introduction by E. G. Mesthene. New York: Cowles, 1968.

Fortune, Editors of. *America in the Sixties.* New York: Harper, 1960.

——. *The Exploding Metropolis.* New York: Doubleday, 1958.

Frank, Phillip G. (ed.). *The Validation of Scientific Theories.* Boston: Beacon Press, 1956.

Franklin, Howard Bruce. *Future Perfect.* New York: Oxford University Press, 1966.

Friedenberg, Edgar Z. *Coming of Age in America.* New York: Random House, 1965.

Friedmann, Georges. *Industrial Society.* Glencoe: The Free Press, 1955.

Friedrich, Carl J., and Brzezinski, Zbigniew. *Totalitarian Dictatorship and Autocracy.* New York: Harcourt, Brace, 1956.

—— (ed.). *Totalitarianism.* Cambridge: Harvard University Press, 1954.

Fromm, Erich. *Escape from Freedom.* New York: Rinehart, 1941.

——. **The Sane Society.* Greenwich: Fawcett, 1965.

—— (ed.). **Socialist Humanism.* New York: Anchor Books, 1966.

Fuller, Buckminster. **No More Secondhand God.* Carbondale: Southern Illinois University Press, 1962.

Fyvel, T. R. *The Troublemakers.* New York: Schocken Books, 1964.

Gabor, Denis. *Inventing the Future.* New York: Knopf, 1964.

Galbraith, John Kenneth. *The Affluent Society.* Boston: Houghton Mifflin, 1958.

——. **The New Industrial State.* Boston: Houghton Mifflin, 1967.

Gans, Herbert. *The Levittowners.* New York: Pantheon, 1967.

Gerth, Hans, and Mills, C. Wright. *Character and Social Structure.* New York: Harcourt, Brace, 1964.

Gettleman, Marvin E., and Marmelstein, David (eds.). *The Great Society Reader.* New York: Vintage, 1967.

Gibney, Frank B., and Feldman, George J. *The Reluctant Space-Farers.* New York: Signet Books, 1966.

Gideon, Sigfried. *Mechanization Takes Command.* New York: Oxford University Press, 1948.

Gilb, Corinne Lathrop. *Hidden Hierarchies.* New York: Harper and Row, 1966.

Gilman, William. *Science: U.S.A.* New York: The Viking Press, 1965.

Gilpin, Robert, Jr. *American Scientists and Nuclear Weapons.* Princeton: Princeton University Press, 1962.

———. *France in the Age of the Scientific State.* Princeton: Princeton University Press, 1967.

———, and Wright, Christopher (eds.). *Science and National Policy-Making.* New York: Columbia University Press, 1964.

Ginsberg, Eli (ed.). *Technology and Social Change.* New York: Columbia University Press, 1964.

Glass, Bentley. *Science and Ethical Values.* Chapel Hill: University of North Carolina Press, 1965.

Goldstein, Richard. *1 in 7: Drugs on Campus.* New York: Walker, 1967.

Goodman, Paul. *Growing Up Absurd.* New York: Vintage, 1960.

———. *People or Personnel and Like a Conquered Province.* New York: Vintage Books, 1968.

Goodwin, Harold Leland. *Space: Frontier Unlimited.* Princeton: Van Nostrand, 1962.

Gordon, T. J., and Helmer, Olaf. *Report on a Long-Range Forecasting Study P–2982.* Santa Monica: RAND Corporation, 1964.

Gottmann, Jean. *Megalopolis.* Cambridge: The M.I.T. Press, 1961.

Gouldner, Alvin W., and Peterson, Richard A. *Notes on Technology and the Moral Order.* Indianapolis: Bobbs-Merrill, 1962.

Gouschev, Sergei, and Vassiliev, Michael (eds.). *Russian Science in the 21st Century.* New York: McGraw-Hill, 1960.

Greenberg, Donald S. *The Politics of Pure Science.* New York: New American Library, 1968.

Grodzins, Morton. *The American System.* Edited by Daniel J. Eleazar. Chicago: Rand McNally, 1966.

———, and Rabinowitch, Eugene (eds.). *The Atomic Age.* New York: Basic Books, 1963.

Gross, Bertram (ed.). *Action Under Planning.* New York: McGraw-Hill, 1967.

———. *Space-Time and Post-Industrial Society.* Bloomington: Comparative Administration Group, American Society for Public Administration, 1966.

Guardini, Romano. *The End of the Modern World.* Translated by J. Thomas and H. Burke. Edited with Introduction by F. D. Wilhelmsen. New York: Sheed and Ward, 1956.

Guilbard, G. T. *What Is Cybernation?* Translated by Valerie McKay. New York: Criterion Books, 1959.

Guzzardi, Walter, Jr. *The Young Executives.* New York: Mentor Books, 1966.

Hagstrom, Warren O. *The Scientific Community.* New York: Basic Books, 1965.

Halacy, D. S., Jr. *The Weather Changers.* New York: Harper and Row, 1968.

Halcrow, H. G. (ed.). *Contemporary Readings in Agricultural Economics.* Englewood Cliffs: Prentice-Hall, 1955.

Haley, Andrew G. *Space Law and Government.* New York: Appleton-Century-Crofts, 1963.

Hammond, J. L. and Barbara. *The Rise of Modern Industry.* Introduction and bibliography by R. M. Hartwell. London: Methuen, 1966.

Harrington, Michael. *The Accidental Century.* New York: Macmillan, 1965.

———. *The Other America.* Baltimore: Penguin Books, 1963.

———. *Toward a Democratic Left.* New York: Macmillan, 1968.

Harrison, Annette. *The Problem of Privacy in the Computer Age: An Annotated Bibliography.* Santa Monica: RAND Corporation, 1967.

Haselden, Kyle, and Hefner, Philip (eds.). *Changing Man: The Threat and the Promise.* New York: Doubleday, 1968.

Haskins, Carlyl P. *The Scientific Revolution and World Politics.* New York: Harper and Row, 1962.

Hatt, Paul K., and Reiss, Albert J., Jr. *Reader in Urban Sociology.* Glencoe: The Free Press, 1951.

Hawkes, Jacquetta, and Wooley, Sir Leonard. *Prehistory and the Beginnings of Civilization.* New York: Harper and Row, 1962.

Hayek, F. A. *The Constitution of Liberty.* Chicago: University of Chicago Press, 1959.

———. *The Counter Revolution of Science.* Glencoe: The Free Press, 1959.

Heady, Ferrel. *Public Administration in Comparative Perspective.* Englewood Cliffs: Prentice-Hall, 1966.

Heckscher, August. *The Public Happiness.* New York: Atheneum, 1962.

Heilbroner, Robert L. *The Future as History.* New York: Grove Press, 1961.

Heineman, F. H. *Existentialism and the Modern Predicament.* New York: Harper, 1958.

Henry, Jules, *Culture Against Man.* New York: Random House, 1963.

Herskovits, Melville J. *Economic Anthropology.* New York: Norton, 1965.

Hillegas, Mark R. *The Future as Nightmare.* New York: Oxford University Press, 1967.

Hoffer, Eric. *The Ordeal of Change.* New York: Harper and Row, 1963.

Hofstadter, Samuel H. and Horowitz, George (eds.). *The Right of Privacy.* New York: Central Book Company, 1964.

Hoggart, Richard. *The Uses of Literacy.* New York: Oxford University Press, 1957.

Horney, Karen. *The Neurotic Personality of Our Time.* New York: Norton, 1937.

Horowitz, Irving Louis (ed.), *The New Sociology.* New York: Oxford University Press, 1964.

———. *The War Game.* New York: Ballantine Books, 1963.

Hoselitz, Bert F., and Moore, Wilbert E. (eds.). *Industrialization and Society.* The Hague: Mouton, 1963.

Huxley, Aldous. *Brave New World* (a novel). New York: Doubleday, Doran, 1932.

———. *Brave New World Revisited.* New York: Harper and Row, 1958.

———. *The Politics of Ecology.* Santa Barbara: Center for the Study of Democratic Institutions, 1964.

———. *Science, Liberty and Peace.* New York: Harper, 1956.

Huxley, Julian. *The Human Crisis.* Seattle: University of Washington Press, 1963.

Hyneman, Charles. *Bureaucracy in a Democracy.* New York: Harper, 1950.

Jacobs, Jane. *The Life and Death of Great American Cities.* New York: Random House, 1961.

Jacobs, Norman. (ed.). *Culture for the Millions.* New York: Vintage, 1966.

Jarrett, Henry (ed.). *Environmental Quality in a Growing Economy.* Baltimore: Johns Hopkins University Press, 1966.

Jennings, Burgess E., and Murphy, John E. (eds.). *Interactions of Man and His Environment.* New York: Plenum Press, 1966.

Josephson, Eric and Mary (eds.). *Man Alone.* New York: Dell, 1962.

Jouvenel, Bertrand de. *The Art of Conjecture.* Translated by Nikita Lary. New York: Basic Books, 1967.

Juenger, Friedrich Georg. *The Failure of Technology.* Chicago: Regnery, 1956.

Jungk, Robert. *Tomorrow Is Already Here.* Translated by Marguerite Waldman. Introduction by Herbert Agar. New York: Simon and Schuster, 1954.

Kahler, Erich. *The Disintegration of Form in the Arts.* New York: Braziller, 1968.

———. *Man the Measure.* New York: Pantheon, 1943.

———. *The Tower and the Abyss.* New York: Braziller, 1957.

Kahn, Herman, and Weiner, Anthony J. *The Year 2000.* New York: Macmillan, 1967.

Kaplan, Norman (ed.). *Science and Society.* Chicago: Rand McNally, 1965.

Kariel, Henry S. *The Promise of Politics.* Englewood Cliffs: Prentice-Hall, 1966.

Kash, Don E. *The Politics of Space Cooperation.* Lafayette: Purdue University Press, 1967.

Kateb, George. *Utopia and Its Enemies.* Glencoe: The Free Press, 1963.

Katz, Elihu, and Lazersfeld, Paul F. *Personal Influence.* New York: The Free Press, 1955.

Kautsky, John. *The Politics of Developing Countries.* New York: Wiley, 1961.

Keller, Suzanne. *Beyond the Ruling Class.* New York: Random House, 1963.

Keniston, Kenneth. *The Uncommitted.* New York: Harcourt, Brace, 1965.

———. *Young Radicals.* New York: Harcourt, Brace, 1968.

Kepes, Gyorgy (ed.). *Education of Vision.* New York: Braziller, 1965.

———. (ed.). *The Man-Made Object.* New York: Braziller, 1966.

———. (ed.). *Module, Proportion, Symmetry, Rhythm.* New York: Braziller, 1966.

———. (ed.). *The Nature and Art of Motion.* New York: Braziller, 1965.

———. (ed.). *Sign, Image, Symbol.* New York: Braziller, 1966.

———. (ed.). *Structure in Art and Science.* New York: Braziller, 1966.

Klapper, Joseph T. *The Effects of Mass Communication.* New York: The Free Press, 1960.

Koestler, Arthur. *The Ghost in the Machine.* New York: Macmillan, 1968.

Kolko, Gabriel. *Wealth and Power in America.* New York: Praeger, 1962.

Kornhauser, William. *The Politics of Mass Society.* Glencoe: The Free Press, 1959.

————. *Scientists in Industry*. Berkeley: University of California Press, 1962.

Kostelanetz, Richard (ed.). *The New American Arts*. New York: Collier Books, 1967.

Kraeling, Carl H., and Adams, Robert M. (eds.). *City Invincible*. Chicago: University of Chicago Press, 1960.

Kranzberg, Melvin, and Pursell, Carroll W. (eds.). *Technology in Western Civilization*. Vols. I and II. New York: Oxford University Press, 1967.

Krutch, Joseph Wood. **And Even If You Do*. New York: Morrow, 1967.

————. *The Measure of Man*. Indianapolis: Bobbs-Merrill, 1954.

Lakoff, Sanford A. (ed.). **Knowledge and Power*. New York: The Free Press, 1966.

Landers, Richard R. **Man's Place in the Dybosphere*. Englewood Cliffs: Prentice-Hall, 1966.

Langmead-Casserly, J. V. *In the Service of Man*. Chicago: Regnery, 1967.

Lapp, Ralph E. **The New Priesthood*. New York: Harper and Row, 1965.

————. *The Weapons Culture*. New York: Norton, 1968.

Larrabee, Eric, and Meyersdorf, Rolf (eds.). **Mass Leisure*. Glencoe: The Free Press, 1958.

Laslett, Peter. *The World We Have Lost*. New York: Scribner's, 1966.

Lawrence, D. H. *The Plumed Serpent* (a novel). New York: Knopf, 1926.

Leakey, L. S. *Adam's Ancestors*. New York: Harper, 1966.

Leary, Timothy. *The Politics of Ecstacy*. New York: Putnam, 1968.

Lenski, Gerhard. *The Religious Factor*. New York: Doubleday, 1961.

Levin, Murray B. *Kennedy Campaigning*. Boston: Beacon Press, 1966.

Levy, Lillian (ed.). *Space: Its Impact Upon Man and Society*. New York: Norton, 1965.

Lewis, Roy, and Stewart, Rosemary. *The Managers*. New York: Mentor Books, 1961.

Lichtheim, George. *Marxism*. New York: Praeger, 1965.

Lifton, Robert J. *Brainwashing and the Psychology of Totalism*. New York: Norton, 1963.

Linton, Ralph. *The Cultural Background of Personality*. New York: Appleton-Century-Crofts, 1945.

Lipset, Seymour Martin. *Political Man*. New York: Doubleday, 1960.

————, and Bendix, Reinhard (eds.). *Social Mobility in Industrial Society*. Berkeley: University of California Press, 1959.

———— (ed.). *Student Politics*. New York: Basic Books, 1967.

Long, Percy (ed.). *Studies in the History of Culture*. Waukesha: Banta, 1942.

Lord, Russell. *The Care of the Earth*. New York: Mentor Books, 1963.

Lorenz, Konrad. *On Aggression*. Translated by Marjorie Wilson. New York: Harcourt, Brace, 1966.

McCarthy, J. D., and Ebling, F. J. (eds.). *The Natural History of Aggression*. London: Academic Press, 1964.

McClelland, David C. *The Achieving Society*. Princeton: Van Nostrand, 1961.

McConnell, Grant. *Private Power and American Democracy*. New York: Knopf, 1966.

Machlup, Fritz. *The Production and Distribution of Knowledge in the United States*. Princeton: Princeton University Press, 1962.

Mack, Raymond W. **Transforming America*. New York: Random House, 1967.

McLanahan, Richard. *Images of the Universe: Leonardo Da Vinci.* Garden City: Doubleday, 1966.

McLuhan, Marshall. *The Mechanical Bride.* New York: Vanguard Press, 1951.

———. **Understanding Media.* New York: McGraw-Hill, 1965.

———, and Fiore, Quentin. **War and Peace in the Global Village.* New York: McGraw-Hill, 1968.

———, and Fiore, Quentin. **The Medium Is the Massage.* New York: Bantam Books, 1967.

McNeill, William H. *The Rise of the West.* Chicago: University of Chicago Press, 1963.

Marcuse, Herbert. *Eros and Civilization.* New York: Vintage, 1962.

———. **One-Dimensional Man.* Boston: Beacon Press, 1964.

Marine Technology Society. *Exploiting the Ocean.* Washington: Marine Technology Society, 1966.

Marsak, Leonard (ed.). *The Rise of Science in Relation to Society.* New York: Macmillan, 1964.

Marshall, T. H. *Class, Citizenship and Social Development.* New York: Doubleday, 1964.

Marx, Karl. **The First English Translation of Marx's Notes on Machines.* Translated by Ben Brewster. Leicester: University Sublation, 1966.

———. **Marx and Engels: Basic Writings on Politics and Philosophy.* Edited by Lewis S. Feuer. New York: Anchor Books, 1959.

Marx, Leo. *The Machine in the Garden.* New York: Oxford University Press, 1964.

Marx, Walter John. *Mechanization and Culture.* St. Louis: B. Herder, 1941.

Matson, Floyd. *The Broken Image.* New York: Braziller, 1964.

Mayo, Elton. *The Human Problems of an Industrial Civilization.* Cambridge: Harvard University Press, 1933.

———. *The Social Problems of an Industrial Civilization.* Cambridge: Harvard University Press, 1945.

Mead, Margaret, (ed.). *Cultural Patterns and Technical Change.* New York: Mentor Books, 1955.

Medewar, P. B. **The Future of Man.* London: Methuen, 1959.

Meehan, Eugene J. *The Theory and Method of Political Analysis.* Homewood: Dorsey, 1965.

Melman, Seymour. *Our Depleted Society.* New York: Holt, Rinehart and Winston, 1965.

Merton, Robert K. *Social Theory and Social Structure.* Glencoe: The Free Press, 1949.

———, Gray, Alisa P., Hockey, Barbara, and Selvin, Hannan G. (eds.). *Reader in Bureaucracy.* Glencoe: The Free Press, 1952.

———, Broom, Leonard, and Cottrell, Leonard S., Jr. (eds.). *Sociology Today.* New York: Basic Books, 1959.

Michael, Donald N. **Cybernation: The Silent Conquest.* Santa Barbara: Center for the Study of Democratic Institutions, 1962.

———. **The Next Generation.* New York: Vintage, 1964.

Michelmore, Peter. *Einstein: Portrait of the Man.* New York: Dodd, Mead, 1962.

Mills, C. Wright. *The Power Elite.* New York: Oxford University Press, 1965.

———. *Power, Politics and People.* Edited by Irving Louis Horowitz, New York: Ballantine Books, 1963.

————. *White Collar*. New York: Oxford University Press, 1951.

Mohan, Robert Paul (ed.). *Technology and Christian Culture*. Washington: Catholic University of America Press, 1960.

Molnar, Thomas. *Utopia: The Perennial Heresy*. New York: Sheed and Ward, 1967.

Montagu, Ashley. *Human Heredity*. New York: Signet Books, 1963.

Moore, Barrington, Jr. *Political Power and Social Theory*. New York: Harper and Row, 1965.

Moore, Wilbert E. *The Impact of Industry*. Englewood Cliffs: Prentice-Hall, 1965.

————. *Man, Time and Society*. New York: Wiley, 1963.

Morse, Dean, and Warner, Aaron W. (eds.). *Technological Innovation and Society*. New York: Columbia University Press, 1966.

Muller, Herbert J. *Freedom in the Modern World*. New York: Harper and Row, 1966.

————. *Issues of Freedom*. New York: Harper, 1960.

Mumford, Lewis. *The Myth of the Machine*. New York: Harcourt, Brace, 1967.

————. *The City in History*. New York: Harcourt, Brace, 1961.

————. *The Culture of Cities*. New York: Harcourt, Brace, 1938.

————. *Technics and Civilization*. New York: Harcourt, Brace, 1934.

Murchland, Bernard L. (ed.). *The Meaning of the Death of God*. New York: Random House, 1967.

Murphy, Earl Finbar. *Governing Nature*. Chicago: Quadrangle Books, 1968.

Murray, John Courtney, S.J. *Freedom and Man*. New York: Kenedy, 1965.

Murray, Michael F. *The Thought of Teilhard de Chardin*. New York: Seabury Press, 1966.

Musgrove, F. (ed.). *Youth and the Social Order*. Bloomington: Indiana University Press, 1965.

Nearing, Scott. *Freedom: Promise and Menace*. Harborside: Social Science Institute, 1961.

Needham, Joseph. *Science and Civilization in China*. Vols. I–IV. Cambridge: Cambridge University Press, 1954–1965.

Nef, John U. *The Conquest of the Material World*. Chicago: University of Chicago Press, 1964.

————. *Cultural Foundations of Industrial Civilization*. Cambridge: Cambridge University Press, 1958.

————. *War and Human Progress*. Cambridge: Harvard University Press, 1950.

Nelson, William R. (ed.). *The Politics of Science*. New York: Oxford University Press, 1968.

Newfield, Jack. *A Prophetic Minority*. Introduction by Michael Harrington. New York: Signet Books, 1967.

New Jerusalem Bible, The. Garden City: Doubleday, 1966.

Newman, William J. *The Futilitarian Society*. New York: Braziller, 1961.

————. *Liberalism and the Retreat From Politics*. New York: Braziller, 1964.

Nieberg, H. L. *In the Name of Science*. Chicago: Quadrangle Books, 1966.

Nisbet, Robert A. *The Quest for Community*. New York: Oxford University Press, 1953.

————. *The Sociological Tradition*. New York: Basic Books, 1966.

Ogburn, W. F. *Social Change*. New York: Huebsch, 1922.

————. (ed.). *Technology and International Relations.* Chicago: University of Chicago Press, 1949.

————, and Nimkoff, M. F. *Technology and the Changing Family.* Boston: Houghton Mifflin, 1955.

————. *The Social Effects of Aviation.* Boston: Houghton Mifflin, 1946.

Oliver, John W. *History of American Technology.* New York: Ronald Press, 1966.

Olsen, Philip (ed.). *America As a Mass Society.* Glencoe: The Free Press, 1963.

Ong, Walter J., S.J. *Frontiers in American Catholicism.* New York: Macmillan, 1957.

————. *In the Human Grain.* New York: Macmillan, 1967.

Ortega y Gasset, Jose. *The Revolt of the Masses.* New York: Norton, 1942.

Orwell, George. *1984* (a novel). New York: Harcourt, Brace, 1949.

Packard, Vance. *The Status Seekers.* New York: McKay, 1959.

————. *The Sexual Wilderness.* New York: McKay, 1968.

Paddock, Paul and William. *Famine 1975!* Boston: Little, Brown, 1967.

Pappworth, M. H. *Human Guinea Pigs.* Boston: Beacon Press, 1968.

Parry, Albert. *The New Class Divided.* New York: Macmillan, 1966.

Parsons, Talcott. *The Structure of Social Action.* Glencoe: The Free Press, 1949.

Pauwels, L., and Bergier, J. *The Morning of the Magicians.* New York: Stein and Day, 1964.

Persons, Stow (ed.). *Evolutionary Thought in America.* New Haven: Yale University Press, 1950.

Petit, Thomas A. *Freedom in the American Economy.* Homewood: Irwin, 1964.

Piggott, Stuart (ed.). *The Dawn of Civilization.* London: Thames and Hudson, 1961.

Platt, John Rader. *The Step to Man.* New York: Wiley, 1966.

Polak, Fred L. *The Image of the Future.* Vols. I and II. New York: Oceana, 1961.

Polanyi, Karl. *The Great Transformation.* New York: Rinehart, 1944.

Polanyi, Michael. *Science, Faith and Society.* Chicago: University of Chicago Press, 1964.

Presthaus, Robert K. *The Organizational Society.* New York: Knopf, 1962.

Price, Don K. *The Scientific Estate.* Cambridge: Harvard University Press, 1965.

Proceedings of the Teilhard Conference 1964. New York: Human Energetics Research Institute, Fordham University, 1964.

Pure, Daniel O. (ed.). *The 99th Hour: The Population Crisis in the United States.* Chapel Hill: University of North Carolina Press, 1967.

Queffelac, Henri. *Technology and Religion.* New York: Hawthorn, 1964.

Quigley, Carroll. *The Development of Civilizations.* New York: Macmillan, 1961.

————. *Tragedy and Hope.* New York: Macmillan, 1966.

Rabinowitch, Eugene. *Dawn of a New Age.* Chicago: University of Chicago, 1963.

Raphaeli, Nimrod (ed.). *Readings in Comparative Public Administration.* Boston: Allyn and Bacon, 1967.

Redfield, Robert. *The Primitive World and Its Transformations.* Ithaca: Cornell University Press, 1953.

Reid, Leslie. *The Sociology of Nature.* Baltimore: Penguin Books, 1962.

Reinow, Robert, and Reinow, Leona Train. *Moment in the Sun. New
    York: Dial, 1967.
Rhodes, Harold V. Utopia in American Political Thought. Tucson: Univer-
    sity of Arizona Press, 1967.
Riesman, David. Abundance for What? New York: Doubleday, 1964.
———. The Lonely Crowd. New Haven: Yale University Press, 1950.
Rimmer, Robert H. The Harrad Experiment (a novel). New York: Bantam
    Books, 1967.
Ripley, S. Dillon (ed.). Knowledge Among Men. Washington and New
    York: Smithsonian Institution and Simon and Schuster, 1966.
Ritchie, Arthur D. Science and Politics. London: Oxford University Press,
    1947.
Rodman, Lloyd (ed.). The Future Metropolis. New York: Braziller, 1961.
Ropke, Wilhelm. A Humane Economy. Chicago: Regnery, 1960.
Rose, Arnold. *The Power Structure. New York: Oxford University Press,
    1967.
Rosenberg, Bernard, and White, David Manning (eds.). *Mass Culture.
    Glencoe: The Free Press, 1957.
Rosenfarb, Joseph. Freedom in the Administrative State. New York:
    Harper, 1948.
Roslansky, John D. (ed.). The Control of Environment. Amsterdam:
    North-Amsterdam, 1967.
———. (ed.). *Genetics and the Future of Man. New York: Appleton-
    Century-Crofts, 1966.
Ross, Ralph, and Van den Haag, Ernest. The Fabric of Society. New York:
    Harcourt, Brace, 1957.
Rostand, Jean. *Peut-on Modifier l'Homme? Paris: Librairie Gallimard,
    1956.
Russell, Bertrand. The Impact of Science on Society. New York: Columbia
    University Press, 1951.
Sackman, Harold. Computers, Systems Science, and Evolving Society.
    New York: Wiley, 1967.
Schmeck, Harold M. The Semi-Artificial Man. New York: Walker, 1965.
Schon, Donald A. Technology and Change. New York: Delacorte Press,
    1967.
Schramm, Wilbur. The Process and Effects of Mass Communications.
    Urbana: University of Illinois Press, 1955.
Science and Law. Special issue of Michigan Law Review, 63 (1965) 1325-
    1422.
Science, Scientists and Politics. Santa Barbara: Center for the Study of
    Democratic Institutions, 1963.
Scientific American. Technology and Economic Development. New York:
    Knopf, 1963.
Seeley, John R., Sim, Alexander, Jr., and Looseley, Elizabeth. Crestwood
    Heights. New York: Basic Books, 1956.
Seidenberg, Roderic. Posthistoric Man. Chapel Hill: University of North
    Carolina Press, 1950.
Seligman, Ben. B. *Most Notorious Victory, Foreword by Robert L. Heil-
    broner. New York: The Free Press, 1966.
Shapley, Harlow. The View from a Distant Star. New York: Basic Books,
    1963.
Shepard, Paul. Man in the Landscape. New York: Knopf, 1967.

Shinn, Roger L. *Tangled World*. New York: Scribner's, 1965.

Shore, William B. (ed.). *The Region's Growth*. New York: Regional Plan Association, 1967.

Silberman, Charles E. *The Myth of Automation*. New York: Harper and Row, 1966.

Simmons, J. L., and Winograd, Barry. *It's Happening!* Santa Barbara: Marc-Laird, 1967.

Simon, Herbert A. *The New Shape of Automation*. New York: Harper and Row, 1965.

Simon, Yves R. *Philosophy of Democratic Government*. Chicago: University of Chicago Press, 1951.

Simpson, George Gaylord. **The Meaning of Evolution*. New Haven: Yale University Press, 1949.

Singer, Charles, Holmyard, E. J., Hall, A. R., and Williams, Trevor I. *A History of Technology*. Vols. I–V. New York: Oxford University Press, 1954–1958.

Skinner, B. F. **Walden Two*. New York: Macmillan, 1962.

Skolnikoff, E. B. *Science, Technology and American Foreign Policy*. Cambridge: The M.I.T. Press, 1967.

Smith, Bruce L. R. *The RAND Corporation*. Cambridge: Harvard University Press, 1966.

Snow, C. P. **The Two Cultures: And a Second Look*. New York: Mentor, Books, 1964.

Society, Science and Technology in Japan. Special issue of *Journal of World History*, IX (1965) 1–437.

Sorokin, P. A. *The Crisis of Our Age*. New York: Dutton, 1941.

Spengler, Oswald. *Man and Technics*. Translated by Charles F. Atkinson. New York: Knopf, 1932.

Stapledon, Olaf. *Last and First Men* (a novel). London: Methuen, 1930.

Stearn, Gerald E. (ed.). *McLuhan: Hot or Cool?* New York: Dial, 1967.

Stein, Maurice R. *The Eclipse of Community*. Princeton: Princeton University Press, 1960.

———, Vidick, Arthur J., and White, David Manning (eds.). **Identity and Anxiety*. New York: The Free Press, 1960.

Stewart, George B. *Not So Rich As You Think*. Boston: Houghton Mifflin, 1967.

Stewart, Harris B., Jr. *The Global Sea*. Princeton: Van Nostrand, 1963.

Stover, Carl F. (ed.). **The Technological Order*. Detroit: Wayne State University Press, 1963.

Strauss, Leo. *Natural Right and History*. Chicago: University of Chicago Press, 1953.

Sussman, Herbert L. *Victorians and the Machine*. Cambridge: Harvard University Press, 1968.

Swados, Harvey. *A Radical's America*. Boston: Little, Brown, 1962.

Sykes, Gerald (ed.). **Alienation*. New York: Braziller, 1964.

———. **The Cool Millennium*. Englewood Cliffs: Prentice-Hall, 1967.

Sypher, Wylie. *Literature and Technology*. New York: Random House, 1968.

Szasz, Thomas. *Law, Liberty and Psychiatry*. New York: Macmillan, 1965.

———. *Psychiatric Justice*. New York: Macmillan, 1963.

Taubenfeld, Howard J. (ed.). *Space and Society*. Dobbs Ferry: Oceana Press, 1964.

Tawney, R. H. *Religion and the Rise of Capitalism*. New York: Harcourt, Brace, 1926.

Taylor, Joshua C. *Futurism*. New York: Doubleday, 1961.

Taylor, Gordon R. *The Biological Time Bomb*. New York: World Publishing Company, 1968.

Technology and the American Economy. Washington, D.C.: Government Printing Office, 1966.

Teilhard de Chardin, Pierre. **The Future of Man*. London: Fontana Books, 1964.

———. *Le Milieu Devin*. London: Fontana Books, 1964.

———. **The Phenomenon of Man*. New York: Harper and Row, 1959.

Theobald, Robert A. **The Challenge of Abundance*. New York: Mentor Books, 1962.

———. (ed.). **Dialogue on Technology*. Indianapolis: Bobbs-Merrill, 1967.

———. (ed.). *The Guaranteed Income*. New York: Doubleday, 1966.

Thompson, Sir George. *The Foreseeable Future*. Cambridge: Cambridge University Press, 1955.

Thorpe, W. H. *Science, Man and Morals*. Ithaca: Cornell University Press, 1966.

Toynbee, Arnold and Veronica (eds.). *Survey of International Affairs, 1939–1946: Hitler's Europe*. London: Oxford University Press, 1954.

*Triple Revolution, The. Santa Barbara: Ad Hoc Committee on the Triple Revolution, 1964.

Trotsky, Leon. *Literature and Revolution*. New York: International Publishers, 1925.

Truman, David. *The Governmental Process*. New York: Knopf, 1951.

Twelve Southerners. *I'll Take My Stand*. New York: Harper, 1930.

Ubbelohde, A. R. *Man and Energy*. Baltimore: Penguin Books, 1963.

Vahanian, Gabrial. *The Death of God*. New York: Braziller, 1961.

Valentine, H. D. *Water in the Service of Man*. Baltimore: Penguin Books, 1967.

Van Dyke, Vernon. *Pride and Power*. Urbana: University of Illinois Press, 1964.

Van Leewven, Arend Theodor. *Christianity in World History*. New York: Scribner's, 1968

———. *Prophecy in a Technocratic Era*. Foreword by Harvey Cox. New York: Scribner's, 1968.

Van Melsen, Andreas G. *Science and Technology*. Vols. I and II. Pittsburgh: Duquesne University Press, 1961.

Vavloulis, Alexander, and Colver, Wayne A. (eds.). *Science and Society*. San Francisco: Holden, Day, 1966.

Veblen, Thorstein. *The Engineers and the Price System*. New York: The Viking Press, 1940.

Von Bertalanffy, Ludwig. *Robots, Men and Minds*. New York: Braziller, 1967.

Von Hoffman, Nicholas. *We Are the People Our Parents Warned Us Against*. Chicago: Quadrangle Books, 1968.

Wagar, W. Warren. *The City of Man*. Baltimore: Penguin Books, 1967.

Wagner, Philip L. **The Human Use of the Earth*. Glencoe: The Free Press, 1960.

Wallace, Anthony F. C. *Culture and Personality*. New York: Random House, 1961.

Waller, Harold. "Natural Scientists and Politics." Unpublished Ph.D. dissertation. Department of Government, Georgetown University, 1968.

Wallich, Henry C. *The Cost of Freedom*. New York: Harper, 1960.

Wall Street Journal. **Here Comes Tomorrow*. Princeton: Dow, Jones, 1967.

Wattenberg, Ben J., in collaboration with Scammon, Richard M. **This U.S.A.* New York: Pocket Books, 1967.

Waterston, Albert J. *Development Planning*. Baltimore: Johns Hopkins University Press, 1965.

Weaver, Richard M. *Ideas Have Consequences*. Chicago: University of Chicago Press, 1948.

Weber, Max. *From Max Weber: Essays in Sociology*. Translated and Edited by H. H. Gerth and C. Wright Mills. New York: Oxford University Press, 1956.

———. *The Protestant Ethic and the Spirit of Capitalism*. Translated by Talcott Parsons. London: Allan and Unwin, 1930.

———. *The Theory of Economic and Social Organization*. Translated by A. M. Henderson and Talcott Parsons. New York: Oxford University Press, 1947.

Weinberg, Alvin M. *Reflections on Big Science*. Cambridge: The M.I.T. Press, 1967.

Weldon, T. H. *The Vocabulary of Politics*. Hammondsworth: Penguin Books, 1953.

Westin, Alan. **Privacy and Freedom*. New York: Atheneum, 1967.

Wheeler, Harvey. **The Restoration of Politics*. Santa Barbara: Center for the Study of Democratic Institutions, 1965.

White, David Manning, and Everson, Richard (eds.). *Sight, Sound and Society*. Boston: Beacon Press, 1968.

White, Hugh C., Jr. (ed.). *Christians in a Technological Era*. New York: Seabury Press, 1964.

White, Leslie A. *The Science of Culture*. New York: Farrar, Straus and Cudahy, 1949.

White, Lynn, Jr. *Medieval Technology and Social Change*. Oxford: Clarendon Press, 1962.

White, Morton A. *Social Thought in America*. Boston: Beacon Press, 1957.

——— and Lucia. *The Intellectuals vs. the City*. Cambridge: Harvard University Press, 1962.

White, Winston. **Beyond Conformity*. New York: The Free Press, 1961.

Whitehead, Alfred North. **Science and the Modern World*. New York: Mentor Books, 1948.

Whyte, Lancelot Law. **The Next Development in Man*. New York: Mentor Books, 1950.

Whyte, William H., Jr. *The Organization Man*. New York: Simon and Schuster, 1956.

Wicker, Brian. *Culture and Liturgy*. New York: Sheed and Ward, 1964.

Wiener, Norbert. **Gods and Golem, Inc.* Cambridge: The M.I.T. Press, 1967.

———. **The Human Use of Human Beings*. Boston: Houghton Mifflin, 1950.

Wilkinson, John. **The Quantitative Society, Or What Are We to Do with Noodle?* Santa Barbara: Center for the Study of Democratic Institutions, 1964.

————, et al. *Technology and Human Values. Santa Barbara: Center for the Study of Democratic Institutions, 1966.

Williams, Raymond. *Culture and Society 1780–1950. New York: Anchor Books, 1960.

————. The Long Revolution. New York: Columbia University Press, 1961.

Winick, Charles E. The New People. New York: Pegasus Press, 1968.

Withers, William. Freedom Through Power. Introduction by A. A. Berle. New York: John Day, 1965.

Wittfogel, Karl A. Oriental Despotism. New Haven: Yale University Press, 1957.

Wolfe, Roy I. Transportation and Politics. Princeton: Van Nostrand, 1963.

Wolfe, Tom. The Kandy-Kolored Tangerine-Flake Streamline Baby. New York: Farrar, Straus and Giroux, 1965.

Wolff, Henry (ed.). Science as a Cultural Force. Baltimore: Johns Hopkins University Press, 1964.

Wolff, Robert, Moore, Barrington, Jr., and Marcuse, Herbert. A Critique of Pure Tolerance. Boston: Beacon Press, 1965.

Wood, Robert C. Suburbia. Boston: Houghton Mifflin, 1958.

Wooten, Barbara. *Freedom Under Planning. Chapel Hill: University of North Carolina Press, 1945.

Worth, Jean S., and Nicolai, Eugene R. Man . . . An Endangered Species? Washington: Government Printing Office, 1968.

Young, Michael. *The Rise of the Meritocracy 1870–2033. London: Thames and Hudson, 1958.

————, and Wilmott, Peter. Family and Class in East London. London: Routledge and Kegan Paul, 1960.

Zollschan, George K., and Hirsch, Walter (eds.). Explorations in Social Change. Boston: Houghton Mifflin, 1964.

Zuckerman, Solly. Science and War. New York: Harper and Row, 1967.

2. Periodicals

Adams, Robert. "The Origin of Cities," Scientific American, 203 (September, 1960), 153–168.

"Anything Goes: The Permissive Society," Newsweek (November 13, 1967), 74–48.

Aron, Raymond. "Social Structure and the Ruling Class," British Journal of Sociology, 1 (1950), 1–16, 126–143.

Barber, Bernard. "Experimenting With Humans," The Public Interest, 6 (Winter, 1967), 91–102.

Barnett, Harold J. *"The Myth of Our Vanishing Resources," Trans-Action, 4 (June, 1967), 6–10.

Basilla, George. "The Spread of Western Science," Science, 156 (1967), 611–622.

Bauer, Raymond A., and Bauer, Alice H. "America, Mass Society and Mass Media," Journal of Social Issues, 16 (1960), 3–66.

————. "The Communicator and His Audience," Journal of Conflict Resolution, 2 (1958), 67–77.

————, and Gleicher, D. "Word-of-Mouth Communication in the Soviet Union," Public Opinion Quarterly, 17 (1953), 297–310.

Bay, Christian. "Politics and Pseudopolitics: A Critical Evaluation of Some Behavioral Literature," *American Political Science Review*, 59 (1965), 39–51.

Bazalon, David T. "The 'New Class,'" *Commentary*, 42 (August, 1966), 48–53.

Beadle, George W. *"Genetics and Cultural Change," *Chicago Today*, 3 (Spring, 1966), 15–23.

Beer, Samuel. "Group Representation in Britain and the United States," *Annals of the American Academy of Political and Social Science*, 319 (1958), 130–140.

Bell, Daniel. "The Disjunction of Culture and Social Structure: Some Notes on the Meaning of Social Reality," *Daedalus*, 94 (1965), 208–222.

———. "Government By Commission," *The Public Interest*, 3 (Spring, 1966), 3–9.

———. *"Notes On the Post-Industrial Society," *The Public Interest*, 6 (Winter, 1967), 24–45, and 7 (Spring, 1967), 102–118.

———. "The Rediscovery of Alienation: Some Notes Along the Quest for the Historical Marx," *Journal of Philosophy*, 56 (1959), 933–952.

———. *"The Study of the Future," *The Public Interest*, 1 (Fall, 1965), 119–130.

———. *"The Year 2000: The Trajectory of an Idea," *Daedalus*, 96 (1967), 639–651.

Bendix, Reinhard. "Bureaucracy and the Problem of Power," *Public Administration Review*, 5 (1945), 194–209.

———, and Fisher, Lloyd. "The Perspectives of Elton Mayo," *Review of Economics and Statistics*, 3 (1949), 312–319.

Berger, Bennett. *"Hippie Morality—More Old Than New," *Trans-Action*, 5 (December, 1967), 10–18.

———. "Self-Hatred and the Politics of Kicks," *Dissent*, 13 (1966), 414–417.

———. *"Suburbia and the American Dream," *The Public Interest*, 2 (Winter, 1966), 80–91.

Bettelheim, Bruno. "Women: Emancipation Is Still to Come," *New Republic*, 151 (November 7, 1964), 48–58.

Boffey, Phil M. "International Biological Program: U.S. Effort Stands on Shaky Ground," *Science*, 159 (1968), 1131–1134.

Bogue, Donald J. "The End of the Population Explosion," *The Public Interest*, 7 (Spring, 1967), 11–20.

Bonjean, Charles M. "Mass, Class and the Industrial Community: A Comparative Analysis of Managers, Businessmen and Workers," *American Journal of Sociology*, 72 (1966), 149–162.

Borghese, Elisabeth M. *"The Republic of the Deep Seas: A Center Report," *The Center Magazine*, 1 (May, 1968), 18–27.

Borkenau, Franz. "Will Technology Destroy Civilization?," *Commentary*, 11 (January, 1951), 20–26.

Born, Max. *"Blessings and Evils of Space Travel," *Bulletin of the Atomic Scientists*, 22 (October, 1966), 12–14.

Boulding, Kenneth. *"Is Scarcity Dead?," *The Public Interest*, 5 (Fall, 1966), 36–44.

———. "Philosophy, Behavioral Science, and the Nature of Man," *World Politics*, 12 (1960), 272–279.

————. *"Where Are We Going If Anywhere? A Look At Post-Civiliza-
tion," *Human Organization*, 21 (1962), 162–167.

Boyle, Edward, et al. "Who Are the Policy Makers?," *Public Administration*, 43 (1965), 251–288.

Braidwood, Robert. "The Agricultural Revolution," *Scientific American*,
203 (September, 1960), 131–148.

Brinckloe, W. D. *"Automation and Self-Hypnosis," *Public Administration Review*, 26 (1966), 149–155.

Bronowski, Jacob. "The Logic of the Mind," *American Scholar*, 35 (1966),
233–242.

Brooks, Harvey. "Physics and the Polity," *Science*, 160 (1968), 396–400.

Brzezinski, Zbigniew. *"America in the Technetronic Age," *Encounter*, 30
(January, 1968), 16–26.

————. *"Toward A Technetronic Society," *Current*, 92 (February, 1968),
33–38.

Burnham, Walter Dean. "The Changing Shape of the American Political
Universe," *American Political Science Review*, 59 (1965), 7–28.

Butterfield, Herbert. "The Scientific Revolution," *Scientific American*, 203
(September, 1960), 173–192.

Calder, Nigel. "Tomorrow's Politics: The Control and Use of Technology,"
The Nation, 200 (1965), 3–5.

Caldwell, Lynton C. "Biopolitics: Science, Ethics, and Public Policy,"
Yale Review, 54 (1964), 1–16.

————. "Managing the Scientific Super-Culture: The Task of Educational
Preparation," *Public Administration Review*, 27 (1967), 128–133.

———— (ed.). "Symposium on Environmental Policy: New Directions in
Federal Action," *Public Administration Review xxviii* (1968), 301–
347.

Carleton, William G. "The Century of Technocracy," *Antioch Review*, 25
(1965–66), 487–508.

Carr, Donald. "Death of the Sweet Waters: The Politics of Pollution,"
The Atlantic, 207 (May, 1966), 93–106.

Carter, Luther J. "Deep Seabed: 'Who Should Control It?,' U.N. Asks,"
Science, 159 (1968), 66–68.

————. "World Food Supply: PSAC Panel Warns of Impending Famine,"
Science, 156 (1967), 1578–1579.

"The Census—What's Wrong With It, What Can Be Done," *Trans-Action*,
5 (May, 1968), 44–56.

Champion, Dean J., and Dager, Edward Z. "Automation Man in the
Counting House," *Trans-Action*, 3 (March-April, 1966), 34–39.

Cleveland, Harlan. "The Political Year of the Quiet Sun," *Department of
State Bulletin*, 50 (1964), 452–456.

Coker, Francis W. "Some Recent Criticisms of Democracy," *American
Political Science Review*, 47 (1953), 1–27.

Cole, La Mont C. *"Can the World Be Saved?," New York *Times Magazine*
(March 31, 1968), 35+.

Coleman, James. "The Possibility of a Social Welfare Function," *American
Economic Review*, 56 (1966), 1105–1122.

Coles, Robert. "Youth: Opportunity to be What?," *New Republic*, 151
(November 7, 1968) 59–64.

Compton, Neil. *"The Paradox of Marshall McLuhan," *New American
Writing*, 2 (1968), 77–94.

Corey, Lewis. *"Marquis de Sade—the Cult of Despotism," Antioch Review*, 26 (1966), 17–31.

Coser, Lewis. *"Nightmares, Daydreams and Professor Shils," Dissent*, 5 (1958), 268–273.

Coser, Rose Lamb. "The Cost of Medical Care," *Dissent*, 6 (1959), 77–80.

Cox, Harvey. "God and the Hippies," *Playboy*, 15 (January, 1968), 93–94+.

Dahrendorf, Ralf. "Recent Changes in the Class Structure of European Societies," *Daedalus*, 93 (1964), 225–270.

Daniels, George H. "The Pure-Science Ideal and Democratic Culture," *Science*, 156 (1967), 1699–1705.

David, E. V., Jr., and Truxal, J. G. "The Man-Made World—A Course for High Schools," *Science*, 156 (1967), 914–920.

Davis, Fred. *"Why All of Us May Be Flower Children Someday," Trans-Action*, 5 (December, 1967), 10–18.

Davis, Kingsley. *"Population Policy: Will Current Programs Succeed?," Science*, 158 (1967), 730–739.

———. "The Urbanization of the Human Population," *Scientific American*, 213 (September, 1965), 41–55.

Davison, W. Phelps. "On the Effects of Communication," *Public Opinion Quarterly*, 23 (1959) 343–360.

Dean, Dwight G. "Alienation, Meaning and Measure," *American Sociological Review*, 26 (1961), 753–758.

de Charms, Richard, and Moeller, Gerald H. "Values Expressed in American Children's Readers: 1800–1950," *Journal of Abnormal and Social Psychology*, 64 (1962), 136–142.

Deevey, Edward S. Jr. *"The Human Population," Scientific American*, 203 (September, 1960), 195–204.

Dennis, Jack. "Support for the Party System by the Mass Public," *American Political Science Review*, 60 (1966), 600–615.

de Rougement, Denis. "Man v. Technics," *Encounter*, 10 (January, 1958), 43–52.

de Sola Pool, Ithiel. "The International System in the Next Half-Century," *Daedalus*, 96 (1967), 930–935.

De Witt, Nicholas. "The Politics of Soviet Science," *American Behavioral Scientist*, 6 (December, 1962), 7–11.

———. "Reorganization of Science and Research in the U.S.S.R.," *Science*, 133 (1961), 1981–1991.

Dobzhansky, Theodosius. *"The Present Evolution of Man," Scientific American*, 203 (September, 1960), 206–217.

Douglas, Justice William O. "An Inquest on Our Lakes and Rivers," *Playboy*, 15 (June, 1968), 96–98+.

Drucker, Peter F. *"Notes on the New Politics," "The Public Interest*, 4 (Summer, 1966), 13–30.

Dubos, Rene J. *"Science and Man's Nature," Daedalus*, 94 (1965), 223–244.

———. "Scientists Alone Can't Do the Job," *Saturday Review*, 50 (December 2, 1967), 68–71.

Du Bridge, Lee A. "Policy and the Scientists," *Foreign Affairs*, 41 (1963), 571–588.

Dupree, A. Hunter. "Central Scientific Organization in the United States Government," *Minerva*, 1 (1963), 455–459.

316 TECHNOLOGICAL MAN

Ehrlich, Paul. "The Fight Against Famine Is Already Lost," Washington Post, March 10, 1968.
Ehrmann, Henry J. "French Bureaucracy and Organized Interests," Administrative Science Quarterly, 5 (1961), 534–555.
Eleazar, Daniel J. *"Are We A Nation of Cities?," The Public Interest, 4 (Summer, 1966), 42–58.
Elliott, George P. "Marshall McLuhan: Double Agent," The Public Interest, 4 (Summer, 1966), 116–122.
Etzioni, Amitai. *"Mixed-Scanning: A 'Third' Approach to Decision Making," Public Administration Review, 27 (1967), 385–392.
———. "On the National Guidance of Science," Administrative Science Quarterly, 10 (1966), 466–487.
Eulau, Heinz. "From Utopia to Probability: Liberalism and Recent Science," Antioch Review, 26 (Spring, 1966), 5–16.
Fackenheim, Emil. J. "On the Self-Exposure of Faith to the Modern-Secular World: Philosophical Reflections in the Light of Jewish Experience," Daedalus, 96 (1967), 193–219.
Ferry, W. H. "Masscomm as Educator," American Scholar, 35 (1966), 293–302.
———. *"Must We Rewrite the Constitution to Control Technology?," Saturday Review, 51 (March 2, 1968), 50–54.
———. "The Technophiliacs," The Center Magazine, I (July, 1968), 45–49.
Fesler, James W. "Approaches to the Understanding of Decentralization," Journal of Politics, 27 (1965), 536–566.
Feuer, Lewis. *"What Is Alienation? The Career of a Concept." New Politics, 1 (1962), 116–134.
Fisher, John. "Why Our Scientists Are About to Be Dragged, Moaning, Into Politics" Harpers, 233 (September, 1966), 16–27.
Fitch, Robert E. "The Scientist as Priest and Savior," The Christian Century, 75 (1958), 368–370.
Frank, Philip. "Philosophical Uses of Science," Bulletin of the Atomic Scientists, 13 (April, 1957), 125–130.
"Freedom from Fear," Time (April 7, 1967), 78–84.
Freyer, Peter. "The Flower Power Structure and the London Scene," Encounter, 29 (October, 1967), 6–20.
Friedenberg, Edgar Z. "The Image of the Adolescent Minority," Dissent, 10 (1963), 149–158.
Frye, Allob. "Politics: The First Dimension of Space: A Review," Journal of Conflict Resolution, 10 (1966).
Fuchs, Victor R. "Redefining Poverty and Redistributing Income," The Public Interest, 8 (Summer, 1967), 88–95.
———. *"The First Service Economy," The Public Interest, 2 (Winter, 1966), 7–17.
Fuller, Buckminster. *"Goddesses of the Twenty-First Century," Saturday Review, 51 (March 2, 1968), 12–14+.
———. *"Vision '65 Summary Lecture," American Scholar, 35 (1966), 206–218.
Furstenberg, Frank F., Jr. *"Industrialization and the American Family: A Look Backward," American Sociological Review, 31 (1966), 326–337.
Gabor, Dennis. "Inventing the Future," Encounter, 14 (May, 1960), 3–16.

Gass, Oscar. "A Washington Commentary," *Commentary*, 40 (October, 1965), 31–36.

Glazar, Nathan. "Paradoxes of American Poverty," *The Public Interest*, 1 (Fall, 1965), 71–81.

Gleason, Ralph J. "The Power of Non-Politics or the Death of the Square Left," *Evergreen*, 11 (October, 1967), 40–45+.

Gomer, Robert. "The Tyranny of Progress," *Bulletin of the Atomic Scientists*, 24 (February, 1968), 4–8.

Goodman, Paul. "The Diggers in 1984," *Ramparts*, 6 (September, 1967), 29–30.

Goodman, Walter. "Doctors Must Experiment on Humans," New York *Times Magazine* (July 2, 1967), 12–13+.

Goran, Morris. "The Literati Revolt Against Science," *Philosophy of Science*, 7 (1940), 379–384.

Gouldner, Alvin P. *"Metaphysical Pathos and the Theory of Bureaucracy," *American Political Science Review*, 49 (1953), 406–507.

Gouldner, Helen P. *"Children of the Laboratory," *Trans-Action*, 4 (April, 1967), 13–19.

Graubard, Allen. "One-Dimensional Pessimism: A Critique of Herbert Marcuse," *Dissent*, 15 (1968), 216–228.

Green, Harold P. "The New Technological Era: A View From the Law," *Bulletin of the Atomic Scientists*, 23 (November, 1967), 13–18.

Greenberg, Donald S., Jr. "Civilian Technology: NASA Study Finds Little 'Spin-off,' " *Science*, 157 (1967), 1016–1018.

———. *"The Myth of the Scientific Elite," *The Public Interest*, 1 (Fall, 1965), 51–62.

Greenfield, Meg. "Science Goes to Washington," *The Reporter*, 29 (September 23, 1963), 20–26.

Greer, Scott. "The Social Structure and Political Processes of Suburbia," *American Sociological Review*, 25 (1960), 514–526.

Grodzins, Morton, "Public Administration and the Science of Human Relations," *Public Administration Review*, 7 (1951), 88–102.

Gross, Bertram. *"National Planning: Findings and Fallacies," *Public Administration Review*, 25 (1965), 263–273.

Gunther, Max. "Computers: Their Built-In Limitations," *Playboy*, 14 (October 1967), 94+.

———. *"Second Genesis," *Playboy*, 15 (June, 1968), 117+.

Gusfield, Joseph R. "Mass Society and Extremist Politics," *American Sociological Review*, 27 (1962), 19–30.

Hacker, Andrew. *"A Country Called Corporate America," New York *Times Magazine* (July 3, 1966), 8–9+.

Hall, Richard H., and Tittle, Charles R. "A Note on 'Bureaucracy and Its Correlates,' " *American Journal of Sociology*, 72 (1966), 267–272.

Handlin, Oscar. *"Science and Technology in Popular Culture," *Daedalus*, 94 (1965), 156–170.

Harrington, Michael. "Marx *vs.* Marx," *New Politics*, 1 (1961), 112–123.

Harris, Chauncey D. "The Cultural Role of Cities," *Economic Development and Cultural Change*, 3 (1954), 55–57.

Harvey, Mary Kersey (ed.). *"Life in the Year 2000," *McCall's*, 95 (March, 1968), 143–144+.

Haskins, Carlyl P. "Technology, Science and American Foreign Policy," *Foreign Affairs*, 40 (1962), 1–20.

Havemann, Ernest. "Computers: Their Scope Today," *Playboy*, 14 (October, 1967), 95+.

Held, Virginia. "The High Cost of Culture," *The Public Interest*, 6 (Winter, 1967), 103–109.

Hentoff, Nat. "The Cold Society," *Playboy*, 13 (Oct., 1966), 133–136+.

———. "Youth—The Oppressed Majority," *Playboy*, 14 (Sept., 1967), 136+.

Hibbard, W. R., Jr. "Mineral Resources: Challenge or Threat?," *Science*, 160 (1968), 143–149.

Hinkle, Warren. "The Social History of the Hippies," *Ramparts*, 5 (March, 1967), 5–26.

Hirschorn, Kurt. "On Re-Doing Man," *Commonweal*, 88 (1968), 257–261.

Hockett, Charles F. "The Origins of Speech," *Scientific American*, 203 (September, 1960), 89–96.

———, and Ascher, Robert. "The Human Revolution," *Current Anthropology*, 5 (1964), 135–168.

Honan, William H. *"They Live in the Year 2000," New York *Times Magazine* (April 9, 1967), 56+.

Hull E. W. Seabrook. "The Political Ocean," *Foreign Affairs* XLV (1967), 492–502.

Huntington, Samuel P. "Interservice Competition and the Political Roles of the Armed Services," *American Political Science Review*, 55 (1961), 40–52.

Hurley, Neil P., S.J. "Satellite Communications: A Case Study of Technology's Impact on Politics. *"The Review of Politics*, 30 (1968), 170–190.

Ingle, Dwight J. *"The Biological Future of Man," *Chicago Today* (Spring, 1966), 36–42.

"Inheritors, The." *Time* (January 6, 1967), 18–23.

Inkeles, Alex, and Rossi, Peter H. "National Comparisons of Occupational Prestige," *American Journal of Sociology*, 61 (1956), 329–339.

Jencks, Christopher, and Riesman, David. *"On Class in America," *The Public Interest*, 10 (Winter, 1968), 65–85.

Jouvenel, Bertrand de. "Letter From France: The Technocratic Age," *Bulletin of the Atomic Scientists*, 20 (October, 1964), 27–29.

———. "The Political Consequences of the Rise of Science," *Bulletin of the Atomic Scientists*, 19 (December, 1963), 2–8.

———. *"Political Science and Prevision," *American Political Science Review*, 59 (1965), 29–38.

Junker, Howard. "Not Gone But Frozen," *The Nation*, 206 (1968), 504–506.

Kadushkin, Charles. "Social Classes and the Experience of Ill Health," *Sociological Inquiry*, 24 (1964), 67–80.

Kahn, Herman, and Weiner, Anthony J. *"The Next Thirty-Three Years: A Framework for Speculation," *Daedalus*, 96 (1967), 705–732.

Kalvin, Harry, Jr. *"The Problems of Privacy in the Year 2000," *Daedalus*, 96 (1967), 17–21.

Kaplan, Norman. "The Western European Scientific Establishment in Transition," *American Behavioral Scientist*, 6 (1962), 17–21.

Kariel, Henry S. "The Political Relevance of Behavioral and Existential Psychology," *American Political Science Review*, 61 (1967), 334–342.

Kass, Leon R. *"A Caveat on Transplants," *Washington Post*, January 14, 1968.

Katz, Elihu. "Communications Research and the Image of Society: Convergence of Two Traditions," *American Journal of Sociology,* 65 (1960), 435–440.

————. "The Two-Step Flow of Communication: An Up-to-Date Report on an Hypothesis," *Public Opinion Quarterly,* 21 (1957), 61–78.

Kecskemeti, Paul. "Totalitarian Communications as a Means of Control," *Public Opinion Quarterly,* 14 (1950), 224–234.

Keniston, Kenneth. *"Youth, Change and Violence," *American Scholar,* 37 (1968), 227–245.

Kepes, Gyorgy. *"The Visual Arts and the Sciences: A Proposal for Collaboration," *Daedalus,* 94 (1965), 117–134.

Kerouac, Jack. "Beatific: On the Origins of a Generation," *Encounter,* 13 (August, 1959), 57–61.

Kerr, Clark. "Clark Kerr Calls It the Exaggerated Generation," New York *Times Magazine* (June 8, 1967), 28+.

Kershner, Lee R. "Cybernetics and Soviet Philosophy," *International Philosophical Quarterly,* 6 (1966), 270–285.

Kesteven, G. L. "A Policy for Conservationists," *Science,* 160 (1968), 857–860.

King, Alexander. "Science and Technology in the New Europe," *Daedalus,* 93 (1964), 434–458.

Klapper, Joseph T. "What We Know About the Effects of Mass Communication: The Brink of Hope," *Public Opinion Quarterly,* 21 (1957-58), 453–471.

Kneese, Allen V. *"Why Water Pollution Is Economically Unavoidable," *Trans-Action,* 5 (April, 1968), 31–36.

Kristol, Irving. "High, Low and Modern," *Encounter,* 15 (August, 1960), 33–41.

————. *"It's Not Such a Bad Crisis to Live In," New York *Times Magazine* (January 12, 1967), 23+.

Krutch, Joseph Wood. *"Epitaph For An Age?," New York *Times Magazine,* (July 20, 1967), 10+.

Lampard, Eric. "The History of Cities in the Economically Advanced Areas," *Economic Development and Cultural Change,* 3 (1955), 81–136.

Landsberg, Hans H. *"The U.S. Resource Outlook: Quantity and Quality," *Daedalus,* 96 (1967), 1034–1057.

Lane, Robert E. *"The Decline of Politics and Ideology in a Knowledgeable Society," *American Sociological Review,* 31 (1966), 649–662.

————. *"The Politics of Consensus in an Age of Affluence," *American Political Science Review,* 59 (1965), 874–895.

Langer, William L. "Europe's Initial Population Explosion," *American Historical Review,* 69 (1963), 1–17.

La Porte, Todd A. "Politics and 'Inventing the Future': Perspectives in Science and Government," *Public Administration Review,* 27 (1967), 117–127.

Laquer, Walter. "It Appears That the New Left is Half-Century Old," Washington *Post,* January 7, 1968.

Lasswell, Harold D. *"The Political Science of Science," *American Political Science Review,* 50 (1956), 961–979.

Lasswell, Thomas (ed.). "Social Class and Social Stratification," special issue of *Sociology and Social Research,* 50 (1966), 227–392.

Lawler, Edward E., III. "How Much Money Do Executives Want?,"
    Trans-Action, 4 (January-February 1967), 23–29.
Leach, Gerald. "Technophobia on the Left: Are British Intellectuals
    Anti-Science?," *New Statesman*, 70 (1965), 286–287.
Lear, John. *"Policing the Consequences of Science," *Saturday Review*, 50
    (December 2, 1967), 65–67.
————. (ed.). "Science, Technology and the Law," *Saturday Review*, 51
    (August 3, 1968), 39–52.
Lederberg, Joshua. *"Experimental Genetics and Human Evolution,"
    Bulletin of the Atomic Scientists, 22 (October, 1966), 4–11, and
    discussion between Lederberg and Leonard Ornstein, 23 (June,
    1967), 57–61.
Leiserson, Avery. *"Scientists and the Policy Process," *American Political
    Science Review*, 59 (1965), 408–416.
Lekachman, Robert. "The Automation Report," *Commentary*, 41 (May,
    1966), 65–71.
Lerner, Max. "Climate of Violence," *Playboy*, 14 (June, 1967), 99+.
Lessing, Lawrence. "Into the Core of Life Itself," *Fortune*, 73 (March,
    1966), 146–51+.
Lindbergh, Charles A. "The Wisdom of Wildness," *Life*, 63 (December 22,
    1967), 8–10.
Lindblom, Charles E. "Economics and the Administration of National
    Planning," *Public Administration Review*, 25 (1965), 274–283.
Lindesmith, Alfred R., and Strauss, Anselm L. "A Critique of Culture-
    Personality Writing," *American Sociological Review*, 15 (1950), 587–
    600.
Litwak, Leo E. "A Trip to Esalen Institute—'Joy Is the Prize," New
    York *Times Magazine* (December 31, 1967), 8–9+.
Lynch, Kevin. "The City As Environment," *Scientific American*, 213
    (September, 1965), 209–219.
Lyons, Gene M. "The New Civil-Military Relations," *American Political
    Science Review*, 55 (1961), 53–63.
McClintock, Robert. "Machines and Vitalists: Reflections on the Ideology
    of Cybernetics," *American Scholar*, 35 (1966), 249–257.
Maccoby, Michael. "Government, Scientists and the Priorities of Science,"
    Dissent, 11 (1964), 55–67.
McLoed, James, Ward, Scott, and Tansill, Karen. "Alienation and the
    Uses of the Mass Media," *Public Opinion Quarterly*, 24 (Winter,
    1965–66), 583–594.
McLuhan, Marshall. *"Address at Vision '65," *American Scholar*, 35
    (1966), 196–205.
————, and Leonard, George B. *"The Future of Sex," *Look*, 31 (July 25,
    1967), 56–63.
Malone, Thomas F. "Weather Modification: Implications of the New
    Horizons in Research," *Science*, 156 (1967), 897–901.
Mann, Georg. "Epitaph for Eros," *Dissent*, 5 (1958), 177–182.
Marquart, Frank. "The Auto Worker," *Dissent*, 4 (1957), 219–233.
Marty, Martin E. *"A Humanist's View of Space Research," *Chicago To-
    day*, 3 (Autumn, 1966), 25–33.
Mead, Margaret. *"The Future as the Basis for Establishing a Shared
    Culture," *Daedalus*, 94 (1965), 135–155.
Means, Richard L. *"Why Worry About Nature?," *Saturday Review*, 50
    (December 2, 1967), 13–15.

Medewar, P. B. "Science and the Sanctity of Life," *Encounter,* 27 (June, 1966), 96–104.
Mencher, Alan G. "Management by Government: Science and Technology in Britain," *Bulletin of the Atomic Scientists,* 24 (May, 1968), 22–27.
Mesthene, E. G. "How Technology Will Shape the Future," *Science,* 161 (1968), 135–143.
————. "The Impacts of Science Upon Public Policy," *Public Administration Review,* 27 (1967), 97–104.
————. "Technology and Religion," *Theology Today,* 23 (1966), 481–495.
Michaelis, Michael. *"Can We Build the World We Want?," *Bulletin of the Atomic Scientists,* 24 (January, 1968), 43–49.
Miller, S. M., and Reissmann, Frank. "Are Workers Middle Class?," *Dissent,* 8 (1961), 507–516.
Minsky, Marvin L. "Artificial Intelligence," *Scientific American,* 215 (September, 1966), 246–260.
Mitzman, Arthur. "Anti-Progress: A Study in the Romantic Roots of German Sociology," *Social Research,* 33 (1966), 47–85.
Morgenthau, Hans J. "Modern Science and Political Power," *Columbia Law Review,* 154 (1964), 1386–1409.
Morison, Elting S. "It's Two-thirds of a Century—We've Made It So Far," *New York Times Magazine* (April 24, 1966), 34–35+.
Morison, Robert S. *"Education for Environmental Concerns," *Daedalus,* 96 (1967), 1210–1223.
————. *"Toward a Common Scale of Measurement," *Daedalus,* 94 (1965), 245–262.
Moulin, Leo. "The Nobel Prizes for the Sciences for 1901–1950: An Essay in Sociological Analysis," *British Journal of Sociology,* 6 (1955), 246–263.
Mowrer, Edgar Ansel, *"Sawdust, Seaweed and Synthetics," *Saturday Review,* 39 (December 8, 1956), 11–13+.
Moynihan, Daniel P. "The Relationship of Federal to Local Authorities," *Daedalus,* 96 (1967), 801–808.
Muller, Hermann J. *"The Prospects of Genetic Change," *The Ameircan Scientist,* 47 (1959), 551–561.
Mumford, Lewis. "Utopia, The City and the Machine," *Daedalus,* 94 (1965), 271–292.
Murray, Rev. George B., S.J., and Huston, Jean. "LSD: The Inward Voyage," *Jubilee,* 15 (June, 1967), 8–17.
Nettler, Gwynn. "A Measure of Alienation," *American Sociological Review,* 22 (1957), 670–677.
Neumann, Franz L. "Approaches to the Study of Political Power," *Political Science Quarterly,* 65 (1950), 161–180.
Newell, Homer E., and Jaffe, Leonard. "Impact of Space Research on Science and Technology," *Science,* 157 (1967), 29–39.
"New Medicine and Its Weapons," *Newsweek* (April 24, 1967), 60–68.
Nieberg, H. L. "The Contract State: Government in the Economy," *Dissent,* 13 (1966), 526–537.
Nisbet, Robert A. "The Year 2000 and All That," *Commentary,* 45 (June, 1968), 60–65.
Novak, Michael. "Christianity: Renewed or Slowly Abandoned?," *Daedalus,* 96 (1967), 238–266.
O'Conner, James. "Concentration and Control," *Dissent,* 7 (1960), 355–361.

O'Dea, Thomas F. *"The Crisis of the Contemporary Religious Consciousness," *Daedalus*, 96 (1967), 116–144.

————. "Technology and Social Change: East and West," *Western Humanities Review*, 13 (1959), 151–162.

Ogburn, William F. "Technology as Environment," *Sociology and Social Research*, 41 (1956), 3–9.

Olsen, Marvin E. "Alienation and Political Opinions," *Public Opinion Quarterly*, 29 (1965), 200–212.

O'Neill, John. "Alienation, Class Struggle, and Marxist Anti-Politics," *Review of Politics*, 17 (1964), 462–471.

Orleans, Leo A. "Research and Development in Communist China," *Science*, 157 (1967), 392–400.

Parsons, Howard L. "Value and Mental Health in the Thought of Marx," *Philosophy and Phenomenological Research*, 24 (1964), 355–365.

Patterson, Robert W. "The Art of the Impossible," *Daedalus*, 96 (1967), 1020–1033.

Perrow, Charles. "The Sociological Perspective and Political Pluralism," *Social Research*, 31 (1964), 411–427.

Pierce, John R. "Communications Technology and the Future," *Daedalus*, 96 (1965), 506–517.

Pi-Sunyer, Oriol, and de Gregori, Thomas. "Cultural Resistance to Technological Change," *Technology and Culture*, 5 (1964), 247–253.

Polanyi, Michael. "Privacy and Behavioral Research," *Science*, 155 (1967), 535–539.

————. "The Republic of Science: Its Political and Economic Philosophy," *Minerva*, 1 (1962), 54–73.

Quarton, Gardner. C. *"Deliberate Attempts to Control Human Behavior and Modify Personality," *Daedalus*, 96 (1967), 837–853.

Rabassiere, Henri. "Some Aspects of Mass Culture," *Dissent*, 3 (1956), 327–332.

Reagan, Michael. "America As a 'Mass Society,'" *Dissent*, 3 (1956), 346–356.

Redfield, Robert. "The Folk Society," *American Journal of Sociology*, 53 (1947), 292–308.

Reeves, Richard. "U.S. Think Tanks," New York *Times*, June 12–16, 1967.

Reich, Charles A. *"The New Property," *The Public Interest*, 3 (Spring, 1966), 57–89.

Reiss, Ira L. *"How and Why America's Sex Standards Are Changing," *Trans-Action*, 5 (March, 1968), 26–32.

Reistrup, J. V. "Davy Jones' Locker Tempts the World," Washington *Post*, November 14, 1967.

"Religion and the New Morality," symposium in *Playboy*, 14 (June, 1967), 55–78+.

Revelle, Roger. "Environment: Land, Air, Water," *New Republic*, 151 (November 7, 1964), 25–32.

————. *"Outdoor Recreation in a Hyper-Productive Society," *Daedalus*, 96 (1967), 1173–1191.

Rice, Berkeley. "Skinner Agrees He Is the Most Important Influence in Psychology," New York *Times Magazine* (March 17, 1968), pp. 27+.

Ridley, F. F. "French Technology and Comparative Government," *Political Studies* (Oxford), 14 (1966), 34–52.

Riesman, David. *"Notes on Meritocracy," *Daedalus*, 96 (1967), 897–908.
————. "Some Observations on the Limits of Totalitarian Controls," *Antioch Review*, 12 (1952), 155–168.
Ripley, S. Dillon, and Buechner, Helmut K. "Ecosystem Science as a Point of Synthesis," *Daedalus*, 96 (1967), 1192–1199.
Rock, Vincent P. "The Politics of Science and Technology," *World Politics*, 18 (1966), 314–333.
Rogers, Carl R. "Freedom and Commitment," *ETC*, 22 (1965), 133–151.
————, and Skinner, B. F. "Some Issues Concerning the Control of Human Behavior: A Symposium," *Science*, 124 (1956), 1057–1066.
Rosenberg, Harold. "Pop Culture and Kitch Criticism," *Dissent*, 5 (1958), 14–19.
Rosenfeld, Albert. *"Will Man Direct His Own Evolution?," *Life*, (October 1, 1965).
Rossi, Peter, and Bauer, Raymond. "Some Patterns of Soviet Communications Behavior," *Public Opinion Quarterly*, 16 (1952), 653–670.
Roszak, Theodore. *"The Counter Culture," *The Nation*, 206 (1968), 400–407, 439–443, 466–471, 497–503.
Rotenstreich, Nathan. "Technology and Politics," *International Philosophical Quarterly*, 7 (1967), 197–212.
Rubenstein, Richard L. "Judaism and the Death of God," *Playboy*, 14 (July, 1967), 69+.
Rustow, Dankwart A. "The Study of Elites: Who's Who, When and How," *World Politics*, 18 (1966), 690–717.
Sagan, Carl, Levinthal, Elliot C., and Lederberg, Joshua. "Contamination of Mars," *Science*, 159 (1968), 1191–1196.
Sahlins, Marshall D. "The Origins of Society," *Scientific American*, 203 (September, 1960), 76–86.
Sapolsky, H. M. "Science Advice for State and Local Government," *Science*, 160 (1968), 280–284.
Sayre, Wallace S. "Science, Scientists and American Science Policy," *Science*, 133 (1961), 859–864.
Schelling, Thomas C. "PPBS and Foreign Affairs," *The Public Interest*, 11 (Spring, 1968), 26–36.
Schiller, Herbert I. *"Social Control and Individual Freedom," *Bulletin of the Atomic Scientists*, 24 (May, 1968), 16–21.
Schilling, Warner R. "The H-Bomb Decision: How to Decide Without Actually Choosing," *Political Science Quarterly*, 76 (1961), 24–46.
————. "Scientists, Foreign Policy and Politics," *American Political Science Review*, 61 (1962), 287–300.
Schnorr, Alvin L. "Selfish Children and Lonely Parents," *The Public Interest*, 4 (Summer, 1966), 8–12.
Seaborg, Glenn T. "Need We Fear Our Nuclear Future?," *Bulletin of the Atomic Scientists*, 24 (January, 1968), 36–42.
Sears, Paul B. *"Utopia and the Living Landscape," *Daedalus*, 94 (1965), 474–486.
Seeman, Melvin. "Alienation, Membership and Political Knowledge: A Comparative Study," *Public Opinion Quarterly*, 30 (1966), 353–367.
————. "On the Meaning of Alienation," *American Sociological Review*, 24 (1959), 783–791.
Senneville, Gerard de. "L'economie contractuelle," *Project*, 15 (January, 1967), 15–25.

Sewall, W. R. Derrick. "Humanity and the Weather," *Chicago Today*, 3 (Spring, 1966), 24–29.

Shils, Edward. *"Daydreams and Nightmares: Reflections on the Criticism of Mass Culture," *Sewanee Review*, 65 (1957), 587–608.

––––––. "Mass Society and Its Culture," *Daedalus* (1960), 288–314.

––––––. "The Sanctity of Life," *Encounter*, 27 (January, 1967), 39–49.

––––––. *"The Theory of Mass Society," *Diogenes*, 39 (Fall, 1962), 45–66.

Shryock, Richard H. "American Indifference to Basic Science During the Nineteenth Century," *Archives Internationaux d'Histoire des Sciences*, 28 (1948–49), 50–65.

Shubik, Martin. *"Information, Rationality and Free Choice in a Future Democratic Society," *Daedalus*, 96 (1967), 771–778.

Sibley, Mulford Q. *"Socialism and Technology," *New Politics*, 1 (1961), 202–213.

Simpson, George. "Western Man Under Automation," *International Journal of Comparative Sociology*, 5 (1964), 199–207.

Sjoberg, Gideon. "The Origin and Evolution of Cities," *Scientific American*, 213 (September, 1965), 55–62.

Skinner, B. F. *"Freedom and the Control of Man," *American Scholar*, 25 (Winter, 1955–56), 47–65.

––––––. "Teaching Science in High School—What Is Wrong?," *Science*, 159 (1968), 704–710.

Smith, Bruce L. R. "The Future of the Not-for-profit Corporation," *The Public Interest*, 8 (Summer, 1967), 127–142.

Smith, G. "Astounding Story: About a Science Fiction Writer," New York *Times Magazine* (March 6, 1966), 28–29+.

Smith, Huston. "This New Age," *University of Chicago Magazine*, 59 (May, 1967), 16–18.

Smith, John Maynard. *"Eugenics and Utopia," *Daedalus*, 94 (1965), 487–505.

Snow, C. P. "The Moral Un-Neutrality of Science," *Science*, 133 (1961), 256–259.

Snyder, Margaret. "Behavioral Sciences and Family Planning," *Science*, 158 (1967), 677–682.

Solow, Robert M., and Heilbroner, Robert L. "The Great Automation Question," *The Public Interest*, 1 (Fall, 1965), 17–36.

Spengler, Joseph J. "The Aesthetics of Population," *Population Bulletin*, 13 (1957), 61–75.

––––––. "Population Threatens Prosperity," *Harvard Business Review* (January–February, 1956), 85–94.

Spilhaus, Athelstan. "The Experimental City," *Daedalus*, 96 (1967), 1129–1141.

––––––. "The Experimental City," *Science*, 159 (1968), 710–715.

––––––. "Oceanography: A Wet and Wondrous Journey," *Bulletin of the Atomic Scientists*, 20 (December, 1964), 11–15.

Spiro, Milford E. "Culture and Personality," *Psychiatry*, 14 (1951), 19–46.

Star, Shirley, and Hughes, Helen MacGill. "Report on an Educational Campaign: The Cincinnati Plan for the United Nations," *American Journal of Sociology*, 55 (1950), 389–400.

Starr, Roger, and Carlson, James. *"Pollution and Poverty: The Strategy of Cross-commitment," *The Public Interest*, 10 (Winter, 1968), 104–121.

Stearn, Gerald Emanuel. "Conversations with McLuhan," *Encounter*, 28 (June, 1967), 50–58.

Stock, Rodney, and Glock, Charles Y. *"Will Ethics Be the Death of Christianity?," *Trans-Action*, 5 (June, 1968), 104–121.

Storer, Norman J. "The Coming Changes in American Science," *Science*, 152 (1963), 464–467.

Strickland, Donald A. "Physicists' View of Space Politics," *Public Opinion Quarterly*, 29 (1965), 223–235.

"Suburbia," special issue of *Look*, 31 (May 16, 1967).

Sutherland, Gordon. "Government and Science in Britain and the United States," *Bulletin of the Atomic Scientists*, 24 (April, 1968), 20–28.

Szasz, Thomas. "Mental Illness Is a Myth," New York *Times Magazine*, (June 12, 1966), 30–31+.

Tarr, David W. "Military Technology and the Policy Process," *Western Political Quarterly*, 18 (1965), 135–148.

"Teen-Agers, The." *Newsweek*, 67 (March 21, 1966), 57–75.

Teller, Azriel. "Air-Pollution Abatement: Economic Rationality and Reality," *Daedalus*, 96 (1967), 1082–1098.

Templeton, Frederic. "Alienation and Political Participation: Some Research Findings," *Public Opinion Quarterly*, 30 (1966), 249–261.

Theobald, Robert. *"Abundance: Threat or Promise?," *The Nation*, 196 (1963), 387–412.

Theones, Piet. "The Provos of Holland," *The Nation*, 204 (1967), 494–497.

Thomas, Keith. "Work and Leisure in Pre-Industrial Society," *Past and Present*, 29 (December, 1964), 50–66.

Thompson, Victor A. "How Scientific Management Thwarts Innovation," *Trans-Action*, 5 (June, 1968), 51–55.

Toch, Hans. "Last Word on the Hippies," *The Nation*, 205 (1967), 582–588.

Toulmin, Stephen. "On Teilhard de Chardin," *Commentary*, 39 (March, 1965), 50–55.

Toynbee, Arnold. "A Sacrificial Generation," *Washington Post*, May 28, 1967.

Trachtenberg, Alan. "Technology and Human Values," *Technology and Culture*, 5 (1964), 359–376.

Van Neumann, John. "Can We Survive Technology?," *Fortune*, 51 (June, 1955), 16–18+.

Volkan, Heinrich N. "Society in the Technical Age," *Diogenes* (Fall, 1966), 16–27.

Von Hoffman, Nicholas. "The Acid Affair," *Washington Post*, October 15–29, 1967.

Vucininch, Alexander. "Science and Morality: A Soviet Dilemma," *Science*, 159 (1968), 1208–1212.

Waldo, Dwight. "Development of Theory of Democratic Administration," *American Political Science Review*, 46 (1952), 81–107.

Walter, E. V. "Mass Society: The Late Stages of An Idea," *Sociological Research*, 31 (1964), 389–399.

Washburn, Sherwood L. "Tools and Human Evolution," *Scientific American*, 203 (September, 1960), 63–75.

Ways, Max. "The Road to 1977," *Fortune*, 75 (January, 1967), 93+.

Weidenbaum, Murray L. "Measurements of the Economic Impact of

Defense and Space Programs," *American Journal of Economics and Sociology*, 25 (1966), 415–426.

Weil, Eric. *"Science in Modern Culture Or the Meaning of Meaninglessness," *Daedalus*, 95 (1965), 171–189.

Weinberg, Alvin M. *"Can Technology Replace Social Engineering?," *University of Chicago Magazine*, 49 (October, 1966), 6–10.

———. "Can Technology Stabilize World Order?," *Public Administration Review*, 27 (1967), 460–464.

Westin, Alan F. *"Science, Privacy and Freedom: Issues and Proposals for the 1970s," *Columbia Law Review*, 66 (1966), 1003–1050, 1205–1253.

———. "The Snooping Machine," *Playboy*, 15 (1968), 130–132.

Wheeler, Harvey. "The Challenge of Bureaucratized Science," *Bulletin of the Atomic Scientists*, 20 (January, 1964), 14–17.

———. "Danger Signals in the Political System," *Dissent*, 4 (1957), 298–310.

———. "Means, Ends, and Human Institutions," *The Nation*, 204 (1967), 9–16.

White, Leslie A. "The Concept of Culture," *American Anthropologist*, 6 (1959), 227–251.

White, Lynn, Jr. *"The Historical Roots of Our Ecological Crisis," *Science*, 156 (1967), 1203–1207.

———. *"St. Francis and the Ecologic Backlash," *Horizon*, IX (Summer, 1967), 42–47.

White, Orion, Jr. "Human Freedom and Bureaucratic Constraint," *Public Administration Review*, 26 (1966), 217–222.

"Why Are We Suddenly Obsessed by Violence?," *Esquire*, 68 (July, 1967).

Wildavsky, Aaron. *"Aesthetic Power or the Triumph of the Sensitive Minority Over the Vulgar Mass: A Political Analysis of the New Economics," *Daedalus*, 96 (1967), 1115–1128.

Wilensky, Harold L. *"Mass Society and Mass Culture: Interdependence or Independence," *American Sociological Review*, 29 (1964), 173–197.

———. *"The Uneven Distribution of Leisure: The Impact of Economic Growth on 'Free Time,'" *Social Problems*, 9 (1961), 32–56.

Wiles, Peter. "Will Capitalism and Communism Spontaneously Converge?," *Encounter*, 20 (June, 1963), 84–90.

Wilson, James Q. "Crime in the Streets," *The Public Interest*, 5 (Fall, 1966), 26–35.

———. "The War on Cities," *The Public Interest*, 3 (Spring, 1966), 27–44.

———. "Why We Are Having a Wave of Violence," *New York Times Magazine* (May 14, 1968), 23–24+.

Winthrop, Henry. "Sociological and Ideological Assumptions Underlying Cybernation," *American Journal of Economics and Sociology*, 25 (1966), 113–126.

———. "Some Roadblocks on the Way to a Cybernated World," *American Journal of Economics and Sociology*, 25 (1966), 405–414.

Wohlstetter, Albert. "Scientists, Seers and Strategy," *Foreign Affairs*, 41 (1963), 466–478.

———. "Technology, Prediction, and Disorder," *Bulletin of the Atomic Scientists*, 20 (October, 1964), 11–15.

Wolfle, Dale. "The Only Earth We Have," *Science*, 159 (1968), 155.

Wollman, Nathaniel. "The New Economics of Resources," *Daedalus,* 96 (1967), 1099–1114.

Wolman, Abel. "The Metabolism of Cities," *Scientific American,* 213 (September, 1965), 178–190.

Zeitlin, Irving. "Some Aspects of the Scientific-Industrial Revolution in America," *Journal of World History,* 9 (1966), 1009–1019.

Zinberg, Norman E. "Facts and Fancies about Drug Addiction," *The Public Interest,* 6 (Winter, 1967), 75–90.

Zoppo, Ciro. "Nuclear Technology, Multipolarity and International Stability," *World Politics,* 28 (1966), 579–606.

Index

Aeropile, 33
Agrarianism, 65–66
Agricultural civilization, 31–35, 47
Albania, 197
Alienation, 74–75, 85, 142, 181–182, 207, 218, 222–223
Altizer, Thomas, 92
Anomie, 71–72
Aquinas, Thomas, 93
Arendt, Hannah, 9, 158
Aristotle, vii, 17, 61, 87, 248
Arnold, Matthew, 64
Arts, 235–236
Astronauts, 3–7, 90, 101
Atomic bomb, 6, 45, 94, 101, 164
Autocreation, 243
Automation, 108, 123–124, 131–135, 142, 157, 240–241

Bach, J. S., 28, 216
Bacon, Francis, 37
Beckmann, Johann, 44
Belgium, 185
Bell, Daniel, 12, 14, 30, 124, 126, 128, 158–160, 181

Bentham, Jeremy, 249
Big Brother, 80
Biosphere, 91
Birth control, *see* contraception
Bismarck, Otto, 43
Black revolution, 16, 164–165
Bogue, Donald, 144
Bonhoeffer, Dietrich, 231
Borsodi, Ralph, 63
Boulding, Kenneth, 268
Bourgeois man, 81, 143, 147, 160, 243–245, 271
Brainwashing, 168, 170
Brown, Harrison, 144
Bryan, William Jennings, 66
Brzezinski, Zbigniew, 14, 78
Burke, Edmund, 61–62
Butler, Samuel, 64

Cage, John, 216
Calvinism, 39
Canada, 185
Carlyle, Thomas, 64
Carnegie Institute of Technology, 44
Castro, Fidel, 59

331